THE PSYCHOLOGY OF
SUPERHEROES

THE PSYCHOLOGY OF SUPERHEROES

EDITED BY
Robin S. Rosenberg, Ph.D.
with Jennifer Canzoneri

AN UNAUTHORIZED EXPLORATION

BENBELLA BOOKS, INC.
Dallas, Texas

"The Positive Psychology of Superheroes" © 2008 by Christopher Peterson and Nansook Park
"The Social Psychology of the Justice League of America" © 2008 by Wind Goodfriend, Ph.D.
"Superman's Personality" © 2008 by Robin S. Rosenberg, Ph.D.
"Anti-Heroism in the Continuum of Good and Evil" © 2008 by Michael Spivey, Ph.D., and Steven Knowlton
"Positive Psychology of Peter Parker" © 2008 by Robert Biswas-Diener
"Prejudice Lessons from the Xavier Institute" © 2008 by Mikhail Lyubansky, Ph.D.
"When I Grow Up I Want to Be a Superhero" © 2008 by Bryan J. Dik, Ph.D.
"Is There a Superhero in All of Us?" © 2008 by Peter A. Hancock and Gabriella M. Hancock
"Mind-Reading Superheroes" © 2008 by William J. Ickes, Ph.D.
"An Appetite for Destruction" © 2008 by Chuck Tate, Ph.D.
"The Stereotypical (Wonder) Woman" © 2008 by Chuck Tate, Ph.D.
"What Would Freud Say?" © 2008 by Andrew R. Getzfeld, Ph.D.
"Coming to Terms with Bizarro" © 2008 by Siamak Tundra Naficy
"Coping with Stress…the Superhero Way" © 2008 by Stephanie R. deLusé, Ph.D.
"Arkham Asylum" © 2008 by Bradley J. Daniels
"The Incredible Hulk" © 2008 by Christopher J. Patrick, Ph.D., and Sarah K. Patrick
"Gender Typicality and Extremity in Popular Culture" © 2008 by Kerri L. Johnson, Leah E. Lurye, and Jonathan B. Freeman
"Cracking the Superhero's Moral Code" © 2008 by Peter DeScioli and Robert Kurzban, Ph.D.
Additional Materials © 2008 by Robin S. Rosenberg, Ph.D.

BenBella Books, Inc.
10300 N. Central Expressway, Suite 530
Dallas, TX 75231
www.benbellabooks.com
Send feedback to feedback@benbellabooks.com

Printed in the United States of America
10 9 8 7 6 5

Library of congress cataloging-in-publication data

The Psychology of Superheroes : an unauthorized exploration / edited by Robin S. Rosenberg, with Jennifer Canzoneri.
    p. cm.
  ISBN 1-933771-31-3
  1. Conduct of life. 2. Heroes—Psychology. 3. Typology (Psychology) 4. Self-actualization (Psychology)
I. Rosenberg, Robin S. ii. Canzoneri, Jennifer.
  BF637.c5p83 2008
  741.5'9019—dc22

                                                                                    2007041418

Proofreading by Kristy D. Dennis and Jennifer Canzoneri
Cover design by Laura Watkins
Cover illustration by Big Time Attic
Text design and composition by John Reinhardt Book Design
Printed by Lake Book Manufacturing

Distributed by Perseus Distribution
perseusdistribution.com

To place orders through Perseus Distribution:
Tel: 800-343-4499
Fax: 800-351-5073
E-mail: orderentry@perseusbooks.com

Significant discounts for bulk sales are available.
Please contact Glenn Yeffeth at glenn@benbellabooks.com or (214) 750-3628.

CONTENTS

THE PSYCHOLOGY OF SUPERHEROES

Robin S. Rosenberg, Ph.D.

INTRODUCTION

WHEN I WAS GROWING UP in New York City in the 1960s and 1970s, I read the comics of lots of different superheroes—whatever I could borrow. But I reserved my allowance money for Superman and Batman comics. As I got older I stopped reading comics, although my admiration for superheroes continued into adulthood—I avidly and repeatedly watched their films.

Time passed, and I had children; as they began to read I introduced them to comics—Batman and Superman, naturally. In turn, they introduced me to the X-Men, which they heard about from their friends. We would read the comics together. Between reading comic books during my childhood and reading them with my children, something happened that altered how I viewed them, something more than becoming an adult—I became a clinical psychologist. In reading the superhero stories with my children, I read the stories not only through adult lenses, but also through psychologist lenses. And what I saw was a surprise.

As an adult, I saw that superhero stories are about morality and loyalty, about self-doubt and conviction of beliefs. I also saw that, like

1

any good fiction, the sagas of superheroes bring us out of ourselves and connect us with something larger than ourselves, something more universal. Moreover, in our superheroes' foibles, struggles, and triumphs, we can see elements of our own foibles and struggles, and hope for our triumphs.

As a psychologist, I spotted the ways in which their stories reflect psychological theories and research findings. For instance, in the wake of witnessing his parents' brutal murder, Bruce Wayne decides to dedicate his life to protecting innocent lives. Thus was Batman born. Psychological research suggests that the underlying process of the birth of Batman isn't farfetched and is, in fact, common: After people have experienced a traumatic event, they often struggle to make meaning of the experience, and one such path is through social action.

Superheroes also serve as models of moral behavior. They try to figure out the "right" path to take in a given situation: When—if ever—is it okay to lie in the service of a greater good? When should violence or the threat of violence be used as a punishment? When should it be used as a deterrent? How much force is "too much?" How can a small band of people fight against the never-ending parade of criminals? And how can people maintain hope in the face of such adversity?

These are questions that most of us have grappled with and tried to answer at various points in our lives; I did as a child, and I still do. As a child, I found it illuminating that Batman and Superman often had different answers to these moral questions. But from each superhero's struggles and actions, I had the opportunity to learn something about myself, as you may have learned about yourself through your favorite superhero's struggles. Their moral journeys serve as models for our own journeys. We get to "try on" a view of morality or style of leadership by immersing ourselves in a superhero's story; in trying it on, we get to see how well it fits or doesn't fit. Psychologists call this process of learning through observing others *observational learning*. Through observing others, we learn something that we can apply to ourselves.

The essays in this volume help to illuminate how superheroes reflect—or don't reflect—what we have learned from psychology. As you read these essays, I hope you discover, as I did, that learning about relevant psychological research and theories and applying them to superheroes can enrich your experiences with the comic book characters.

This book investigates psychological theories and research results as applied to superhero phenomena large and small. On the "small" scale, this volume includes essays that focus on the psychology of the person, or in this case, the superhero. Many of these essays examine the psychological implications of having superpowers:

- What it is like to live with super-senses, super-abilities, and superpowers ("Is There a Superhero in All of Us?"; "Mind-Reading Superheroes"; "The Incredible Hulk");
- Living and coping with Superstresses ("The Positive Psychology of Superheroes"; Positive Psychology of Peter Parker"; "Coping with Stress . . . the Superhero Way");
- Ways that the environment shapes and motivates superheroes ("Superman's Personality"; "An Appetite for Destruction"; "Coming to Terms with Bizarro"; "Cracking the Superhero's Moral Code");
- Ways that super-abilities and superpowers influence the superhero's mission in life ("When I Grow Up I Want to Be a Superhero") and the moral dilemmas faced ("Anti-Heroism in the Continuum of Good and Evil").

In fact, in our own way, each of us experiences a version of these same qualities and experiences, as these essays point out.

Other essays in this volume focus on larger elements—on the psychology of groups, institutions, and societies:

- How groups, such as the Justice League of America, function ("The Social Psychology of the Justice League of America");
- Issues of discrimination ("Prejudice Lessons from the Xavier Institute");
- Issues related to gender ("The Stereotypical [Wonder] Woman"; "Gender Typicality and Extremity in Popular Culture");
- Issues related to mental illness and its treatment ("What Would Freud Say?"; "Arkham Asylum").

In terms of specific superheroes, this book has something for everyone. The psychologist authors cast a wide net and included many different characters. Within these essays are discussed (in alphabetical order): Aquaman, the Avengers, Batman, Blade, Captain Marvel, Daredevil, Fantastic Four, the Flash, Green Arrow, Green Lantern, Hellboy, the Hulk, the Incredibles, Justice League of America, Mystery Men, Plasticman, the Punisher, Spider-Man, Star Trek and Star Wars characters, Superman, Thor, Wonder Woman, and the X-Men.

Enjoy!

Christopher Peterson
and Nansook Park

THE POSITIVE PSYCHOLOGY OF SUPERHEROES

Do superheroes live positive psychology's vision of a "good life"? Are superheroes happy? And if they're not happy, why should we want to be like them? In their essay, Peterson and Park examine whether superheroes have lives "well lived." Peterson and Park focus on the superhero character, on the *hero* in superhero, and how a superhero's morality makes him or her different from the villains. Peterson and Park also discuss the ways in which a superhero's character is not like that of us humans—through connections with other people.

IF COMIC BOOKS CAN BE EXAMINED from the vantage of literature, cultural history, and philosophy (Fingeroth, 2006; Morris & Morris, 2005; Wright, 2001), then they can also be looked at in terms of psychology. A psychological interpretation of comic books can provide the framework for understanding the characters as well as the readers.

5

Comic books have been extremely popular since their inception in the 1930s, and while comic book sales may have decreased in their absolute numbers, the popularity of superheroes is on the rise. Witness Hollywood films, television cartoons, lunch boxes, T-shirts, and U.S. postage stamps that feature familiar superheroes from Superman and Batman to Spider-Man and the Incredible Hulk. Why have superheroes appealed to so many people for so many years? Psychology may provide an answer. We propose that superheroes allow us to see ourselves in stark and entertaining ways and to dream of what we might be.

As self-identified positive psychologists, we are interested in people being well and doing well (Peterson, 2006). Part of our research program entails identifying what we call natural homes for positive psychology—settings in which excellence is recognized, celebrated, and nurtured (Park & Peterson, 2006). Studies of those who excel in these settings can teach the rest of us something about what makes life most worthwhile. Such natural homes include schools, businesses, the performing arts, sports, and the military.

Are comics an additional natural home for positive psychology? Never mind that the superheroes who live there are fictional. Our heroes and heroines have always resided in stories, from Biblical parables to the Harry Potter saga (Burrell, 1997). Those who attempt to teach about good character invariably use stories to make their points (Kilpatrick, Wolfe, & Wolfe, 1994). The stories may be real, apocryphal, or mythic. But we do not think it makes much difference if the point is to provide us with examples of a life well-lived.

Positive psychology has several topics of central concern: (a) positive subjective experiences (pleasure and happiness), (b) positive traits (values, talents, and good character), (c) rewarding social relationships (friendship and love), and (d) institutions that enable optimal functioning (the natural homes) (Peterson, 2006; Seligman, 2002; Seligman & Csikszentmihalyi, 2000). According to positive psychology, the good life results when these factors align themselves (Park & Peterson, 2003). In this essay, we examine comic book superheroes in terms of these concerns and assess whether superheroes are also "super" people in terms of positive psychology's vision of the good life.

THE HAPPINESS OF SUPERHEROES

Are superheroes happy? It certainly would seem fun to do what they can do. From decades ago, comic book ads hawked special devices that would allow purchasers to see through clothing or eavesdrop through walls. But Superman is not a voyeur, and one would be hard-pressed to find a superhero whose guiding orientation is hedonism. Indeed, a number of superheroes—the early and late Batman and many characters from the Marvel stable—were brooding and neurotic. Even the most affluent of superheroes were not materialistic in a Scrooge-like way, which is probably good for their own well-being (Kasser, 2002). One of the features of pleasure is that we adapt to it rather quickly, and superheroes appear no different from the rest of us except that they have figured this out. How many lumps of coal can be squeezed into diamonds before the experience becomes old hat (Csikszentmihali, 1999)?

In contrast, the villains with whom superheroes battle are always having fun. These archenemies are frequently mad scientists bent on world domination, immortality, and other goals that never seem to lose their appeal. Villains pursue their goals with obvious relish. The Joker not only looks like a clown but also enjoys killing for its own sake, playing whimsical pranks, and matching wits with Batman. According to one storyline, the Joker was a failed comedian (Moore, Bolland, & O'Neill, 1988)! Other villainous motivations include Superman's nemesis, Lex Luthor's selfish desires to control the world while pretending to be a philanthropist. The enemy of Thor, his brother Loki, is the god of lies and mischief. The Black Manta (from Aquaman) seeks personal power. Captain Cold, one of the villains who battled the Flash, is motivated by money and—unusual for a comic book character—lechery. As Billy Joel sung, "the sinners are much more fun," but that does not mean we root for them. Good *should* triumph over evil, especially evil pleasure.

Positive psychology states that pleasure is but one ingredient of what happiness entails (Peterson, Park, & Seligman, 2005). A second important ingredient is engaging in what one does and thereby experiencing the psychological state of flow (Csikszentmihalyi, 1990). Superheroes are highly involved in what they do, so much so that when they occasionally and temporarily walk away from their callings, this becomes a plot line of significance.

Yet another route to happiness entails a life of meaning, being connected to something larger than the self (Seligman, 2002). For many people, religion provides meaning to their lives (Peterson, Ruch, Beerman, Park, & Seligman, 2007), although there are secular equivalents, including deep relations with others or an abiding concern with nature or humanity writ large. Other than the handful who themselves are deities—Thor, Wonder Woman—few superheroes practice a conventional religion. Few are married, and fewer still have children. Superheroes have sidekicks and protégés, but rarely friends in the way that the term is usually used to describe a reciprocal relationship between peers. When superheroes occasionally band together, as in DC's Justice League or Marvel's Avengers, what we have is an all-star team of individuals. However, one of the defining features of a superhero is an over-riding mission to serve the larger world and to defend it. In this sense, superheroes have profoundly meaningful lives.

Our own research shows that engagement and meaning consistently trump pleasure in terms of their importance in leading a satisfied life (Peterson, Park, & Seligman, 2005), which means that superheroes are probably happier than most everyday people. However, we have also learned that the happiest people are those who experience engagement, meaning, *and* pleasure—what we can call a full life. Superheroes do not have the fullest possible lives. They do not stop and smell the roses, eat a good meal, or savor a soothing shower. They do not have hobbies. They are connected to humanity but not to specific individuals.

THE CHARACTER STRENGTHS OF SUPERHEROES

Our particular research interest within positive psychology is moral character (Park 2004; Peterson & Seligman, 2004). Our concern is with the "hero" component of superheroes and not with the "super" component. The extraordinary powers of superheroes are of course interesting and compelling to readers, but we believe that the real appeal of superheroes stems from their moral qualities as opposed to their talents. After all, not all superheroes have powers that transcend what is humanly possible—read: Batman—and many of the villains who figure prominently in comic books have their own super powers.

Virtually all superheroes have character strengths, usually to such a degree that we can describe them as paragons of one virtue or another. Iron Man is a fierce patriot. Wonder Woman is compassionate and empathic, as wise as Athena, and always able to discern what is true. Spider-Man has a self-deprecating sense of humor. And when Captain Marvel utters the magical acronym SHAZAM, he summons several virtues and abilities, those that are possessed by Solomon (wisdom), Hercules (physical strength), Atlas (stamina), Zeus (power), Achilles (courage), and Mercury (speed).

That superheroes have conspicuous strengths of character sets them apart from many other potential role models in today's society, even in the fictional realm where the anti-hero has ascended in recent decades (Bostic et al., 2003). Where have all the heroes and heroines gone? One explanation for their scarcity is that contemporary journalism has thoroughly undressed most potential candidates. Past sports heroes no doubt abused drugs and past government leaders no doubt cheated on their spouses, but the general public did not see their misdeeds unfold in real time on twenty-four-hour cable television like we do today. We have few heroes except in comic books because now everyone else has such well-documented feet of clay.

However, the general public, if not the media, is usually sophisticated enough to know that even very good people are not saints and no reasonable person expects them to be (cf. Wolfe, 1982). Good character is not a present-or-absent monolith that can be vetoed by a single error or fault. Rather, character is a family of positive traits, and our research consistently shows that no one consistently possesses all such traits (Park & Peterson, 2006). It is enough to possess one or two notable strengths of character—what we term signature strengths—to be morally praiseworthy (Walker & Pitts, 1998). Collectively, superheroes have all of the virtues that positive psychologists have identified and studied; although no given superhero has them all (cf. Dahlsgaard, Peterson, & Seligman, 2005). Their character is most accurately described in terms of a profile of greater and lesser strengths. The same is true for the everyday people to whom we have administered our surveys (Park, Peterson, & Seligman, 2006).

Consider the character flaws of superheroes. As we see them, Captain Marvel can be immature, and Spider-Man can be peevish. Batman, at least in his early days, was much more angry and self-righteous than we would want even our casual acquaintances to be, and of all the possible Superman spin-offs, one featuring the Man of Steel doing standup comedy is simply not going to happen. But there is a notable difference between the profiles of more versus less typical character strengths of superheroes and everyday people. With some exceptions, everyday people seem *more* likely than superheroes to have what we call *strengths of the heart* that connect them to specific other people: love, kindness, gratitude, and humor. Furthermore, everyday people seem *less* likely than superheroes to display strengths of temperance like self-regulation and persistence, *less* likely to be courageous and hopeful, and *less* likely to have a sense of purpose and zest for life.

So, most superheroes are not like most real people in terms of their specific character strengths. This is hardly surprising with respect to the strengths conspicuously possessed by superheroes. These strengths provide ample grounds for readers to admire superheroes. But less obvious, our positive psychology perspective additionally reveals some strengths of character to be conspicuously missing among most superheroes. The absence of these strengths may preclude envy and resentment on the part of readers.

Tradeoffs are inevitable among strengths of character (Schwartz & Sharpe, 2006), and superheroes have struck a different moral bargain than real people. Superman can retreat to his Fortress of Solitude and be content, but if and when everyday people isolate themselves from others, they are simply miserable.

THE PERSONAL RELATIONSHIPS OF SUPERHEROES

We have already noted the absence of personal relationships in the lives of superheroes and the scarcity of character strengths that focus on specific individuals. For real people, close relationships with friends and family are perhaps the single biggest contributor to a satisfied life (Reis & Gable, 2003). Superheroes are therefore anything but super in these terms.

The Fantastic Four are a notable exception to these generalizations. Reed Richards (Mr. Fantastic) is married to Susan Richards (The Invisible Woman), who is the sister of Johnny Storm (The Human Torch). Ben Grimm (The Thing) is the long-time friend and former college roommate of Reed Richards. However, these relationships were established before their acquisition of super powers, during an outer space mission, and the Fantastic Four differ in other ways from the superhero template, lacking secret identities and—at least in the beginning—special costumes.

Psychology provides two major perspectives on personal relationships. The first, equity theory, views relationships in economic terms and proposes that close relationships—friendships or romances—are established and persist to the degree that both people involved believe that what they are getting out of the relationship is proportional to what they are putting into it (Walster, Walster, & Berscheid, 1978). Given the talents and abilities of superheroes, with whom could they have an equitable relationship? Other superheroes are the obvious answer, but the field is narrow, especially for romance and marriage. Even a causal reader of comic books knows that superheroes are predominantly male and predominantly heterosexual.

The second psychological perspective in personal relationships is provided by attachment theory, which emphasizes the feelings that bind people together and traces them to the initial attachment between infant and mother (Bowlby, 1969). Securely attached infants become securely attached adults and capable of reciprocal relationships (Hazan & Shaver, 1987, 1994). Those without a history of secure attachment are socially challenged throughout life. In this area superheroes appear no different than real people. Consider how many superheroes were orphans—Superman, Captain Marvel, Batman, Spider-Man, and Beast Boy—or victims of early neglect and abuse—Professor X, Blade, and Venom. Other superheroes did not even have human parents in the first place: Hell Boy and Wolverine.

Psychology often contrasts these two theories of relationships (Clark & Mills, 1979), but in the case of superheroes, each theory predicts what we actually find in the comics: a paucity of personal relationships. A common plot device in superhero sagas is the thwarting of romance ostensibly by the need of the superhero to keep his identity secret and protect the Lois Lanes of the world. (From what, we ask, given the powers of the superhero?) This is a noble rationale that may appeal to readers grappling with their own lack of close relationships, but the deeper psychological truth may be that superheroes (and their fans) are missing the point that real relationships are inherently imperfect yet infinitely rewarding.

SUPERHEROES AND SOCIETAL INSTITUTIONS

Unlike their cousins in fantasy and science fiction stories, superheroes live in a world that is familiar to readers. The same societal institutions—police departments, schools, and churches—are found in comic books as in real life, along with the same historical timeline and events—World War II, the Civil Rights movement, and space exploration. The chief difference between comic books and real life is of course the presence of one or more superheroes, which means that it is unsurprising that they are the focus. The larger world is simply the assumed and often unexamined backdrop. The focus on individual superheroes makes for a good comic book, which are not just stories but *illustrated* stories. People's attention—at least in the Western world—is immediately drawn to the people in pictures and not to the background (Chua, Boland, & Nisbett, 2005).

Nonetheless, this feature of comic books works against our goal of understanding the psychological good life. Real people—their happiness, their character, and their relationships—do not exist in a vacuum. Context is always critical, and one of the most important contexts in which people need to be placed and understood is provided by societal institutions like the family, the school, the workplace, the community, and the nation. Positive psychology holds that given institutions can make it more or less easy for someone to have the good life. The characterization of what we call enabling institutions can be difficult, in large part because institutions are complex and have all sorts of effects on what people feel and do, from very good to very bad. Consider organized religion, and the equally valid arguments for both its benefits and its costs throughout history.

Given the complexity of all institutions, "positive" institutions are the weakest link of positive psychology. Although efforts are ongoing to characterize them and understand how they influence the good life (e.g., Cameron, Dutton, & Quinn, 2003). Comic books have traditionally sidestepped the role of institutions. Consider that superheroes do not try to remake the world in profound ways. They do not try to cure cancer, eliminate poverty, or promote universal literacy. They are hardly revolutionaries. Superman and Batman fight corruption but not the system that allows it to exist. World War II was an exception, and many superheroes helped the Allied war effort. But even in this case, few superheroes directly battled the Germans or the Japanese. Instead, they fought crime on the home front. Exceptions existed, of course, including Captain America and Wonder Woman, but these superheroes took on specific individuals and not entire nations or their armies.

Partly explaining why superheroes do not deal with larger societal institutions are the comic codes of 1948 and 1954. Among other things, they prohibited the presentation of "policemen, judges, government officials, and respected institutions... in such a way as to create disrespect for established authority," (Nyberg, 1998). But the code, to which comic book creators adhered to in varying degrees, certainly did not mandate against the presentation of the positive roles played by institutions.

More deeply, therefore, we believe that superheroes existed apart from societal institutions because a literary decision was made to portray them as exaggerated individualists as opposed to collectivists (Triandis, 1995). Superheroes are Horatio Alger in tights, and as such they convey the thoroughly incorrect message that one can live and achieve something important with little help or influence from others (Murray, 2003). When larger social institutions are occasionally on focus in the comics, they are not depicted as the source of good but rather as obstacles and challenges to overcome.

There is one feature of the larger social world of superheroes that is worth noting, and that is the existence of obvious good and obvious evil. Positive psychology is based on the premise that both are genuine and worthy of study, but it can be difficult to make the same distinctions in the real world, which is so often morally gray. People want—indeed perhaps need—to see the world in moral terms (Wright, 1994) and comic books readily afford such perceptions. Superheroes are morally just, and villains are thoroughly wicked.

Is the stark simplicity of the comic book world a drawback in conveying moral examples? We think not. One of the truisms from the legal and legislative world is that difficult cases make for bad laws. It is better to start with a simple case and proceed to the complex, rather than starting with the complex and proceed to nowhere. Perhaps the same principle has been adopted by comic book creators.

CONCLUSIONS

We have examined superheroes in light of what positive psychology has learned about the life worth living, asking if superheroes are also super people. Our major conclusion is of the "yes-but" variety. Yes...much about superheroes resonates with the lessons of positive psychology. They are engaged in what they do, and they have lives of meaning. They possess extraordinary talents (obviously) but also certain strengths of character rare in the real world and thus all the more praiseworthy. But...superheroes are also incomplete. Mundane pleasures are largely absent from their lives, personal relationships and related strengths of character are almost nonexistent, and the role of societal institutions in shaping a satisfying life is for the most part missing. At the beginning of this essay, we proposed that superheroes allow us to see ourselves in stark and entertaining ways and to dream of what we might be. The dream apparently needs to be fleshed out.

Why then are comic book heroes so popular? We believe we have an answer. You may not have noticed, but throughout our discussion, we deliberately focused on the superhero as superhero and said little about his or her secret identity. The secret identity may be more than a plot device. It may also be the rest of the story, at least in psychological terms. From Bruce Wayne to Diana Price to Bruce Banner to Peter Parker, the secret identity is necessarily a more mundane individual than the superhero, even if the individual in question is affluent and talented. But it is in this role that the superhero experiences everyday pleasures, goes to school, holds a job, has friends, and participates as an ordinary member of the larger society.

In discussing Superman and Clark Kent, it is observed that the powers of Superman make him capable of saving the world but that the grounding of Clark Kent in the American heartland makes him want to do it (Engle, 1987). Simply put, the Superman saga would not work without Clark Kent, and we would argue that the same is true of other superhero stories.

For many superheroes, the secret identity is primary in the sense of predating the superhero role, although there are exceptions. It may not matter much if we recognize that the superhero is both super and ordinary, and *that* is a primary lesson of positive psychology that all of us should heed. No one can have it all, at least not simultaneously and not in all roles played. Superheroes—as heroes and everyday people—may have it all sequentially, and that is pretty super if it teaches readers patience and flexibility.

Christopher Peterson is a social and clinical psychologist and professor of psychology at the University of Michigan. He has been studying character strengths and virtues and their positive outcomes on health, well-being, and work. He is the author of *A Primer in Positive Psychology* (Oxford University Press, 2006).

Nansook Park is a clinical and school psychologist and associate professor of psychology at the University of Rhode Island. She is interested in good character among children and youth and how it is related to well-being, family functioning, health, and education.

Both **Peterson** and **Park** are Fellows at the Positive Psychology Center of the University of Pennsylvania and Consulting Editors of the *Journal of Positive Psychology*.

REFERENCES

J. Q. Bostic, S. Schlozman, C. Patakim, C. Ristuccia, E. Beresin, and A. Martin, "From Alice Cooper to Marilyn Manson: The Significance of Adolescent Antiheroes," *Academic Psychiatry* 27 (2003): 54–62.

Bowlby, J. *Attachment and Loss, Vol. I. Attachment.* New York: Basic Books, 1969.

Burrell, B. *The Words We Live By.* New York: Free Press, 1997.

Cameron, K. S., Dutton, J. E., and Quinn, R. E. (Eds.) *Positive Organi-*

zational Scholarship: Foundations of a New Disciple. San Francisco: Berrett-Koehler, 2003.

H. F. Chua, J. E. Boland, and R. E. Nisbett, "Cultural Variation in Eye Movements During Scene Perception," *Proceedings of the National Academy of Science of the United States of America* 102 (2005): 12629–12633.

M. S. Clark and J. Mills, "Interpersonal Attraction in Exchange and Communal Relationships," *Journal of Personality and Social Psychology* 37 (1979): 12–24.

Csikszentmihalyi, M. *Flow: The Psychology of Optimal Experience.* New York: Harper & Row, 1990.

M. Csikszentmihalyi, "If We Are So Rich, Why Aren't We Happy?" *American Psychologist* 54 (1999): 821–827.

K. Dahlsgaard, C. Peterson, and M. E. P. Seligman, "Shared virtue: The convergence of valued human strengths across culture and history," *Review of General Psychology* 9 (2005): 209–213.

G. Engle, "What Makes Superman so Darned American?" In D. Dooley & G. Engle (Eds.), *Superman at Fifty: The Persistence of a Legend* (pp. 79–87). Cleveland, OH: Octavia Press, 1987.

Fingeroth, D. *Superman on the Couch: What Superheroes Really Tell us about Ourselves and Our Society.* New York: Continuum, 2006.

C. Hazan and P. R Shaver, "Romantic Love Conceptualized as an Attachment Process," *Journal of Personality and Social Psychology* 52 (1987): 511–524.

C. Hazan and P. R. Shaver, "Attachment as an Organizational Framework for Research on Close Relationships," *Psychological Inquiry* 5 (1994): 1–22.

Kasser, T. *The High Price of Materialism.* Cambridge, MA: Bradford, 2002.

Kilpatrick, W., Wolfe, G., and Wolfe, S. M. *Books that Build Character.* New York: Simon & Schuster, 1994.

Moore, A., Bolland, B., and O'Neill, D. *The Killing Joke.* New York: DC Comics, 1988.

Morris, T., and Morris, M. (Eds.) *Superheroes and Philosophy: Truth, Justice, and the Socratic Way.* Chicago: Open Court, 2005.

Murray, C. *Human Accomplishment: The Pursuit of Excellence in the Arts and Sciences, 800 B.C. to 1950.* New York: HarperCollins, 2003.

Nyberg, A. K. *Seal of Approval: History of the Comics Code.* Jackson. MI: University Press of Mississippi, 1998.

N. Park, "Character Strengths and Positive Youth Development," *The*

Annals of the American Academy of Political and Social Science 591 (2004): 40–54.

Park, N., & Peterson, C. "Virtues and Organizations." In K. S. Cameron, J. E. Dutton, & R. E. Quinn (Eds.), *Positive Organizational Scholarship: Foundations of a New Discipline* (pp. 33–47). San Francisco: Berrett-Koehler, 2003.

Park, N., & Peterson, C. "Methodological Issues in Positive Psychology and the Assessment of Character Strengths." In A. D. Ong & M. van Dulmen (Eds.), *Handbook of Methods in Positive Psychology* (pp. 292–305). New York: Oxford University Press, 2006.

N. Park, C. Peterson, and M. E. P. Seligman, "Character Strengths in Fifty-four Nations and the Fifty U.S. States," *Journal of Positive Psychology* 1 (2006): 118–129.

Peterson, C. *A Primer in Positive Psychology.* New York: Oxford University Press, 2006.

C. Peterson, N. Park, and M. E. P. Seligman, "Orientations to Happiness and Life Satisfaction: The Full Life versus the Empty Life," *Journal of Happiness Studies* 6 (2005) 25–41.

C. Peterson, W. Ruch, U. Beerman, N. Park, and M. E. P. Seligman, "Strengths of Character, Orientations to Happiness, and Life Satisfaction," *Journal of Positive Psychology* 2 (2007): 1–8.

Peterson, C., & Seligman, M. E. P. *Character Strengths and Virtues: A Handbook and Classification.* New York: Oxford University Press/ Washington, DC: American Psychological Association, 2004.

Reis, H. T., & Gable, S. L. "Toward a Positive Psychology of Relationships." In C. L. M. Keyes & J. Haidt (Eds.), *Flourishing: Positive Psychology and the Life Well-lived* (pp. 129–159). Washington, DC: American Psychological Association, 2003.

B. Schwartz and K. E. Sharpe, "Practical Wisdom: Aristotle Meets Positive Psychology," *Journal of Happiness Studies* 7 (2006) 377–395.

Seligman, M. E. P. *Authentic Happiness.* New York: Free Press, 2002.

M. E. P. Seligman and M. Csikszentmihalyi, "Positive Psychology: An Introduction," *American Psychologist* 55 (2000) 5–14.

Triandis, H. C. *Individualism and Collectivism.* Boulder, CO: Westview Press, 1995.

L. J. Walker and R. C. Pitts, "Naturalistic Conceptions of Moral Maturity," *Developmental Psychology* 34 (1998): 403–419.

Walster, E., Walster, G. W., and Berscheid, E. *Equity: Theory and Research.* Boston: Allyn & Bacon, 1978.

S. Wolf, "Moral Saints," *The Journal of Philosophy* 79 (1982): 419–439.

Wright, B. W. *Comic Book Nation: The Transformation of Youth Culture in America*. Baltimore: The Johns Hopkins University Press, 2001.

Wright, R. *The Moral Animal: The New Science of Evolutionary Psychology*. New York: Random House, 1994.

THE PSYCHOLOGY OF SUPERHEROES

Wind Goodfriend, Ph.D.

THE SOCIAL PSYCHOLOGY OF THE JUSTICE LEAGUE OF AMERICA

Why is the Justice League of America such an effective superhero team? Although they have their occasional differences, by and large they function well as a group to get the job done—to protect Earth and its inhabitants. In this essay, Goodfriend shares the secrets of their success and how it mirrors what is known from psychological research about how groups function best—and the factors that prevent them from functioning well.

AFTER WORLD WAR II, everything changed. The worlds of politics, economics, and culture would never be the same. Individual lives were also altered in many different ways. Within this massive shift between the past and the future, two other realms would change as well. These two fields would experience an era of great importance to each—a time that everyone involved would remember as being extremely influential. These two fields were the worlds of superheroes and of social psychology.

Psychology before World War II was dominated, at least in the United States, by a perspective called "behaviorism." This perspective was that the field of psychology should focus only on actual behaviors of individuals, with no focus on thoughts or emotions. Part of this theoretical trend was the general belief that all animals—including humans—were essentially the same, and thus psychology spent several decades doing research with apes, rats, and pigeons. The central idea of behaviorism was that psychology could only be "scientific" if it studied observable, objective behaviors; thoughts and emotions were subjective, and therefore difficult to measure. However, the war changed psychology in a profound way: psychologists were called upon to explain the horrors of the Holocaust. Clearly, insight into thoughts and emotions was necessary to understand the evils of the world. In addition, the Nazi regime led to a renewed interest in the psychology of groups—conformity, obedience to authorities, and how a powerful group leader could affect the lives of millions. Social psychology was thus born. This sub-field of psychology proper focuses on interactions between people and how one's thoughts and behaviors are influenced by these *social* situations. Therefore, the process, motivation, and success or failure of groups is the heart of social psychology.

At the same time in history, a monumental event occurred in the world of comics. In 1960, the DC anthology series *The Brave and the Bold* revealed the greatest superhero team of all time—the Justice League of America. In volume #28 of this series, Gardner Fox updated the older, original team (the Justice Society of America) to write an adventure that would be a pioneer event in comics history. We saw in this volume, Starro the Conquerer!, the original JLA team: Aquaman, Wonder Woman, Superman, Green Lantern, Batman, Flash, and J'onn J'onzz (the Martian Manhunter). In this first adventure, the JLA must fight Starro the Conqueror, who is quite an impressive enemy. He's psychic. He's extraterrestrial. And he's a really, really big starfish. How does the JLA defeat this mighty foe? Their plan of attack is one we would see many times over the years: they split up to take on different aspects of the overall threat, then come together again as a united force to finally stop the evil of the day. At a time in history when everyone was concerned with fighting evil, we could look to the League to defend freedom and liberty for all. We can also count on this group of superheroes to display many of the central theories and phenomena of social psychology.

THE BENEFITS OF A GROUP

Folk wisdom teaches that more will be accomplished by a group than by an individual. However, social psychology actually calls this to question. There's actually quite a bit of research showing that if you took the added efforts of ten individuals working alone and you compared this to the total work of a group of ten people working together, the work of the individuals would be both bigger and better. Why is it that some groups fail in this way? One problem well known in social psychology is *social loafing*. The idea here is that when put in a group, individuals will feel a "diffusion of responsibility" such that when a task appears, each member of the group will think, "Why should *I* be the one to take care of that? Someone else will do it." In other words, individual responsibility is greatly decreased and therefore so is individual effort. Another problem with work in groups is that individuals do not always share all of the information they have. They might assume that the other team members know the information already, or that the information is not important. Unfortunately, this means that often the other team members begin the task ignorant of information that may be essential for success.

So why is the Justice League of America such a good example of a successful team? The first answer is that they do not make the mistakes mentioned above, so common to other groups. Each member of the JLA takes individual responsibility for contributing to every task put before them. Part of the reason that the JLA is successful in this is because each member has his or her own abilities, forcing individual action. As mentioned above, the general strategy of the group is to come together at the beginning, but then split up into smaller teams of two or three. In these smaller groups everyone knows that he or she must step up and engage the enemy. An example is seen in *Justice League of America* #5, "When Gravity Went Wild!" Here, there are two groups of enemies to fight, so Flash, Wonder Woman, and Green Arrow (a later member of the team) work together, while Aquaman, Green Lantern, and J'onn J'onzz separate to stop the other enemies. Finally, on many occasions, it's the case that only one of the heroes has the specific skills needed for that occasion. If an evildoer must be stopped with super speed, Flash is your man. If the villain is hiding something in a wall, Superman will need to use his X-ray vision. And if you need somebody to talk to a fish, there's only one candidate for the job.

Of course, although certainly the heroes within the JLA each have an individual role to play, what makes the JLA truly great is that it is, ultimately, a successful *group effort*. The JLA demonstrates teamwork while simultaneously allowing each individual to shine in *Justice League of America* #7, "The Cosmic Fun House!" Here, the JLA is frozen from action by energy-sapping spirals of power. To escape, Green Arrow throws a boomerang designed to catch Wonder Woman's magic lasso and bring it to her. However, The Flash sees that the boomerang is not going to make it all the way to the lasso, so he moves his hand super-quickly to create the necessary gust of wind. Wonder Woman then uses the lasso to release Green Arrow from his frozen and powerless state; finally, Green Arrow saves the rest of the team from being killed.

In a similar way, the JLA is good at avoiding the second mistake common in groups: not sharing information. The members of the JLA always fully divulge all the relevant facts to everyone on the team. Through the different volumes, different members are the ones to first learn about the various evil threats; each member always fully briefs the others before each fight. Even Snapper Carr, the annoying power-less human who is an "honorary" member of the JLA, does his part to inform the heroes of dangers on Earth (then he "helps" by snapping his fingers in the most irritating way possible). Clearly the members of the JLA value this brotherhood. They come together not only to fight evil, but they also gather for informal parties to celebrate occasions such as the anniversary of their first adventure together. What was the adventure, and why is it important for the team, according to social psychology?

MEMBERSHIP HAS ITS PRIVILEGES

Researchers in social psychology have studied the effects of initiation to groups. What makes someone value a group and willing to make sacrifices for that group? One answer is a brutal and effortful initiation. A famous study by Aronson and Mills in 1959 (just one year before the appearance of the Justice League of America) examined this question in a creative way. College women were asked to come into a research lab if they were interested in joining a discussion group about sex. In 1959, this was certainly not a common opportunity. The women were then assigned by the experimenters to go through either a light interview, a moderately annoying and lengthy interview, or a long and embarrassing series of ceremonies before being allowed access to the group. When all of the women were finally allowed to hear the group discussion, the researchers had designed the discussion to in actuality be excessively boring and dry (not exciting and controversial, as the women had expected). What happened? The women who had been allowed to join quickly and easily agreed that the group was uninteresting and were negative about continuing membership. However, the women who had been put through the long and effortful initiation stated that the discussion was exciting and interesting, and that they wanted to continue membership in this valuable group.

Other examples of this phenomenon can be seen in the hazing traditions typical of fraternities and sororities, as well as the harsh basic training required of new military personnel. Social psychology would praise these rituals (as long as they don't become illegal or unethical), because the field has established that the harder it is to join a group, the more the members of the group will value it and show loyalty. For the Justice League of America, this is easy to see. In *Justice League of America* #9, readers finally got to see the origin story of the group. On the planet Appellax, the ruler died leaving several beings who wanted to take over. To settle this, they decided to battle it out on Earth (so as to not destroy their own planet), with the winner being named the new Kalar (emperor) of Appellax. So each candidate headed to Earth in a meteor to take claim on a region of our planet. This led our individual superheroes to unknowingly fight just one being from this alien planet, risking life and limb as usual. However, it all changes when they each head off to fight the last being. Here, the evil alien uses his powers to cover the heroes with tree bark so that they can't move. It is only with teamwork that they win the day: Aquaman uses his strength to lurch against Green Lantern's tree-finger to scrape off the wood covering the power ring. Green Lantern then aims a beam of powerful light onto the Martian Manhunter, who blows his awesome Martian breath onto Wonder Woman, which gives her the strength needed to reach the magic lasso she uses to bind the nymph-like wood alien, and to swing at such a speed that the lasso breaks up the wood around the heroes into kindling.

Such a dangerous and frightening experience leads the heroes to affiliate with each other and appreciate each other, and to acknowledge the fact that it is the combination of group effort and individual powers that would make them unbeatable if they were to make the group official. Through the remaining adventures, the team is loyal, brave, and always concerned about the League itself—they value their membership and take pride in being a part of the greatest superhero group of all time. The group is a constant success. But the question arises in all groups: will the members feel lost in the crowd? Social psychology has an answer to this as well, in the theory called *optimal distinctiveness*.

NOT ALL GROUPS ARE CREATED EQUAL

Psychology suggests that there are just a few basic human motivations. One of these is the need to be recognized and respected as a unique individual. Another, however, is the need to be loved and be part of a group. How can these two motivations co-exist when they are essentially opposites of each other? The answer comes from a popular theory in social psychology called *optimal distinctiveness*. Marilyn Brewer, the creator of this theory, suggests that we can satisfy both needs simultaneously by becoming a member of a small, elite group.

By keeping the group small, we do not get lost in the crowd. We can see that the Justice League of America is very small, only admitting new members one at a time and only with a unanimous vote from the existing members ("Doom of the Star Diamond!" #4). In addition, each member wears a unique uniform. The fact that they all have a uniform shows that they are in an elite crowd (superheroes in general), but all the uniforms are different, establishing each member's independence and uniqueness.

Social psychology research on optimal distinctiveness has also shown that we prefer to be members of groups in which the other members share our basic values and beliefs, because this validates ourselves (Hogg and Mullin, 1999). Everyone in this group shares the motivation to fight evil, and they all agree that it is worth risking life itself to protect others. Finally, people enjoy being the member of a group that is recognized as positive and successful. Many educated people on Earth acknowledge that the JLA is the ultimate team of superheroes. However, the JLA's fame is not so limited—in several of their adventures they are targeted by extra-terrestrials who have also heard of their fame. A nice example is seen in *The Brave and the Bold* #29, "Challenge of the Weapons Master!" Here, the evil genius Xotar from the year 11,960 is fighting the police of his time, and he knows that only one of his fabulous weapons will work. Unfortunately, he doesn't know which weapon that is. Fortunately, however, he does have a time machine! So, he cleverly decides to travel back in time to fight the Justice League of America with his various weapons, knowing that if one of them can defeat the JLA, it should be no problem to use that weapon to stop the police. Why does Xotar choose the JLA? Because even 10,000 years in the future on a far distant planet, he knows that they are "the greatest team of crime-fighters in the history of the universe!" (2).

CONCLUSION

What makes the Justice League of America the "greatest crime-fighting team in the history of the universe?" There are certainly other teams of superheroes, such as the X-Men or the Fantastic Four. This leads us to social psychology's final contribution to this analysis: a discussion of leadership. What form of leadership guides the JLA, and how is it different from other superhero teams?

First, recall that social psychology was largely inspired by attempting to explain the atrocities that occurred before and during World War II. Immediately before the war, a man named Kurt Lewin immigrated to the U.S. and became (what is now widely accepted) the "father" of social psychology. Lewin wanted to understand how the German people could have been led astray by the powerful leadership of Hitler and the psychology of his regime. To do this, Lewin set up a now-famous experiment. He created three groups of boys who did similar tasks under three different types of leaders: autocratic (or fascist), democratic, and laissez-faire (or non-directive). Much to the delight of Americans, the democratic group of boys showed the best work and the best attitudes during the task and the autocratic group did the worst.

Interestingly, groups such as the X-Men or the Fantastic Four are more *autocratic* in their style—Professor Charles Xavier and Mr. Fantastic are clearly in charge, they made the decisions and they ordered around the other members. Granted, these leaders are wise and beneficent; however, the individual members who are not the leader feel the effects of this hierarchical system. In fact, social psychology would suggest that these groups are doomed to have problems such as infighting and group members feeling that they are not respected for their own individual efforts and talents. However, the Justice League of America is unique in that there is *no* single leader. In fact, the bylaws of the JLA require that the Chair position rotates for each assignment they take. In this way, every member of the League feels equal, promoting a truly supportive and empowering atmosphere. Although some members are considered to be more powerful than others—such as Superman—Superman in fact is often the *least* important member of the team, typically too busy doing his own missions to join the JLA, much less lead them. Instead, every single member has his or her chance to shine and to lead the entire group to success. This truly democratic and equal treatment of all members is certainly the ideal of the American way, and it is what makes the Justice League of America the unquestioned greatest superhero team of all time. The description we are given in *Justice League of America* #2, "Secret of the Sinister Sorcerers!" is therefore both accurate and compelling:

Crime-fighters beyond compare! Foes of all evil,
whether it comes from land, sea, or air!
Enemies of injustice and the terror of all wrong-doers—
these are the members of the Justice League of America!

Wind Goodfriend, Ph.D., is an assistant professor of psychology at Buena Vista University. She earned her Ph.D. in social psychology in 2004 from Purdue University. Her areas of research expertise are gender stereotypes and romantic relationships, focusing specifically on positive and negative predictors of relationship stability over time. In her final year of graduate school, Dr. Goodfriend received both the "Outstanding Teacher of the Year Award" and the "Outstanding Graduate Student of the Year Award" for her research. Since then, she has been nominated for and won several more research and teaching awards.

ACKNOWLEDGMENTS

Dr. Goodfriend would like to thank Clint Hughes and Ryan Harder for their help with this essay.

REFERENCES

E. Aronson and J. Mills, "The Effect of Severity of Initiation on Liking for a Group," *Journal of Abnormal and Social Psychology* 59 (1959): 177–181.

M. B. Brewer, "The Social Self: On Being the Same and Different at the Same Time," *Personality and Social Psychology Bulletin* 17 (1991): 475–482.

Fox, Gardner F. (w), Mike Sekowsky (p), and Bernard Sachs, Joe Giella, & Murphy Anderson (i). "Starro the Conquerer!" *The Brave and the Bold* #28. National Comics Publications (DC Comics): Mar.–Apr. 1960.

Fox, Gardner F. (w), Mike Sekowsky (p), and Bernard Sachs (i). "Secret of the Sinister Sorcerers!" *The Justice League of America* #2. National Comics Publications (DC Comics): Dec. 1960–Jan. 1961.

Fox, Gardner F. (w), Mike Sekowsky (p), and Bernard Sachs (i). "Doom of the Star Diamond!" *The Justice League of America* #4. National Comics Publications (DC Comics): Apr.–May 1961.

Fox, Gardner F. (w), Mike Sekowsky (p), and Bernard Sachs (i). "When

Gravity Went Wild!" *The Justice League of America* #5. National Comics Publications (DC Comics): June–July 1961.

Fox, Gardner F. (w), Mike Sekowsky (p), and Bernard Sachs (i). "The Cosmic Fun-House!" *The Justice League of America* #7. National Comics Publications (DC Comics): Oct.–Nov. 1961.

Fox, Gardner F. (w), Mike Sekowsky (p), and Bernard Sachs (i). "The Origin of the Justice League!" *The Justice League of America* #9. National Comics Publications (DC Comics): Feb. 1962.

M. A. Hogg and B. A. Mullen, "Joining Groups to Reduce Uncertainty: Subjective Uncertainty Reduction and Group Identification," In D. Abrams and M. A. Hogg (Eds.), *Social Identity and Social Cognition* (pp. 249–279). Malden, MA: Blackwell, 1999.

K. Lewin, R. Lippit, and R. K. White, "Patterns of Aggressive Behavior in Experimentally Created Social Climates," *Journal of Social Psychology* 10 (1939): 271–301.

THE PSYCHOLOGY OF SUPERHEROES

Robin S. Rosenberg, Ph.D.

SUPERMAN'S PERSONALITY: FROM KRYPTON, KANSAS, OR BOTH?

How much of Superman's—and Clark Kent's—personality arises from innate qualities he inherited from his Kryptonian parents and how much of his personality was formed by his upbringing with the Kents on a farm in Kansas? What would Superman be like if his rocket had landed near New York City and he was raised there—how different would he be? In this essay, Rosenberg explores the answers to these and related questions about Superman's personality as seen through the lens of psychological research on these topics and provides an explanation for why Superman's simplistic morality: good versus evil, right versus wrong. She examines the influence of his biology, his adoptive family, his peers, and the community in which he was raised.

AFTER VIEWING *SUPERMAN RETURNS* with my children and their friends, we got to talking about Superman's character. I mused, "Imagine if Superman had been raised in New York City—what

would he be like?" How much of Superman's—and Clark Kent's—
personality was shaped by his biology, his *temperament*—his innate
tendencies to respond to emotional stimuli in particular ways? How
much of his personality was shaped by the values of his adoptive parents, Martha and Jonathan Kent, and of his rural Kansas upbringing?
How did his temperament and environment interact?

As a clinical psychologist, I've spent time reading and thinking
about how people become who they are, and how much of who people are can be modified. Let me review some psychological research
that tells us about how people's personalities are formed, and then
examine how such knowledge might apply to Superman's personality.

First, though, let's address the matter of the different versions of
Superman that have arisen over the years: the various incarnations
born in different eras, with different storylines from more than sixty
years of comics, radio, television shows, and movies. I'm going to focus on the important common elements among most versions:

- Kal-el—as Superman was known on Krypton—was well-loved
  by his very smart birth parents, Jor-el and Lara. His father, Jor-
  el, had a strong moral sense, valued life, and tried to use his talents for the good of his planet.
- Kal-el had the good fortune to be adopted by loving, sensible
  people—Martha and Jonathan Kent—who named him Clark. By
  all accounts, Clark was a well-behaved, responsible boy, an only
  child who listened to his parents, both about how he should behave, and also about the life lessons they tried to impart. He was
  close to his adoptive parents, confiding in them, spending time
  with them as a family and as a team member working the farm.
- The bulk of Clark's powers emerged with the onset of puberty,
  although the specific age varies with each origin story. During
  his teenage years, Clark's father gave him two important pieces
  of advice:

  (1) "You must uphold law and order, and those in need, and
  save lives!" (*Superman* #146) or more generally, as Martha Kent
  said in 1939, "assist humanity" (*Superman* #1).

  (2) Clark should "hide his strengths from others so they won't

be afraid of him" (*Superman* #1). Other versions of this admonition are that he should develop a different identity when doing good, so that people wouldn't try to threaten his family as a way to manipulate him.

- Superman didn't come into being until Clark moved to Metropolis.[1]

In this essay, I will focus on ways that psychological research can address the degree to which Clark's—and Superman's—personality was relatively fixed (versus malleable). In other words, in what ways would he be the same and different had he grown up in New York or some other place?

TEMPERAMENT: BEHAVIORAL ACTIVATION AND INHIBITION SYSTEMS

As anyone who's ever taken care of an infant knows, infants are not born blank slates. They come with their own character. Some babies are "fussy" or "difficult," some are "easy" or "mellow." Some babies are interested in meeting new people, others are shy. Some children respond best to reward, others respond best to punishment. All of these characteristics arise from temperaments—innate tendencies to respond to stimuli in particular ways. These qualities frequently endure over time.

From where does an individual's temperament arise? The biggest influence on temperament is biology—how our brains and bodies respond to stimuli—and genetics play a substantial role (Bouchard et al.; Bouchard; Loehlin). Biology sets the range of possible temperaments an individual can have, and the environment (that is, life's experiences) nudges the individual in one direction or another along his or her set range (Kagan et al.).

The most fundamental types of temperament involve the behavioral activation system and the behavioral inhibition system, each of

---

[1] I am not considering Superboy in this essay, nor will I address which is the "real" person–Clark or Superman–and which is the alter ego. As originally conceived by Siegel and Shuster, Superman was generally considered to be the authentic self and Clark Kent the alter ego. This reversed in 1986 with John Byrne's "reboot" of the series (*Man of Steel*).

which involve different neurotransmitter systems and specific brain areas (Davidson, 1992a, b; Gray, 1982, 1987, 1991). The *behavioral activation system* (BAS) is the biological system that motivates us to approach stimuli—to seek out and engage with the world; the BAS also initiates positive feelings and is activated when we respond to rewards or incentives. Some people have a BAS that is more easily activated than others—such people are more responsive to rewards and incentives—even small ones (Meyer et al.). The BAS is associated with sociability, a tendency to prefer to be in the company of others versus to be alone; people who have an easily activated BAS are more likely to be outgoing people and seek out novel stimuli.

In contrast, the *behavioral inhibition system* (BIS) is the biological system that motivates us to withdraw from or avoid stimuli; the BIS also initiates anxiety and is activated when we respond to punishment or threats. Some people have a BIS that is more easily activated than others—such people are more responsive to punishment or threatening stimuli; they are more likely to become distressed or anxious in response to even small threats and may be generally anxious or depressed (Johnson et al.; Kasch et al.). People with a relatively unresponsive BIS are not likely to feel much distress, even when the threat is considerable (Carver & White; Carver et al.; Heponiemi et al.; Meyer et al.). Even in infancy it is possible to discern individual differences in responsiveness (Fox et al.; Kagan, et al.).

Let's examine what might apply to Superman's BAS, assuming that Kryptonian temperament is similar to that of humans: Superman is not generally depicted as a social butterfly. He more than tolerates spending time alone in his apartment, in the Fortress of Solitude, or flying about in outer space. Although he responds to particular rewards, such as the thanks of those he's helped and the knowledge that he's done the right thing, he's not responsive to all rewards. As his biological mother, Lara, remarks in the movie, *Superman II*:

> "You have been given a higher form of happiness. The happiness you feel by serving others..."

He can't be corrupted by the lure of other incentives that work for most people: pleasure, power, money, fame. This suggests that he doesn't have an *over-responsive* BAS. Moreover, Superman responds well to other people's faith and trust in him. For instance, in one comic book issue, Superman—temporarily blind and without superpowers—was treated as a slave and had given up hope. Another blind slave admonished him not to give up hope; he'd heard that a Super-man would free all the slaves.

> "The faith of that blind man suddenly gives Superman new courage, new determination." (*Superman* #155)

What about his BIS? Superman isn't prone to depression or anxiety; his emotions are generally on an even keel (thank goodness— imagine an impulsive, irritable, or depressed Superman!), indicating that his BIS isn't over-responsive. Of course he displays annoyance and irritation—even anger, but it's clear that he's in control of his anger. No road rage from this superhero.

Moreover, like most superheroes, Superman tends to seek out— rather than run away from or avoid—situations that most of us would consider threatening, indicating an *under-responsive* BIS. You may be saying to yourself that situations that humans consider threatening *aren't* threatening to Superman, so his reactions to those situations aren't a valid indicator of his BIS. Here's the thing, though: Even when Superman knows that he might be harmed (e.g., when there's kryptonite involved), he *still* seeks out threatening situations if someone is in danger.[2]

ATTACHMENT STYLE

One area of personality development that isn't particularly influenced by biology, but rather by the family environment, is social closeness—a desire for intimacy with others (Tellegen et al.). Our style of relating to other people we are close to, our *attachment style* (Bowlby), begins in infancy and continues into adulthood.

---

[2] A temperament is a *tendency* to behave in certain ways, not a guaranteed forecast. Someone with an easily activated BIS can, when motivated, learn to overcome his or her innate tendency to withdraw or avoid threatening stimuli. Perhaps Bruce Wayne (Batman's alter ego) had an over-responsive BIS, but learned to counteract this tendency. That question, however, is beyond the scope of this essay.

In the 1970s, psychologist Mary Ainsworth (Ainsworth et al.) developed a method—called the "Strange Situation"—to assess children's style of attachment to their mothers. Mother and toddler come to the researcher's lab; in this novel situation, the mother leaves briefly, and the child is either alone or left with a stranger. How the child handles her departure and her return determine the attachment style. Researchers noted three attachment styles, each of which persists into childhood (Hazan and Shaver):

1. *Secure attachment*: The child will leave mother's side to explore the toys in the room; when mother leaves, the child can't be soothed by a stranger, but is quickly soothed by her upon her return. In adulthood, people with a secure attachment desire closeness and aren't preoccupied by whether the relationship might end at some point.
2. *Resistant/anxious attachment*: The child stays close to mother, and becomes angry when she leaves and when she returns— even hitting her upon her return. The child isn't quickly soothed when she returns. In adulthood, such people both want but fear closeness in a relationship.
3. *Avoidant attachment*: Whether the mother is present or absent, the child behaves the same—neither noticing nor caring whether she or a stranger is there. Because the child isn't agitated when the mother leaves, there is no need for soothing. In adulthood, people with this attachment style aren't comfortable with intimacy and closeness, and so they avoid it.

The attachment style guides what the child—and later the adult— pays attention to and remembers, and how the child—and later adult—interprets and makes sense of the world. If the parent is responsive, the child comes to expect others to be responsive; if the parent is neglectful or abusive, that's what the child comes to expect of others.

How does this apply to Clark? We can infer that he was securely attached to his Kryptonian mother, Lara; had he not been, he would not have become similarly attached to the Kents and had such a loving relationship with them. Clark seems to have been an easy child to love, also indicating a secure attachment. As an adult, Clark doesn't fear or avoid closeness: he has friends, and very much desires an emotionally—and sexually—intimate relationship with Lois.[3]

The Kents's powerful influence on Clark's personality was clear from the very first issue of *Superman* comics (#1) in 1939:

> "The love and guidance of his kindly foster-parents was to become an important factor in the shaping of the boy's future."

BIRTH ORDER

Another environmental factor that impacts personality is birth order. On Krypton, Kal-el was an only child, and in the Kent household he continued to be an only child—how might this have shaped his personality? Only children are similar to first-borns in that they are more likely to support the status quo, in contrast to younger-borns, who are generally more open to new ideas, including political and scientific revolutions. Eldests see things as their parents do, and they are more assertive and dominant, more responsible and conscientious, and more ambitious (Beer and Horn; Sulloway 1996, 1999); they are also more anxious. Older and younger children tend to be closer with their families than middle-borns (Salmon; Salmon and Daly). However, these birth order-related personality characteristics are not true in all cases—they are modified by the particulars of a child's temperament and relationship with family members (Sulloway, 1996).

Many of these characteristics apply to Clark/Superman: he's generally polite (even while rounding up the bad guys), assertive, and can dominate situations (even among his superhero colleagues in the Justice League). He supports the existing social order, and his belief in the criminal justice system is touching, if naïve. And Superman is conscientious. As villains sometimes joke, he is a super-boy scout. Somehow it's hard to imagine him turning out the same were he a younger brother.

---

[3] Since the reboot, such a relationship does evolve, and Lois and Clark married in 1996.

GROWING UP INVULNERABLE

What might it be like to go through the teenage years knowing you are invulnerable? To know, as Clark did, that you're smarter, stronger, and faster than everyone else, and that you can't get hurt? How might such knowledge have affected his developing personality? In order to answer these questions, let's examine the closest that psychological research can come: studying "gifted" children—children who are exceptionally bright. According to studies that have compared gifted children in regular classrooms (where they are, metaphorically, big fish in small ponds) to those in special programs or schools for gifted children, the gifted students in regular classrooms ("big fish") have a better academic self-concept than their counterparts in gifted programs (Chessor and Whitton; Marsh and Hau; Marsh et al.; Zeidner and Schleyer, 1999a). This phenomenon is called the *big fish little pond effect*, and similar results have been found in the athletic realm, with athletically gifted people (Chanal et al.).

How might this effect come about? Gifted students, like all of us, compare their abilities to those of people around them, and they use these comparisons to create their self-concept—their view of themselves. When around people who are less able, their self-concept will be higher than when around people who are more able. Those who feel that they are more able are likely to perform better, and persevere more often (Marsh; Parker).[4]

But being gifted—and being *aware* of being gifted—comes at a cost: the high likelihood of being ostracized and rejected by peers. Children and adolescents tend to value conformity, and so gifted children and adolescents hide the full extent of their abilities, holding themselves back; they wear a "mask" that makes them appear less able (Gross; Swiatek). In one study, for instance, academically gifted middle-schoolers avoided activities in which their abilities would stand out, instead undertaking activities in the arts or athletics, where they weren't particularly gifted (Buescher and Hingham).

---

[4] Although some people interpret these results to mean that gifted students are better off in regular classrooms than gifted classrooms or programs, there are other factors to consider, such as a gifted student's likelihood of boredom, and resulting underachievement, when in a regular classroom (Plucker et al.).

Often the mask works, then, but it leaves the gifted child hesitant to reveal his or her true gifted self for fear of rejection.

In almost any version of Superman's origins, some of Clark's superpowers emerge with puberty, and his powers—or his discovery of them—increase with his age: "By the time young Clark is a grown boy, he has learned that he is different from others," leaping over buildings, outrunning fast animals, and "a thousand other startling feats" (*More Fun Comics* #101). When contemplating his abilities, Clark realized (*More Fun Comics* #101),

> "I can't let people know how different I am! I'll just have to hold myself in check and go along like all the other kids."

Later, in his room, Clark reflected,

> "Super strength! It's a little frightening…my powers give me the chance to do a lot of good—but I can't let people know that Clark Kent can do these things…the knowledge might be dangerous."

His mask continues into adulthood. College student Clark looked at the college football team practicing and lamented,

> "I could be the world's greatest football player…but I can't join the team and reveal my super-powers! Besides, it would be unfair to win that way! I'll have to pretend I'm 'meek' and 'unathletic' all my life!" (*Superman* #146)

The experience of being gifted among peers likely leads Clark to be aware that, as Superman—someone with superior abilities—he can never be fully accepted. In the movie, *Superman Returns*, he says as much to his sleeping son,

> "You will be different, sometimes you'll feel like an outcast."

Humans can become envious of his abilities. Although citizens may be grateful for his interventions and assistance, Superman isn't human. He lives "in the closet," acting a part much of the time. Yet he wants to be connected to others—wants to belong. Perhaps this is why Superman is generally so humble. As Superman explained to Batman about why he didn't join a version of the Justice League (*Batman & Superman: World's Finest* #69):

> "…sometimes I wish I **had** joined. To have people to **talk** to….to share my problems and worries with…someone who would **understand** them. Colleagues. **Friends**. I think that's what **all** of us want— don't **you**?" [emphasis in original]

Later he added that he didn't join,

> "Not because I was too **busy**…but because if I joined, they'd be **too powerful**. People fear anything…anyone who's too powerful. I work…**so hard** to make sure people trust me…." [emphasis in original] (75)

Perhaps his moral simplicity is part of his mask, making him seem predictable and trustworthy so humans aren't afraid of him.

GIFTED MORALITY

Children who are intellectually gifted also have a more advanced sense of moral development (Gross, 1993; Silverman; Terman). They can empathize and feel compassion and be concerned about moral and ethical issues at a younger age. Yet one of the remarkable aspects of Superman, superpowers aside, is his two-dimensional moral view of the world—good versus evil. He rarely appears to wrestle with the moral implications of his crime-fighting behavior. Perhaps this *apparent* overly simplistic morality is a holdover from his youth: He saw complexity in moral situations when his peers couldn't, so now he frames moral situations for others as he believes they'll be able to understand them—in black and white.

Superman leaves no doubt about his morality in this first "interview" of Superman by Lois, in a version of the script for *Superman I*:

> LOIS: Let's just say your average Joe can't deliver an airmail letter without putting a stamp on it.
> SUPERMAN: I wouldn't do that. It's against the law.

LOIS (to herself): I don't believe this...
SUPERMAN: I never lie.

Maybe he just doesn't realize that many adults are capable of complex moral reasoning.

Or perhaps Superman—by virtue of his giftedness—perceives that the best way for him to lead by example is by providing a simple, crystal clear guide so that the "right path" is easy for humans to figure and apply in their own lives. As Jor-el says to him in the Fortress of Solitude (*Superman I*):

"They [humans] can be a great people, Kal-el, they wish to be. They only lack the light to show the way. For this reason above all, their capacity for good, I have sent them you... my only son."

Maybe Superman's simplistic morality is a façade, providing a "light to show the way." His actions are straightforward, predictable, and clear, and provide moral guideposts that are easy to remember. In an episode from the *Lois and Clark* television series, ("Big Girls Don't Cry"), when Superman is about to leave Earth for an indefinite period he says to the world:

"Emerson said, 'self-trust is the essence of heroism.' Inside each of you is a hero. And so, I leave knowing that a world full of heroes has nothing to fear."

Were his moral behavior more nuanced, it would be difficult for humans to discern right from wrong and behave accordingly in a given situation.

I would also argue that his intellectual gifts have allowed him to learn a lot about human nature. He realizes that he "serves" at the will of the people. Humans allow Superman free reign *because* his moral behavior is simplistic and, therefore, predictable. People aren't nervous that he will become a super-vigilante; if they were, Superman might well become an alien specimen in a lab.[5]

---

[5] A version of this occurred in *Superman #3*, "Secret Identity" 2004, K. Busiek.

YOU ARE WHERE YOU LIVE: CULTURE AND VALUES

So far, we can see how Clark's personality has been influenced by biology (his temperament), by his family (his birth order, his attachment style), and his peers (the effects of being gifted and then wearing a "mask" around others). Let's examine how the community he grew up in may have influenced his personality: as a member of a farm family in Kansas, versus as a New Yorker. Could Clark, or Superman, have become the same person if he grew up in New York?[6]

One area of research that sheds some light on the subject is personality differences across cultures. What constitutes "ideal" personality traits aren't the same in each culture. Social scientists have classified two different types of ideal personalities, depending on the culture (Hui and Triandis): *Collectivist* cultures value getting along with others. The individual is expected to defer his or her own goals to those of the group. Asian, Latin American, and Middle Eastern countries are generally considered to have collectivist cultures.

At the other end of the continuum are *individualist* cultures, which value autonomy, self-reliance, assertiveness, and independence. The individual's goals take precedence over the goals of the group. Australia, Canada, the United Kingdom, and the United States are generally considered to have individualist cultures.

Kansas

Within a country, different regions can differ on where they fall on the individualist-collectivist continuum. For instance, Midwestern farming communities, like the one in which Clark grew up, tend to value collectivist qualities—otherwise the crops would never be brought in. Teenagers from farm families report that they value hard work, self-reliance, a sense of responsibility, a commitment to family, and trust in others (Elder and Conger). Sound like Clark?

There are a host of differences between farm children and their urban or suburban counterparts: Farm children report feeling more positively toward their siblings and parents (Elder and Conger), they're less likely to have adolescent "rebellions" (Salamon, 1992),

---

[6] My comment is not meant *at all* as an insult to New York City, where I was born and raised.

they're less materialistic (Friedberger), and they're less likely to be depressed (Elder, King, and Conger). How might these values and preferences be instilled in teenagers?

- *Children have many opportunities to absorb the values of their families.* Farm children, compared to other children, spend more time with their families—even in teenage years (Larson and Dearmont). Grandparents and other extended family members are more likely to help with childcare than their urban counterparts, making formal childcare less necessary (King and Elder). This higher level of family time provides more opportunities for adults to model, teach, and support the values they care about: honesty, loyalty, hard work, and self-reliance (Ayalon; Salamon, 1995).
- *Children's efforts on the farm make a meaningful contribution and are appreciated.* They begin helping out on the farm at a young age, and as they get older their responsibilities increase (Elder and Conger). They are seen—and see themselves—as integral members of a team.
- *Collectivism in action.* Farm children, and farm families generally, are expected to make personal sacrifices for the sake of the family business. For instance, during planting and harvesting times, everyone puts all other activities aside in order to complete these high-priority tasks (Elder, King, and Conger; Larson and Dearmont). And when members of other farm families fall ill, a child may be asked to help that family with their farm temporarily (Conger and Elder).

It's easy to see the influence of these farm family values on Superman's personality. He clearly has many collectivist values—he puts the needs of others (the entire planet!) ahead of his own.

New York City

But what about a New York Clark Kent? I envision him as cosmopolitan, worldly wise, and world-weary. A New York-raised Superman would know better than to let his worst criminals live—he wouldn't be the naïve, moralistic superguy from Kansas, but would instead be a pragmatist, a realist who believes:

- *truth* can be a relative term, and sometimes withholding the truth serves a greater good;
- *justice*, although a great guiding principle, doesn't always materialize;
- *the American way* can be an amorphous concept, and is there really national consensus about what that would be anyway?

This New York Superman that I envision reminds me a little bit of— Batman! Weird!

It turns out, though, that New York City, with its diverse socioeconomic groups (and ethnic groups, which I won't go into here), has no single "New York" set of values. The personality traits that are valued and encouraged vary across families, depending on the social class, personal and religious beliefs, and values that a particular family holds. Neighborhoods can be proxies for those values.

One study investigated the values that mothers from three different New York City neighborhoods wanted to impart to their preschool children (Kusserow):

Upper East Side, Manhattan. This was an upper-middle and upper class professional neighborhood. Most mothers in the study had professional degrees and worked at least part time, and the children were always supervised by adults (versus older children). These mothers wanted their children to:

- Have self-confidence;
- Be assertive, and not back down when they thought they were right;
- Be aware of their own uniqueness;
- Be aware of their preferences, desires, and feelings.

Compared to the other two groups, the mothers in this group were particularly attentive to the children's emotional life; they believed that as children discover their passions, they will be motivated to do work that they love, leading them to be happy and fulfilled. Rather than command the children, they preferred to explain and suggest, letting children arrive at their own conclusions; the preschool teachers did the same thing. These mothers and teachers worried about hurting their children's feelings, and didn't view the children as emotionally resilient.

Beach Channel, Queens. At the time the study was done, this community was generally a white, working class neighborhood where families were often distantly related to each other. These mothers wanted their children to:

- Forge their own path;
- Succeed;
- Have self-confidence;
- Persevere and give their all—to school work and to athletics.

These mothers believed that through hard work, their children could achieve. Specific parenting behaviors to meet these goals included encouragement, empathy, and trying to ensure that their children got into a good school, which the children could then utilize to the fullest.

South Rockaway, Queens. This was a "rough" racially mixed, lower-middle class neighborhood; the mothers in this group were frequently single mothers who had overcome various hardships—substance abuse, maltreatment—and believed that, for them and for their children, life was a struggle. These mothers wanted their children to:

- Remain safe in a rough neighborhood; in order to do so, they believed that the children should:
  - learn the hard truths about the world around them;
  - mind their own business;
  - toughen up, persevere, and become self-reliant;
  - not trust anyone but themselves;
- Respond to strict discipline.

These mothers limited their praise because they didn't want their children to get "too full" of themselves. It was the same with the pre-school teachers: they teased the children so that the kids would learn to defend themselves, not melt into tears. Both mothers and teachers didn't necessarily respond immediately to children's cries, and children were praised when they did things on their own.

Of the values in the three New York neighborhoods, the South

Rockaway one seems most likely to yield personality traits of the jaded, worldly wise Clark Kent I envisioned; but this assumes that his adoptive parents would have similar values to the South Rockaway mothers. In order to have a jaded Clark Kent, then, he couldn't have been raised by the Kents—at least not the way they have been portrayed in the Superman material. It's also clear, though, that there is no monolithic "New York Superman."

CONCLUSION

So how different would Superman be if he had grown up in a different part of the country?[7] It would depend on the personal and moral values of his adoptive parents, influenced, in part, by their socioeconomic status. These values would influence which behaviors are modeled, explicitly taught, and reinforced.

If the Kents were his parents, I propose that his personality wouldn't be too different. His temperament, birth order position, attachment style, and "giftedness" would all remain the same. The Kents' values—and the values they would instill in Clark—would undoubtedly remain the same no matter where they lived. The key, then, is the Kents, not the locale.

> **Robin S. Rosenberg, Ph.D.**, is a clinical psychologist and co-author of *Psychology in Context* and *Fundamentals of Psychology* (introductory psychology textbooks) and *Abnormal Psychology: The Neuropsychosocial Approach* (abnormal psychology textbook). Her first foray into applying psychological theories and research to popular culture figures was for *The Psychology of Harry Potter: An Unathorized Exploration of the Boy Who Lived.* She has taught psychology courses at Lesley University and Harvard University and has a private practice in the Boston area. She can be found at drrobinrosenberg.com.

---

[7] People at DC Comics have also wondered about what Superman would be like if he grew up elsewhere. In 2004, they published *Superman: Red Son*, which places the Kryptonian rocket's landing site in the Ukraine, in a Soviet Union led by Stalin. Superman's powers begin to emerge with puberty, and he grows up to fight "a never-ending battle for Stalin, socialism, and the international expansion of the Warsaw Pact."

ACKNOWLEDGMENTS

The author wishes to thank David Kosslyn, Justin Kosslyn, Neil Kosslyn, and Irene Segal Ayers for their incisive and helpful comments on an earlier version of this essay.

REFERENCES

Ainsworth, Mary D. S., M. C. Blehar, E. Waters, and S. Wahl. *Patterns of Attachment: A Psychological Study of the Strange Situation.* Hillsdale, NJ: Erlbaum, 1978.

A. Ayalon, "Does Multicultural Education Belong in Rural White America?," *Rural Educator* 16.3 (1995): 1–6.

J. M. Beer and J. M. Horn, "The Influence of Rearing Order on Personality Development within Two Adoption Cohorts," *Journal of Personality* 68 (2000): 789–819.

Bernstein, Robert (w), George Papp (i). "The Secret of Mon-el." *Superboy* #89. National Comics Publications (DC Comics): 1961. "Big Girls Don't Cry." *Lois & Clark: The New Adventures of Superman.* Episode 22, Dirs. Neal Ahern, Jr. and Michael Vejar. ABC, 1996.

Binder, Otto (w), Al Plastino (i). "The Complete Story of Superman's Life." *Superman* #146. (DC Comics): 1961.

T. J. Bouchard, Jr., "Genes, Environment, and Personality," *Science* 264 (1994): 1700–1701.

T. J. Bouchard, Jr., D. T. Lykken, M. McGue, N. L. Segal, and A. Tellegen, "Sources of Human Psychological Differences: The Minnesota Study of Twins Reared Apart," *Science* 250 (1990): 223–228.

Bowlby, J. *Attachment.* Vol. 1 of *Attachment and Loss.* New York: Basic Books, 1969.

T. M. Buescher, and S. J. Hingham, "A Developmental Study of Adjustment Among Gifted Adolescents," in *Patterns of Influence on Gifted Learners: The Home, the Self, and the School*, eds. J. L. VanTassel-Baska and P. Olszewski-Kubilius (New York: Teachers College Press, 1989), 102–124.

Busiek, Kurt (w) and Stuart Immonen (i) *Superman: Secret Identity.* National Comics Publications (DC Comics): 2004.

Byrne, John and Dick Giordano. *Superman: The Man of Steel, Volume 1.* DC Comics. October 1986.

C. S. Carver, B. Meyer, M. H. Antoni, "Responsiveness to Threats and Incentives Expectancy of Recurrence and Distress and Disengagement: Moderator Effects in Early-stage Breast Cancer Patients," *Journal of Consulting and Clinical Psychology* 68 (2000): 965–975.

C. S. Carver, and T. L. White, "Behavioral Inhibition, Behavioral Activation, and Affective Responses to Impending Reward and Punishment: The BIS/BAS Scales," *Journal of Personality and Social Psychology* 67 (1994): 319–333.

J. P. Chanal, H. W. Marsh, P. G. Sarrazin, J. E. Bois, "Big-Fish-Little-Pond Effects on Gymnastics Self-Concept: Social Comparison Processes in a Physical Setting," *Journal of Sport & Exercise Psychology* 27 (2005): 53–70.

D. Chessor, and D. Whitton, "The Impact of Grouping Gifted Primary School Students on Self-Concept, Motivation and Achievement from Parents' Perspectives," *Australian Journal of Guidance & Counselling* 15 (2005): 93–104.

Conger, R. D. and G. H. Elder, Jr. *Families in Troubled Times: Adapting to Change in Rural America.* New York: Aldine de Gruyter, 1994.

R. J. Davidson, "Emotion and Affective Style: Hemispheric Substrates," *Psychological Science* 3 (1992a): 39–43.

R. J. Davidson, "A Prolegomenon to the Structure of Emotion: Gleanings from Neuropsychology," *Cognition and Emotion* 6 (1992b): 245–268.

Elder, G., and R. Conger. *Children of the Land: Adversity and Success in Rural America.* Chicago: University of Chicago Press, 2000.

G. H. Elder, Jr., V. King, and R. D. Conger, "Intergenerational Continuity and Change in Rural Lives: Historical and Developmental Insights," *International Journal of Behavioral Development* 19 (1996): 433–455.

Friedberger, M. *Shake-out: Iowa Farm Families in the 1980s.* Lexington, KY: University Press of Kentucky, 1989.

Finger, Bill (w) and Wayne Boring (i). *Supeman* #155. National Comics Publications (DC Comics): 1962.

E. Fox, R. Russo, R. Bowles, and K. Dutton, "Do Threatening Stimuli Draw or Hold Attention in Subclinical Anxiety?," *Journal of Experimental Psychology General* 130 (2001): 681–700.

J. A. Gray, "Précis of the Neuropsychology of Anxiety: An Enquiry into the Functions of the Septo-hippocampal System," *Behavioral & Brain Sciences* 5 (1982): 469–534.

J. A. Gray, "Perspectives on Anxiety and Impulsiveness: A Commentary," *Journal of Research in Personality* 21 (1987): 493–509.

J. A. Gray, "The Neuropsychology of Temperament," in *Explorations in*

Temperament: International Perspectives on Theory and Measurement, eds. J. Strelau and A. Angleitner (New York: Plenum Press, 1991), 105–128.

J. R. Gray, "A Bias toward Short-term Thinking in Threat-related Negative Emotional States," *Personality and Social Psychology Bulletin* 25 (1999): 65–75.

Gross, M.U.M. *Exceptionally Gifted Children*. New York: Routledge, 1993.

M. U. M. Gross, "The 'Me' behind the Mask: Intellectually Gifted Students and the Search for Identity," *Roeper Review* 20 (1998): 167–174.

C. Hazan, and P. R. Shaver, "Romantic Love Conceptualized as an Attachment Process," *Journal of Personality and Social Psychology* 52 (1987): 511–524.

T. Heponiemi, L. Keltikangas-Järvinen, S. Puttonen, and N. Ravaja, "BIS/BAS Sensitivity and Self-rated Affects During Experimentally Induced Stress," *Personality & Individual Differences* 34 (2003): 943–957.

C. H. Hui, and H. C. Triandis, "Individualism-collectivism: A Study of Crosscultural Researchers," *Journal of Cross-cultural psychology* 17 (1986): 225–248.

S. L. Johnson, R. J. Turner, and N. Iwata, "BIS/BAS levels and Psychiatric Disorder: An Epidemiological Study," *Journal of Psychopathology & Behavioral Assessment* 25 (2003): 25–36.

J. Kagan, J. S. Reznick, and N. Snidman, "Biological Bases of Childhood Shyness," *Science* 240 (1988): 167–171.

Kagan, J., Snidman, N., Arcus, D., and J. S. Reznick. *Galen's Prophecy: Temperament in Human Nature*. New York, NY: Basic Books, 1994.

K. L. Kasch, J. Rottenberg, B. A. Arnow, and I. H. Gotlib, "Behavioral Activation and Inhibition Systems and the Severity and Course of Depression," *Journal of Abnormal Psychology* 111 (2002): 589–597.

A.S. Kusserow, "De-homogenizing American Individualism: Socializing Hard and Soft Individualism in Manhattan and Queens," *Ethos* 27 (1999): 210–234.

M. Lamont, J. Kaufman, and M. Moody, M., "The Best of the Brightest: Definitions of the Ideal Self among Prize-winning Students," *Sociological Forum* 15 (2000): 187–224.

N. C. Larson and M. Dearmont, "Strengths of Farming Communities in Fostering Resilience in Children," *Child Welfare Journal* 81 (2002): 821–835.

Loehlin, J. C. *Genes and Environment in Personality Development*. Newbury Park, CA: Sage, 1992.

D. T. Lykken, "The Mechanism of Emergenesis," *Genes, Brain & Behavior* 5 (2006): 306–310.

H.W. Marsh, "Multidimensional Physical Self-concept: A Construct Validity Approach to Theory, Measurement, and Research," *Psychology, The Journal of the Hellenic Psychological Society* 9 (2002): 459–493.

H. W. Marsh, K. Hau, "Big-Fish—Little-Pond Effect on Academic Self-concept: A Cross-Cultural (26-country) Test of the Negative Effects of Academically Selective Schools," *American Psychologist* 58 (2003): 364–376.

H. W. Marsh, J. Hey, L. A. Roche, and C. Perry, "Structure of Physical self-concept: Elite Athletes and Physical Education Students," *Journal of Educational Psychology* 89 (1997): 369–380.

H. W. Marsh, C. Perry, C. Horsely, and L. Roche, "Multidimensional Self-concepts of Elite Athletes: How Do They Differ from the General Population?," *Journal of Sport & Exercise Psychology* 17 (1995): 70–83.

B.Meyer, L. Olivier, and D. A. Roth, "Please Don't Leave Me! BIS/BAS, Attachment Styles, and Responses to a Relationship Threat," *Personality and Individual Differences* 38 (2005): 151–162.

Millar, Mark. *Red Son.* DC Comics: 2004.

More Fun Comics #101. DC Comics: 1945.

Kesel, Karl. *Batman & Superman: World's Finest.* DC Comics: 2003.

S. K. Parker, "Enhancing Role Breadth Self-efficacy: The Roles of Job Enrichment and Other Organizational Interventions," *Journal of Applied Psychology* 83 (1998): 835–852.

J. A. Plucker, N. M. Robinson, T. S. Greenspon, J. F. Feldhusen, D. B. McCoach, and R. F. Subotnik, "It's Not How the Pond Makes You Feel, but Rather How High You Can Jump," *American Psychologist* 59 (2004): 268–269.

Salamon, S. *Prairie Patrimony: Family, Farming, and Community in the Midwest.* Chapel Hill, NC: University of North Carolina Press, 1992.

Salamon, S., "The Rural People of the Midwest," In E. Castle (Ed.), *The Changing American Countryside: Rural People and Places* (pp. 352–365). Lawrence: University Press of Kansas, 1995.

C. A. Salmon, "The Evocative Nature of Kin Terminology in Political Rhetoric," *Politics and the Life Sciences* 17 (1998): 51–57.

C. A. Salmon, and M. Daly, "Birth Order and Familial Sentiment: Middleborns are Different," *Evolution and Behavior* 19 (1998): 299–312.

Siegel, Jerry and Joe Shuster. *Superman* #1. DC Comics: 1939.

Silverman, L.K. *Counseling the Gifted and Talented.* Denver; Love, 1993.

Sulloway, F. J. *Born to Rebel: Birth Order, Family Dynamics, and Creative Lives.* New York: Vintage, 1996.

Sulloway, F. J. "Birth order," In M. A. Runco & S. Pritzker (Eds.) *Encyclopedia of Creativity* 1. 1999. 189–202.

Superman I. Dir. Richard Donner. Perf. Christopher Reeve, Margo Kidder, Gene Hackman. Warner Bros. 1978.

Superman II. Dir. Richard Lester. Perf. Christopher Reeve, Margo Kidder, Gene Hackman. Warner Bros. 1980.

Superman Returns. Dir. Bryan Singer. Perf. Brandon Rouse, Kate Beckinsdale. Warner Bros. 2006.

M. A. Swiatek, "An Empirical Investigation of the Social Coping Strategies Used by Gifted Adolescents," *Gifted Child Quarterly* 39(3) (1995): 154–161.

M. A. Swiatek, "Social Coping among Gifted High School Students and its Relationship to Self-concept," *Journal of Youth and Adolescence* 30 (2001) 19–39.

A. Tellegen, D. T. Lykken, T. J. Bouchard, K. J. Wilcox, N. L. Segal, and S. Rich, "Personality Similarity in Twins Reared Apart and Together," *Journal of Personality and Social Psychology* 54 (1988): 1031–1039.

Terman, L.M. "Genetic Studies of Genius," (Vol. I). *Mental and Physical Traits of a Thousand Gifted Children.* Stanford, California: Stanford University Press, 1925.

M. Zeidner and E. J. Schleyer, "The Big-Fish-Little-Pond Effect for Academic Self-concept, Test Anxiety, and School Grades in Gifted Children," *Contemporary Educational Psychology* 24 (1999a): 305–329.

M. Zeidner and E. J. Schleyer, "The Effects of Educational Context on Individual Difference Variables, Self-perceptions of Giftedness, and School Attitudes in Gifted Adolescents," *Journal of Youth and Adolescence* 28 (1999b): 687–703.

THE PSYCHOLOGY OF SUPERHEROES

Michael Spivey, Ph.D.,
and Steven Knowlton

ANTI-HEROISM IN THE CONTINUUM OF GOOD AND EVIL

Although the world of some superheroes is filled with black-and-white caricatures—the classic superheroes and their evil villains—Spivey and Knowlton shine the spotlight on the anti-hero: a person who on occasion does "bad things for the right reasons." Their essay plumbs the workings of various anti-heroes who have undertaken dark deeds when they believed the end justified the means. Spivey and Knowlton even provide a three-dimensional grid so that you can determine how close your favorite character comes to being a tragic hero, an anti-hero, or a sympathetic villain!

"No one knows what it's like to be the bad man, (…) behind blue eyes."

—THE WHO

THE ANTI-HERO CONCEPT

Too good to be a villain, too evil to be a hero, the anti-hero occupies an all too realistic gray area in between those idealized extremes. This *good guy who does bad things for the right reasons* has not always been appropriately appreciated in literature, or in psychology for that matter. Take, for example, one recently uncovered version of the story of Judas Iscariot, where Jesus is interpreted as *asking* Judas to betray him so that his martyrdom can fulfill the plan and cause Christianity to bloom. Had Judas not committed that betrayal, the story of Jesus (and his teachings of peacefulness) would likely have had far less impact on the world. Yet poor Judas is widely thought of as nothing more than a traitor who sold out his best friend for thirty pieces of silver.

However, over the last few hundred years—at least as far back as Milton's portrayal of a justifiably indignant Lucifer in *Paradise Lost*—the anti-hero has been slowly emerging as a popular hard-to-put-your-finger-on character in fiction. In homage to Lord Byron's knavery, such a character in literature is sometimes called a "Byronic hero." In professional wrestling, when a character is neither a "face" nor a "heel," he is called a "tweener" or a "gray." But nowhere is this bad good-guy—or is he a good bad-guy?—more adored than in the comic book-superhero genre, where in between the fine classics and professional wrestling, the anti-hero has risen to his highest pedestal.

There are many comic book characters whose personalities cluster around this difficult-to-define prototype: partly good, partly evil, partly likeable, and partly repellent. As we discuss these wrecked souls, it will become clear that sometimes a good guy does more than *dress like a bad guy*. Sometimes he *does bad things*. And yet those bad things that the anti-hero does are often arguably...the right thing to do. There is a rich array of broken men (and some women) who make up the multi-dimensional construct we call the anti-hero. In this essay, we will ·compare and contrast a handful of these shady characters and explore what makes them tick. As a result, we will find it necessary to carve up the anti-hero category into a few psychological sub-partitions, and we may even have to face up to the "gray areas" of a relativistic morality in a complex world.

In Western culture, we often prefer formal logical predicates for our folk wisdom, or our "folk-psychology." We pretend that there are good people like Superman, and there are evil people like Lex Luthor. The anti-hero, however, is not so easily pigeonholed, blurring the line between good and evil. Or rather, he shines his flashlight on that line, revealing that it was already blurred when he got there.

Sympathetic villains also find themselves slightly "off the grid" when it comes to good versus evil. They are exceedingly well represented in science fiction and fantasy, with archetypal characters including Frankenstein's monster, Darth Vader, and Gollum from the Lord of the Rings. In comic books, notable examples include Dr. Octopus, who fell in love with Peter Parker's aunt and worked to save her from Hammerhead. Then there is Professor Xavier's old friend and arch nemesis, Magneto. At one point Magneto reluctantly agreed to take over running Xavier's mutant training academy in Xavier's absence. For several issues of *The New Mutants* (#31–40), the "good" Magneto struggles with self-doubt and barely inhibits his urge to be a tyrannical teacher. For example, as he battled the Avengers, who mistakenly assumed he was still evil, Magneto thought, "[I]t is so hard to restrain myself. I want to unleash my full fury—teach these self-righteous louts once and for all that Magneto is not to be trifled with. That would be my ultimate betrayal. First, Charles Xavier's faith in me. Then, the new mutants'. And now, lastly, my faith—my belief—in myself." Magneto's journey from villain to sympathetic villain to anti-hero is anything but complete.

Then there are tragic heroes, with such classic examples as Oedipus and Hamlet, whose undoing arises from foul luck or the curses of the gods or even their own self-doubt. In comic books, the story arc generally prevents the permanent death of the main character, but the tragic hero can still be tortured by the loss of loved ones, rendered powerless by uncertainty, or crushed under the weight of responsibility. Most superhero stories have elements of tragedy—even Superman lost his parents (and his home world) tragically, and his relationships are often strained by his dual identity. However, Spider-Man is the classic tragic hero of comic books—although he's not quite Achilles, he has a much rougher time of it than most superheroes. His uncle is killed as a result of Peter Parker's careless and selfish lapse in the very first Spider-Man comic (*Amazing Stories* #15), and his first fiancé, Gwen Stacy, is killed by his very attempt to save her from falling off the Brooklyn Bridge—her neck snapped by the sudden stop even though his web prevents her from falling all the way to the water (*The Amazing Spiderman* #121). Prior to her death, Gwen blamed Spider-Man for the death of her father, who was killed by falling debris from a battle between Spider-Man and Doctor Octopus (*The Amazing Spiderman* #90). Peter's various relationships, career, money, and other woes make him doubt the wisdom of being Spider-Man, to the point where he actually does give up twice (*The Amazing Spiderman* #50, #100). In the end, though, his belief that with great power comes great responsibility always brings him back.

The anti-hero, by contrast, is not always motivated by such noble principles, and is frequently placed in the position of choosing among several evils. Take, for example, Gene Wolfe's protagonist from *The Book of the New Sun*. Severian is a professional torturer and headsman, whose first genuine act of kindness was to deliver poison to a prisoner with whom he had fallen in love, so that she may kill herself. Or consider Travis Bickle from *Taxi Driver*. Determined to free twelve-year-old Iris against her will from a life of prostitution, he premeditatedly murdered her pimp, the hotel manager, and a client in cold blood. Then there's the *Man with No Name* from the spaghetti westerns that made Clint Eastwood famous, Riddick from *Pitch Black*, Leon from *The Professional*, McMurphy from *One Flew Over the Cuckoo's Nest*, or even Peter from *Office Space*. On TV, we've had Kerr Avon from *Blake's 7*, Vick Mackey from *The Shield*, Mal Reynolds from *Firefly*, and Jane Tennison from *Prime Suspect*, to name just a few. These and other anti-heroes from literature, movies, and TV are simultaneously loved and feared for performing the precarious give-and-take of high-stakes moral bargaining.

THE ANTI-HEROES THEMSELVES

Here we focus on comic book superheroes that fit the anti-hero mold, starting with the most hero-like and going downhill from there. **Batman** is, for comic books, the original anti-hero, getting his start in comic books less than a year after Superman. Unlike Superman, however, he is "a creature of the night.... Elusive as a smear of smoke..." (*Detective Stories* #47). His city, which was New York long before it became Gotham, is much darker and more criminal than Superman's Metropolis. Although he primarily punches and kicks his foes into submission, he is shown brandishing a pistol on the cover of one very early story (*Detective Stories* #35) and actually kills two vampires with silver bullets in another (*Detective Stories* #32). Over time he adds the gas capsules, the *batarang*, the utility belt, and eventually a wide variety of other toys, while the pistol quickly vanishes from his repertoire. He almost always avoids lethal force and makes Robin swear to "fight... against crime and corruption and never swerve from the path of righteousness" (*Detective Stories* #38). Batman's reputation as an anti-hero comes almost solely from his preference for striking from the shadows, using fear as a weapon against his enemies, and willingness to work slightly outside the law in order to catch villains. Although he can come across as a brooding, shadowy figure, as a hero the "Dark Knight" is more super than anti.

Slightly more gritty is the anti-hero who is genuinely willing to *kill* bad guys, not just subdue them. Take **Wolverine**, for example: here we have a short, boozing loner from Canada, yet he is incredibly strong and agile, has heightened senses, nearly instant healing ability, and adamantium plating on his skeleton. Moreover, his retractable claws can cut through just about anything. Wolverine started out as a loose cannon with a very short fuse, about as likely to attack his fellow mutant X-Men as he was the enemy. As his story grew—both forward and backward in time—his own lost memories came back to him, and his motivations became more understandable. Nonetheless, he always stood out from his teammates. While Professor Xavier's other X-Men usually take great pains to avoid actually killing enemies, Wolverine does not so limit himself: "I got no stomach for guttin' animals. People though—that's another matter" (*Wolverine* vol. 1, #1). Although he does avoid causing the deaths of innocent people, Wolverine is not above jamming a pistol into the face of a relatively innocent gun dealer in order to find out to whom he sold some submachine guns (*Wolverine* vol. 3, #2). Moreover, in a very recent issue (*Wolverine* vol. 3, #50), while in mortal combat with his long-time foe Sabretooth (who now works for the X-Men), Wolverine silently pondered over the morality of murder. He concluded that there is indeed a time and a place for it: "Sabretooth's a killer. Just so we're clear, I've killed too. But I never *liked* it. And I might hate myself in the morning, but I'm going to enjoy *this*."

Although the original **Magik** never quite admits to enjoying murder, the evil of her methods is undeniable. Even at the young age of fourteen, she already knew how dangerous she was: "I am Illyana Rasputin...humanity's savior...or the means of its eternal damnation" (*Magik* #1). Magik uses her evil powers (e.g., command over certain demons) to eradicate bad guys on Earth, and yet she is constantly struggling with her urge to fully embrace her evil nature. She has such immense potential for evil that, while in Limbo, transformed versions of Storm and Kitty Pryde actually considered killing her to prevent the demon lord Belasco from controlling her. In the end, it is Illyana who killed Kitty in self-defense, then also Storm—to save her soul from Belasco's gods. This demon sorceress later joined Professor Xavier's School for Gifted (mutant) Youngsters, but she struggled with relating to her cohorts. When she and Danielle Moonstar traveled to the future and witnessed their fellow mutants having turned evil, Magik watched Danielle cry over the ruination of her comrades: "I wish I could cry like that, Dani—feel the pain and grief you do. Then, maybe, we could comfort each other. But I have to keep my heart locked up tight—to protect it from the evil in my soul." Silently she admitted to herself that "part of me wanted so much to stay with those future mutants" (*New Mutants* #32). Later, when Magik was brain-washed by the Beyonder (a power-hungry supreme being who claims to be "the sum and substance of what is"), the illustration in which this took place might be a poster for the anti-hero concept itself (*New Mutants* #36). This very frame shows the ultimate transposition of good and evil that is faced by anti-heroes: the kind-looking man emanating light with outstretched arms is the bad guy, while the red woman with horns and a tail is the good guy.

As complex as Magik is for her use of evil to promote good, **Venom** trumps her in the complexity department. Venom is actually two minds: one an alien symbiote that was imprisoned by its civilization for believing that it should bond with its host instead of consuming it, the other mind was originally Spider-Man, who rejects the living "suit" that is the form of the venom symbiote when he realizes it is alive. The rejected symbiote found a kindred spirit in Eddie Brock, a former journalist who lost his job as the result of Spider-Man solving a case. The resulting combination (Venom) genuinely believes in saving innocents, but also believes they may at times be sacrificed for the greater good. Unfortunately, his desire to kill Spider-Man for having ruined/rejected him is generally lumped into the "greater good." So, after suffocating one prison guard with the web-like substance he could create, he said "innocent death is always unpleasant...but nothing must block our righteous revenge" (*The Amazing Spiderman* #300). Despite this claim, Venom refused to fight in the presence of innocents on a number of occasions, preferring to schedule safe times and places with Spider-Man to avoid unnecessary deaths. He even allowed Spider-Man to escape from a helpless position during one fight in order to save a baby that fell into a river (*The Amazing Spiderman* #332). Venom eventually transformed from a negative anti-hero to a more positive one upon a realization that killing Spider-Man would in effect be killing all the potential innocents that Spider-Man would save in the future. After his conversion, although Venom can still at times be quite brutal, he shows even more of a "soft" side. For example, Venom is at one point imprisoned by the Punisher and left to die. He managed to escape and found the Punisher about to be ambushed. Despite some misgivings, he chose to save the Punisher from certain death (*Venom*, "Funeral Pyre" #2).

The Punisher acknowledges his debt to Venom by grudgingly agreeing to spare one person he thinks he should kill. However, the Punisher (a.k.a. Frank Castle) is not the sort of anti-hero to turn over a new leaf. After seeing his wife and son murdered by the Mafia, Frank Castle is, to use the technical term, damaged goods. If *Wolverine* calls you a "brainless hothead," you should know that something is not right (*Wolverine/Punisher* #5). Astonishingly, the Punisher calls Wolverine a "limp-wristed liberal" in return, for wanting the bad guys to receive due justice rather than lethal punishment. Frank spends little time concerning himself with the risks of collateral damage, assuming that anyone near a criminal is also a criminal. For example, after the Punisher killed a group of drug dealers, a man that the gangsters had been torturing for fun begged him for protection. The Punisher answered with a deadpan, "This is white phosphorous." The frightened man scampered away from the grenade's explosion while the Punisher sauntered out the front door (*The Punisher*, "Barracuda"). Later in the same story, a CEO for a power company took his top shareholders on a yacht to celebrate his plan to fake power shortages in Florida and artificially raise the price of electricity. Standing in a nearby dinghy, Frank blew up the yacht, and everybody on it began to get eaten by sharks. When the chief bad guy looked like he might swim to safety, Castle shot him and watched as the sharks dismembered him. Then the CEO's hired killer, Barracuda, who in the end turned coat and helped Castle with the explosives on the yacht, started to climb back into their dinghy. "Now, I's thinking all this put you an' me on the same side, Homes," said Barracuda with a profanely hopeful smile. Without saying a word, the Punisher shot him, too, launching his body into the shark-infested waters.

The Punisher has been known to say, "Frank Castle is dead." In the case of **The Crow**, his former self (Eric) really *is* dead. The Crow is the first of our anti-heroes whose universe is itself profoundly "dark." If Batman's Gotham City is filled with crime and dark alleys, at least the crime is generally a means to an end rather than an end in itself. The crime that spawns the Crow, multiple murder with sexual assault committed for entertainment value, is bleak in the extreme. The Crow's vengeful response is similarly extreme: he seems to enjoy primarily mental torture as part of reaping vengeance. The Crow generally starts by reciting nursery rhymes, poems, prayers, or jokes, often ending with a warning of approaching death as he waits for his victims to attack. For example, he decapitated one of Tom Tom's associates with a sword, and when Tom Tom saw the lifeless body, said, "Bed time! Lights out!!" and then cut the lights. Between Tom Tom's wild pistol shots in the dark, the Crow recited "Now I lay me down to sleep...," followed it with a crucifixion joke, and then cut Tom Tom's legs off at the knees. The Crow finished the scene by questioning Tom Tom, while he bleeds out, on the whereabouts of the others involved in his and his fiancée's murders. The many internal interludes focusing on his gentle nature in life, combined with the occasional positive intervention with a relative innocent, amply demonstrate the Crow's tortured spirit; but in terms of actions, the Crow himself is essentially a being of pure vengeance.

That said, the Crow's stomach for torture cannot hold a candle (or should we say a cattle prod?) to that of **Marv** from Sin City. Although Marv is definitely one of the most "evil" anti-heroes we examine here, his universe is chock full of people whose motives, intent, and day-to-day actions are far worse. In fact, Marv generally tries to avoid trouble. At times, this is because he realizes that he really should try to restrain himself. Marv is a bigger, stronger, and better fighter than almost anyone he comes across. He is virtually unaffected by pain, and can take inhuman levels of physical punishment. In addition, Marv sometimes tries to avoid trouble because he worries that he is hallucinating: "It's OK when I smell things that aren't there or even when I hear things, but it's pretty serious when I see things.... I would've been all right if I took my medicine when I should have.... When you've got a condition it's bad to forget your medicine." But that isn't the whole story. As Dwight said in *Sin City: A Dame to Kill For*, "Marv's a guy you've got to be careful around—he doesn't mean any harm but he causes plenty." What really separates Marv from other anti-heroes is that once Marv can't avoid trouble, dealing with it through physical violence or torture is pure bliss for him. Unlike the Crow, for example, who seems to enjoy brief *psychological* torture as part of revenge, Marv has a sense of fulfillment and joy regarding *physical* torture that places him in a subcategory all his own. About his killing of the primary villain (Rourk), Marv said, "it's loud and nasty, my kind of kill. I stare the bastard in the face and I laugh as he screams to God for mercy, and I laugh harder when he squeals like a stuck pig, and when he whimpers like a baby, I'm laughing so hard I cry." Although he is generally careful not to harm those he considers innocent, Marv's actions toward his enemies are limited only by his imagination.

The last comic book anti-hero to be profiled here is the infamous **Judge Dredd**. His duty—and duty is everything to him—is to clean up crime on the streets of post-nuclear Mega-City One by acting as judge, jury, and executioner on the spot. He has no time for the sophistry of individual freedom or human dignity, often quoted as saying "Democracy is *not* for the people," and, "I *am* the law." While he is a bit like the Punisher in doling out death sentences with little rumination, a key difference is that if the Punisher is after you, the legal system will at least *try* to protect you, but if Judge Dredd is after you, he *is* the legal system. Moreover, Dredd is quick to choose what he sees as the lesser of two holocaust-level evils with little or no remorse about collateral damage. For example, in one story arc, the demented necromagus, Sabbat, started turning all the dead people on Earth into zombies. Five mega-cities lost all their judges while defending their city walls from millions of zombies (*Judge Dredd: Judgment Day*). In a meeting of chief judges, it was noted that the inhabitants of those overrun mega-cities would soon be killed and become zombies. Without hesitation, Judge Dredd offered a solution: "Then we nuke 'em." Even the Texan judge was scandalized, "Y'all crazy, Dredd? That's 2 billion people!" "Those cities are gone," Dredd replied, "They're nothing but zombie factories now." A few frames later, the inhabitants of those five mega-cities were vaporized along with their attacking zombies: "Living and dead fry together in the greatest act of genocide the world has ever seen." And the world has Judge Dredd to thank for it. Thus, on the sheer *scale* of atrocities, Judge Dredd is by far the most destructive of our anti-heroes.

THE ANTI-HERO SPACE

As far as the "psychology of the anti-hero" goes, there does not appear to be a set of necessary and sufficient conditions for diagnosing someone with the anti-hero syndrome. Some of our anti-heroes are clearly *psychopaths* (e.g., The Punisher, Marv), while others might only have a mild form of *antisocial personality disorder* (e.g., Wolverine) or *schizoid personality disorder* (e.g., Batman), and still others are generally quite sociable (e.g., Magik). Some of them appear to suffer from a form of *multiple personality* (or *dissociative identity*) *disorder* (e.g., Venom, Magik), but most do not. Judge Dredd exhibits some of the symptoms of *narcissistic personality disorder*, and the Crow is almost certainly *clinically depressed*. However, rather than shoe-horning distinct psychiatric labels on them, better progress in understanding our anti-heroes might be made by comparing them to heroes, tragic heroes, villains, and sympathetic villains along a few continua that together form a volumetric state space. For example, on a scale from zero to one, how evil are the methods (or means) used by the individual in question? Also, on the same scale, how evil are the consequences (or ends) that tend to result from his actions? Finally, how much self-doubt does the character exhibit? If you estimate these three numbers for a fictional character, you can treat them as coordinates in a three-dimensional space. How close various characters are to one another in that space is thus an indicator of how similar they are to one another.

Figure 1 on the next page shows estimated values for these coordinates for our anti-heroes, as well as for several other characters. Superman and Lex Luthor are treated as the quintessential forthright hero and unwavering villain, respectively. This provides a pair of idealized anchors (or basis functions) from which the rest of the layout can more readily make sense. Our anti-heroes form a cluster in this space, with most of them near a region with substantially evil means and somewhat good ends—and they run the gamut of low to high self-doubt. Batman is at a far edge of that cluster because he is more like the standard hero. We might call him the "Dark Defender" type of anti-hero. Judge Dredd is at another edge of the cluster, near the villain region, which we call the "Resolute Destroyer" type. Quantitatively, Magik and Venom are the closest to the Tragic Hero region, so we call them the "Tortured Protector" type of anti-hero. Finally, Marv is the closest to sympathetic villains, so we call his type the "Muddled Revenger." At either extreme of destructiveness and/or at either extreme of internal struggle, we can thus imagine two dimensions *inside the anti-hero category* that allow us to loosely associate them into subcategories. Our other anti-heroes live somewhere in the middle of those four extreme types.

BETWEEN GOOD AND EVIL

When analyzed in a continuous state space, it becomes clear that the anti-hero concept is flexible enough to accommodate some rather intriguing variations on a theme. By having the guts and moral ambiguity to commit astounding acts that require anything from intimidation to mass murder as the means to an end, anti-heroes

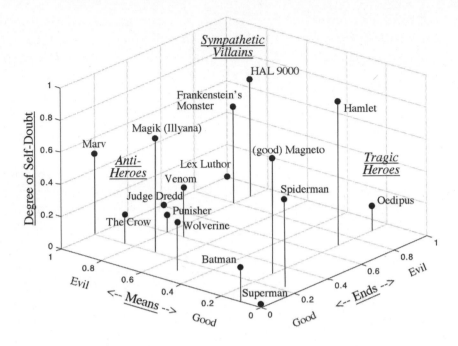

Figure 1. In the 3-D space of *means, ends,* and *self-doubt,* anti-heroes cluster in an interesting location, actually quite far from tragic heroes. They are a weighted mixture of villain and hero. (Note that the coordinates for each character are approximations, and surely have distributions associated with them.)

blaze trails in the uncharted territory between the categories of obvious goodness and unmitigated evil. Thus, any attempts to categorize them (including those presented here) are best treated as an affiliation with regions along a continuum, rather than as a set of discrete classifications that are either applied or not.

However, what all anti-heroes have in common is that they capture our imagination by attempting to balance their evil methods with their good intentions. Sometimes the results are purely gratifying; sometimes purely horrifying. More often, the results are a strange but compelling mixture of the two. Indeed, it is those mixed results that endear them to us. We see our flawed selves in anti-heroes, and this allows us to understand their humanity, even when their deeds are unquestionably evil.

"But my dreams, they aren't as empty as my conscience seems to be."

—THE WHO

Michael Spivey, Ph.D., is full professor of cognitive science at the University of California, Merced, and author of *The Continuity of Mind*. He received his B.A. in psychology from the University of California, Santa Cruz, and his Ph.D. in brain and cognitive sciences at the University of Rochester.

Steve Knowlton is a senior research analyst with Kaiser Foundation Health Plan. He received his B.A. in rhetoric from the University of California, Berkeley, his M.A. in communications from the University of California, Davis, and his M.A. in psychology from the University of Pennsylvania.

Robert Biswas-Diener

POSITIVE PSYCHOLOGY
OF PETER PARKER

Too frequently, Spider-Man gets the crap beaten out of him. But he doesn't give up—he keeps looking for an angle, a solution. What keeps him going day after day, whatever his personal crises? In this essay Biswas-Diener explains what sustains Spider-Man; how he uses his superpowers for good, and in doing so, he enhances his strength of character. For Spider-Man, and for us, when we do good, we feel good. Biswas-Diener explains how, in the dark times, Peter Parker's positive characteristics see him through. And the strengths of his character affect the reader (or viewer); we feel better by sharing his adventures.

MOST FOLKS ARE FAMILIAR with the secret origin of Spider-Man: wallflower Peter Parker was bitten by a radioactive spider on a school field trip to The Science Hall. The atomic properties of the spider gave Parker the proportionate strength and agility of a spider, a "spider-sense" warning him of impending danger, and the ability to stick to surfaces. But, that is really only the beginning of the story. Further events had to take place in order for the newly powerful Peter Parker to transform into a wall-crawling superhero. One fateful evening Peter refused to stop a petty thief, citing the frequent excuse, "I've got my own problems." Returning home later that evening, Peter was horrified to discover that his Uncle Ben had been shot and killed by this very same thief. Wracked with guilt, and with his uncle's admonition "With great power comes great responsibility" ringing in his ears, Peter set out to use his powers to capture the villain, and Spider-Man was born.

But have you ever wondered why Peter Parker continues to be a superhero? Why would he make such enormous sacrifices and expose himself to repeated danger? Why not take a night off? Is his guilt really that strong, even years later? Let's be honest, even the most noble and motivated people have the tendency to rationalize their actions. Why wouldn't Spider-Man say to himself, "I've battled Doc Oc, Electro, and the Sandman this week. I have done enough. I think the next few nights will be Peter Parker time!"? Why wouldn't Parker use his extraordinary abilities to earn some much needed cash and a more luxurious life in addition to fighting crime? I propose that there is another motive behind Parker's superheroism, and it can be explained by positive psychology.

Positive psychology is a new field that looks at what is going right, rather than what is going wrong with people. It is the science of human flourishing and success, and it rests on research in such topics as creativity, happiness, and optimism. Abraham Maslow, the humanist famous for his "Hierarchy of Needs," used the term positive psychology in the 1960s. More recently, Martin Seligman, the former president of the American Psychological Association, made positive psychology an integral part of his presidency, arguing that the field of psychology needs to pay more attention to people's strengths rather than only focusing on their weaknesses. What's more, this strengths-based focus is more than American-style happiology. Businesses, therapists, and coaches are adopting a positive psychology mindset because the research shows that a positive focus is widely beneficial. One study of a speed reading program in Nebraska, for example, showed that it was the best, rather than the worst readers who made the largest gain in skills during the program. Similarly, a study of a British brewery that manages more than 7,000 bars showed that investing extra money to refurbish the most successful establishments reaped seven times more profit than the same investment made to shore up the weaknesses in the least successful bars. Not only is a strengths-based orientation effective, it is attractive. People the world over hunger for opportunities to put their best skills and talents to work. Most folks, including your friendly neighborhood Spider-Man, want the chance to shine.

The appeal of positive psychology certainly wouldn't be lost on Peter Parker, a teenager to whom life seems to have dealt a poor hand. Parker is an orphan, living a low income existence with his aunt, and a person for whom high school holds few social prospects and the promise of daily ridicule by Flash Thompson and other members of the "in-crowd." Even before the miraculous spider bite, Parker looked to his personal strengths to overcome the hardships he faced. For instance, although he is not naturally athletic, Peter is an excellent student, and focuses on his intelligence to help him achieve the things he wants in life. What he lacks in social acumen among his peers, he compensates for through his relationships with his intellectual mentors. In fact, Peter enjoys a healthy enough dose of self-esteem from his academic performance that it even gives him the courage to stand up to bullies at school. In *Amazing Spider-Man* #2 Parker doesn't let himself be pushed around by Flash, saying "At least my brain isn't muscle-bound, like that fat head of yours!" This is an uncharacteristically brave thing to say, and evidence that a strengths-based focus can be beneficial. If anything, Peter Parker's alter ego Spider-Man is the positive counterpoint to all of Peter's failings: Spidey is strong and athletic, outgoing and witty, adventuresome and risk-taking. No wonder Parker wants to put his life on the line night after night; in Spider-Man Peter Parker at last gets the opportunity to use the full range of his strengths. There are three topics central to positive psychology that crop up time and again in Spider-Man: character strengths, resilience, and hope.

SPIDER STRENGTH AND STRENGTHS OF CHARACTER

Most people have private fantasy lives in which they play the hero in their day-dreams. They imagine that they are courageous soldiers, wealthy philanthropists, award-winning parents, or movie stars. These rosy internal monologues serve an important psychological purpose, they can be a boost to self-esteem. Peter Parker is lucky in that he can actually live his idealized life through his powerful alter-ego, Spider-Man. Take a moment and consider how liberating it would feel to swing across town on webs, how gratifying to stop a mugging, how fortunate to be able to use super-strength to loosen even the tightest peanut butter jar lids. In *Amazing Spider-Man* #3 Parker arrives at the conclusion that having super-powers is a great confidence booster, thinking to himself, "These suction fingers of mine will get me up the wall in no time. Boy, its great being Spider-Man! I can do almost anything!" In no time at all Parker comes to realize that Spider-Man is his ideal self precisely because the web-slinger is so capable. In *Amazing Spider-Man* #96 Parker sees police speeding down the road and thinks, "Here's my chance to do what Peter Parker does best. I dunno—it must be a compulsion or something. I guess I'm really hooked on turning into Spider-Man."

Spider-Man is about much more than speed, agility, and a metal-crunching left hook. Spidey also gives Parker the opportunity to strut his stuff where character strengths are concerned. As a superhero Peter Parker has the chance to be generous, funny, self-sacrificing, courageous, humble, and persistent. Employing these virtues can be just as ego-boosting as physical powers. One of the most exciting aspects of Positive Psychology research has been the study of character strengths. Researchers Chris Peterson and Martin Seligman set out to identify virtues that existed and were valued in every culture. They read religious texts, novels, philosophical treatises, self-help books, the Boy Scout Law, and even the Klingon Code from Star Trek. From this background material they were able to identify twenty-four character strengths—such as leadership, compassion, and wisdom—that were viewed as highly desirable around the globe. In fact, in a study I conducted, I took this list of twenty-four virtues to tribal people in Kenya, university students in America, and to a remote Inuit village in Northern Greenland, and found that people widely recognized and valued these traits, and hoped their children would have them. Peterson and Seligman used this list to develop a free, online measure called the Values in Action (VIA) assessment of character strengths. (You can take the VIA by going to: www.viastrengths.org.) The VIA does not compare your generosity or bravery with that of other people but orders your virtues against one another, and tells you your top five "signature strengths"—those that come very naturally. The VIA is an interesting intellectual counter-point to traditional diagnosis, in which therapists and psychiatrists take stock of client symptoms to identify the exact malady from which they suffer. The VIA, by contrast, pinpoints personal assets that can be used to enhance functioning. Think of it as positive diagnosis.

How important is the VIA, and the concept of positive diagnosis? Imagine going to the doctor and being told what you were doing well, and the factors that were promoting your health. This information would be useful to you, encouraging, and reassuring. Similarly, Seligman and his colleagues conducted a study in which they asked college students to take the VIA, identify their strengths, and then to "use one of these top strengths in a new and different way every day for one week." What benefit did an extra helping of gratitude or generosity have for the research sample? Just after this exercise, and at a one week follow-up, there were few differences in happiness between the strengths group and a placebo control group. However, one month later the strengths group was significantly happier, and this emotional boost appeared to last for as long as six months! In addition, the strengths group showed far fewer signs of depression than the control group at one, three, and six month follow-ups! No wonder Peter Parker is hooked on being Spider-Man! Every time he uses his super-powers, and every time he puts them toward a virtuous cause, he buys himself additional happiness, and protects himself from mental anguish.

THE PROPORTIONAL HUMOR OF A SPIDER?

You wouldn't happen to be the new home ec teacher, would you?

—SPIDER-MAN, TO THE GREEN GOBLIN,
WHEN THE VILLAIN ATTACKS HIS HIGH SCHOOL (*ULTIMATE SPIDER-MAN* #1)

Psychological research has shown that humans have an enormous capacity to adapt to new circumstances, including new jobs, schools, relationships, and even homes. In fact, our natural resilience extends even to adverse circumstances. Most folks, given time, can adjust to unemployment, the death of a loved one, and even a serious injury. People are quite creative in how they overcome life's pitfalls. Some fall back on social support, others tap religious beliefs, and still others harness their personal strengths. Peter Parker is a perfect example of using a character strength—humor in his case—to deal with hardships. Of course, hardships for Spider-Man are more along the lines of bank robbers and super-villains, but all the more reason why his humor is useful.

Take the famous instance of the days leading up to the death of Peter Parker's friend Gwen Stacy. It was a dark period for Parker. He was arguing with his best friend Harry Osborn, was having girl troubles, and his arch-enemy the Green Goblin had learned his secret identity. In a series of battles the Goblin outsmarted and outgunned Spider-Man, leaving him weak and web-less. For the vast majority of us, it would have been time to throw in the towel and hang up the superhero cape for good. But, in a free fall from a Manhattan skyscraper, Spidey is quick to use his sense of irony. "Oh great," he tells himself, "I am out of web-fluid, can't stick to walls anymore, and facing a murderous madman who's out to destroy me. Well, anyone can be a hero with the odds in his favor.... But why am I always the one who has to do it the hard way?"

Positive psychologists have conducted research on humor and discovered that it is more than idle entertainment, it is beneficial. Humor, according to researchers, buffers a good mood against life's stresses, promotes health, and is a sign of creativity and intelligence. Psychologists tell us that playfulness is at the heart of humor. In short, humor is the ability to recognize and delight in incongruity, to see the light side of adversity, and to make others smile or laugh. It is likely that humor helps bond relationships, as most folks are attracted to others who are in a good mood. The other major function of humor is overcoming stress. In fact, while Spidey uses humor to take the edge off the life or death situations he finds himself in, we—the readers—feel increasingly connected to him because we are drawn in by his wit.

One of the great appeals of Spider-Man is his humor. Not only is the web slinger witty, but it is exciting and awesome to see him use his sharp tongue in even the toughest situations. Humor, where Spider-Man is concerned, seems to hint at silliness, a level head, and a bright mind. For instance, in *Ultimate Spider-Man* #10, Spidey squares off against the hulking Kingpin. The Kingpin grabs Spider-Man and holds him tight. "Who sent you?" the Kingpin demands. Instead of screaming or wetting his costume, Parker responds with characteristic bravado, "Cason Daly." "I don't know who that is," the Kingpin growls. "Sure ya don't," retorts Spidey, "You wanna know why? Because he didn't invent a line of pre-packaged pastries. If he did I bet you'd know everything about him—you big fat fatty of a fat man." And with that, Spider-Man kicks the Kingpin and is free. Of course, poking fun at people's size is generally frowned upon, but in the case of the Kingpin, Spider-Man expertly uses his humor to offset nervousness, belittle his enemy, and buy time for a successful escape.

An unintended side-effect of Spider-Man's humor is the admiration it inspires in the rest of us. What reader hasn't sat back after reading *Ultimate Spider-Man* #6 and wished he would have said to a bomb throwing Green Goblin, "I don't mean to tell you your business, but that's kind of a fire hazard isn't it?" Positive psychologists have also studied this feeling of awe that frequently arises when we witness someone do something great. Psychologist Jon Haidt calls this feeling *elevation*, and describes it as a warm sense in the chest, sometimes accompanied by tingles, and an expansive good mood. When we listen to Martin Luther King, Jr.'s "I Have a Dream" or read Lincoln's Gettysburg Address, it is easy to feel elevated by their greatness. Similarly, Spider-Man evokes the same uplifting sense of admiration. It is precisely because Peter Parker is—super-powers aside—a regular youngster with everyday problems that we can relate to him, and be so moved by his good example. When Spidey refuses to lose his cool, or give in to despair, we all learn a lesson in resilience that can guide us in our own lives.

SPIDEY'S OTHER SUPER-POWER: HOPE

Perhaps one of the least appreciated aspects of all varieties of super-heroes is their consistent optimism. Spider-Man wouldn't get out of bed in the morning, let alone rush into knock-down drag-out fights with the likes of Venom and the Hobgoblin, if he did not feel an overwhelming sense of optimism. By definition, Peter Parker must hold out hope for a positive outcome or he would turn tail and flee the majority of the challenges he faces. What gives Spider-Man this uniquely positive outlook? Is he simply a foolish, risk-seeking teen-ager? Is he too cocky, begging to be knocked down a peg? Is he stupid, unable to accurately assess the risks he faces? Indeed not. Spider-Man has a good handle on his life, and his hope—as we have witnessed through countless victories—is well-founded. What gives Peter Parker this dynamic ability to keep his psychological fingers crossed? How can the rest of us tap this source? Fortunately, positive psychology has the answers.

The late psychologist Rick Snyder spent most of his career study-ing hope, and trying to understand what makes some people hopeful and others more pessimistic. Snyder came to see hope not as a feel-ing, but as a way of thinking about personal goals. He identified two major components that form the foundation of hopeful thinking: *agency* and *pathways* thinking. By "agency" Snyder meant feelings of self-efficacy and competence. The more confident an individual is in his or her ability to achieve a goal, the more hopeful he or she will be that it will be achieved. Spider-Man, by virtue of his super-pow-ers and experience beating super-villains, shows a level of self-confi-dence that can only promote hopeful thinking. After beating aliens, defeating the Vulture, and saving an astronaut from a runaway rock-et, Peter Parker—in *Amazing Spider-Man* #3—lets slip his private thoughts, "The only problem is my jobs are too easy. I'd welcome a little competition once in a while." Although this sentiment sounds dangerously close to conceit, it is easy to see how such an attitude would help a person take risks, exert effort, and persevere at difficult tasks.

The other part of the hope equation is "pathways thinking," by which Snyder meant a person's ability to find multiple routes to a goal. We often call this "thinking creatively" or "thinking outside the box." The better people are at thinking of multiple solutions to a problem, the more hopeful they will be that they can achieve their goal. When a hurdle presents itself, good pathways thinkers can simply go around. Take the time in *Amazing Spider-Man* #2 when the Vulture traps Spider-Man in a water tank on the roof of a New York brownstone. Spidey tries the obvious escape tactics but, unfortunately, his web-shooter is empty, and the walls of the tank are too wet and slimy for him to stick to. He grows tired, and knows that he cannot tread water forever. How will he escape? Always resourceful, Spider-Man dives to the bottom of the tank and lunges upward from the floor, using his exceptional strength to propel him through the hatch in the ceiling. Rather than be dismayed at his early failures Spidey continued to look for solutions, knowing that he would stumble onto a novel answer to the problem at hand. In his consistently hopeful attitude Spider-Man provides yet another imitable example of positive psychology. By following his lead, we understand that increasing self-confidence and expanding problem solving skills are vital to increasing hope.

HAPPILY EVER AFTER?

Some critics of positive psychology have expressed concern that it is a one sided philosophy. Might a positive-focus ignore the very real problems of everyday life? Indeed. Positive psychology is not a Pollyanna science, suggesting that there are no ills or that life should always be rosy. There will always be a Scorpion or Bullseye waiting for Spidey around some dark corner and pining for an epic battle. Positive psychology acknowledges everyday hardships, and realizes the value in growing through adversity. In *Amazing Spider-Man* #122, after Gwen Stacy is killed, and Spider-Man defeats the Green Goblin, the mood remains heavy. Peter Parker says, "I thought seeing the

Goblin die would make me feel better about Gwen. . . . Instead, it just makes me feel empty, washed out, a little more alone." There is an appropriate time and place for hardship, and it is a fact of life. But, by the same token, positive psychology also suggests that a problem-focus overlooks the many positives in life. By emphasizing strengths, employing them effectively—as Spidey does with his humor—and working to maintain a hopeful attitude, it is possible to boost health, happiness, and strengthen social bonds. Spider-Man is an inspiring example of a person who rises to challenges on a consistent basis, and flourishes because he has the opportunity to use his greatest talents and strengths. He inspires all of us to harness our virtues so that we too can say, "Big time superhero comin' through!"

Robert Biswas-Diener is known as the "Indiana Jones" of positive psychology. His studies on culture and happiness have taken him to such far-flung places as Greenland, India, Kenya, and Israel. He is also a career coach and is Program Director for Education and Learning for the Center for Applied Positive Psychology (CAPP). He lives in Portland, Oregon.

THE PSYCHOLOGY OF SUPERHEROES

Mikhail Lyubansky, Ph.D.

PREJUDICE LESSONS FROM THE XAVIER INSTITUTE

Anyone who has read X-Men comics or seen X-Men movies can't help but be aware of the detrimental role that prejudice plays. In this essay, Lyubansky shows us the ways in which the prejudice experienced by the X-Men—in particular Professor Xavier and Magneto—reflects what psychologists have learned about prejudice. This essay provides the reader with a clear sense of how prejudice against X-Men in the X-universe isn't so dissimilar to prejudice that occurs in our world. Lyubansky explains theories and research regarding *why* such prejudice arises, as well as different types of prejudice.

THE X-MEN[1] AREN'T YOUR TYPICAL SUPERHEROES. Sure, both the comics and the films are loaded with the typical clashes of super-powers that have long been a comic mainstay, but at their soul, the X-Men are less about superpowers and more about human tendencies to fear and hate those who are different, and the various ways we deal with such tendencies. In the words of long-time X-Men writer Chris Claremont, "The X-Men are hated, feared, and despised collectively by humanity for no other reason than that they are mutants. So what we have here, intended or not, is a book that is about racism, bigotry, and prejudice" (Claremont, 1982).

The remark about "intentionality" is noteworthy, and it's quite possible that prejudice was far from the minds of writer Stan Lee and illustrator Jack Kirby when they first introduced the X-Men in 1963. At the very least, given that the original ensemble of X-Men was entirely racially and ethnically homogeneous (as per the comic industry's standard of the time), the themes of prejudice were most likely not very well thought out at first. Nonetheless, the seeds of these themes were planted in the very first issue when Charles Xavier, a mutant telepath responsible for creating the X-Men, observed that human beings are not yet ready to accept super-powered individuals in their midst (The X-Men #1). By 1975, the X-Men were ethnically and racially diverse, featuring Canadian (Wolverine), Russian (Colossus), German (Nightcrawler), and African (Storm) characters that reflected the comic's ideology of tol-

---

[1] Writing about the X-Men poses certain challenges. For starters, who exactly should one write about? The original five-member team, formed in 1963, consisted of Cyclops, Marvel Girl (Jean Grey), Angel, Beast, and Iceman. The more familiar (to most casual readers) 1975 team featured Cyclops (the only holdover from the original), Wolverine, Colossus, Nightcrawler, and Storm. At various points, other X-teams were formed, including The New Mutants, X-Factor, Excalibur, and Alpha Flight, and membership in these teams, as well as in the original X-Men, was constantly shifting as new characters joined and familiar faces came and went. The films had their own unique ensemble of the popular mutant heroes, as did two different animated TV shows: X-Men Animated Series and X-Men: Evolution. On top of all that, the comics introduced several alternative timelines, such as Days of Future Past, a reality in which the mutants were incarcerated in concentration camps, and Age of Apocalypse, in which a young Xavier gave up his life to save Magneto, who later formed the X-Men. Indeed, the number of known mutants in the X-Universe is so vast (at least 160 according to http://en.wikipedia.org/wiki/List_of_X-Men_characters) and group alliances so fluid that even diligent fans sometimes have a hard time keeping track of who is part of which X-team at any point in time. For the purpose of this essay, I avoid the alternative timelines and focus mainly on the X-Universe itself, giving special attention to X-Men founder Charles Xavier and his long-time friend and adversary, Magneto, whose contrasting visions of human-mutant relations provide the backdrop for much of the series's commentary on group relations. As in the real world, the specific ensemble of individuals is not especially relevant to understanding group dynamics.

erance and multiculturalism—an ideology that was a good decade ahead of its time.[2]

The X-Men comics, however, do more than merely model an ideology of tolerance and diversity. Rather, they examine the causes of prejudice and intolerance and pit competing perspectives against each other as different characters try to come to terms with the ethical and psychological implications brought on by the dawn of a new evolutionary phase, in which genetic mutations have given a handful of humans a variety of different superpowers.

Mutants, of course, are intended as an allegory for oppression in general. X-Men readers/viewers are intended to generalize Professor Xavier's philosophy of tolerance and assimilation to other oppressed groups, including racial and ethnic minorities and the Lesbian-Gay-Bisexual-Transgendered (LGBT) community. Unfortunately, the analogies are not always adequate. In this essay, I first examine whether the depiction of anti-mutant prejudice in the X-Universe is consistent with what psychologists have learned about the development of prejudice and group conflict and then turn my attention to the intended analogy to the African American Civil Rights Movement.

PREJUDICE IN THE X-UNIVERSE

Although humans initially seemed pleased by the X-Men's contributions to law enforcement (*The X-Men* #1), anti-mutant sentiment quickly developed. Within approximately two years' time, the government deployed giant robot Sentinels, programmed to detect mutants and capture or kill them (*The X-Men* #14). In subsequent issues, the government continued to reflect society's prejudice through whatever means it had at its disposal, including the Mutant Registration Act[3] (*The X-Men* #181), and the development of the technologi-

---

[2] A few years after this shift to multiculturalism, writer and artist John Byrne introduced the first gay superhero, Northstar, although Marvel did not allow him to actually "come out" formally until 1992 (*Alpha Flight* #106). Despite restrictions imposed by the Comics Code Authority, other gay, lesbian, and bisexual characters followed, including long-time friends and lovers, Mystique and Destiny (*Uncanny X-Men* #265). A list of gay and lesbian comic book characters is available at http://www.gayleague.com/gay/characters/.

[3] The Mutant Registration Act (MRA) is a controversial legislative bill in the X-Universe which mandated the registration of all mutants with the government. The specific terms of the MRA are not consistently described in the films or comics. However, it is generally assumed that the MRA would require all mutants to reveal their real names to the government and possibly also to obtain governmental approval in order to use their abilities.

cal "cure" for the X-gene (*Astonishing X-Men* #1–4). Although there are periods when tensions ease, human-mutant relations in the X-Universe are uneasy at best and often in a state of open conflict.

At the center of this conflict are two mutants, Erik Lehnsherr (a.k.a. Magneto) and his old friend, Charles Xavier, each with a different explanation for the anti-mutant sentiments. I will take up Xavier's position later (when I discuss the analogy to the Civil Rights Movement), but first let's take a look at Magneto's thesis and see if it's consistent with psychological research and real human history.

Magneto, a child Holocaust survivor who lost his entire family, believes that humans inevitably rise up against those who are different and that it is "just a matter of time before mutants are herded off to camps"[4] (X-Men). The following dialogue with Rogue,[5] during the first film's climactic scene at the Statue of Liberty, provides a glimpse of Magneto's worldview:

MAGNETO: I first saw her in 1949. America was going to be the land of tolerance. Peace.
ROGUE: Are you going to kill me?
MAGNETO: Yes.
ROGUE: Why?
MAGNETO: Because there is no land of tolerance. There is no peace. Not here, or anywhere else that women, children, whole families are destroyed simply because they were born different from those in power.

From a historical perspective, Magneto certainly seems to have a point. Inter-ethnic group conflict has been around for thousands of years, and the United States, the self-proclaimed "land of immigrants" and "leader of the free world" is no exception. In addition to enacting the slave trade, the Jim Crow laws that followed, and the forced internment of more than 100,000 Japanese Americans during

---

[4] This is a reference to Nazi concentration camps, as well as to the popular 1981 story arc set in an alternate future in which the Brotherhood of Evil Mutants' assassination of a U.S. senator led to the incarceration of mutants in concentration camps (*Uncanny X-Men* #141–142).

[5] Rogue is a mutant member of the X-Men. Her mutation, which she often considers a curse, forces her to involuntarily absorb the memories and life energies, and in the case of other mutants, super abilities of anyone with whom she makes skin contact, preventing her from physically touching others, including her friends and romantic interests.

WWII, the U.S. government also engaged in a variety of other unsavory activities that were clearly motivated by prejudice and/or fear. While many of these[6] are less familiar to the general public, they are nevertheless an important part of U.S. history, a history that Lehnsherr seems to know well, particularly the U.S. compulsory sterilization program.[7]

Although the Nazis forcefully sterilized more people than any other country (more than 450,000 people in less than a decade), the United States is second on the list! More importantly, the U.S. sterilization program, as well as its eugenics program in general, not only preceded the Nazis but actually served as their inspiration (Kuhl). In 1907, Indiana became the first U.S. state to enact sterilization legislation, followed by Washington and California in 1909. In 1927, the U.S. Supreme Court legitimized the practice in *Buck v. Bell*, and the number of forced sterilizations increased each year until 1942, when another Supreme Court case, *Skinner v. Oklahoma*, ruled that forced sterilization of criminals was unconstitutional (eugenic sterilizations were still permitted). Although the mentally retarded and mentally ill were the groups most frequently targeted, Native Americans were also forcefully sterilized against their will, often without their knowledge, when they were hospitalized for some other reason.

Thus, when Magneto warns that "the cure" for the X-gene, initially offered on a voluntary basis, will be forced upon mutants, he certainly has historical precedent. But times do change. It is not unreasonable to argue that not only do genes evolve, but so do societies. Is it not possible for different groups to live peacefully together now, even if they have struggled to do so historically? To answer this question, we have to turn to the psychological literature on prejudice and group conflict. Like the topics themselves, the body of knowledge is complex and multi-dimensional, with a variety of competing theories. A comprehensive review of all the relevant theories is

---

[6] For example, in the late 1800s and early 1900s, tens of thousands of American Indian children were forcefully removed from their families and placed into Federal or Christian boarding schools in order to facilitate the assimilation of American Indians into mainstream society. Upon arrival to the schools, children were given American names, prohibited from speaking their native language, and forced to learn and practice Christianity instead of their native religion.

[7] Compulsory sterilization programs are government policies which force people to undergo surgical sterilization, usually as part of eugenics programs intended to prevent the reproduction and multiplication of members of the population considered to be undesirable (Wikipedia).

beyond the scope of this essay, but the following four theoretical frameworks provide a good testing ground for both Magneto's claims about human nature and for the depiction of prejudice development in the X-Universe.

AUTHORITARIAN PERSONALITY THEORY

When psychologists tried to make sense of the Holocaust perpetrated by the Nazis, one of the first theories offered was that the Germans, with their emphasis on efficiency and organization, were characterized by an authoritarian personality that caused them to (1) think in "us vs. them" categories, rather than make more inclusive categorizations that might have, for example, considered the local Jews as Germans, and (2) follow orders from authority figures without engaging in a self-reflective or critical-thinking process regarding the moral implications of those orders.[8] Thus, the Holocaust, according to the authoritarian personality theory, occurred because Germans were predisposed to not think of Jews as German and to obey Nazi-authority demands, even if such demands required immoral behavior. In the context of the X-Universe, this theory suggests that anti-mutant prejudice developed because humans were predisposed to not recognize the humanity of the mutants and to follow the demands of the fanatical few who, like Senator Kelly, deliberately stirred people's fears and pushed an anti-mutant agenda.

For many years, this theory, which essentially locates the cause of prejudice in a person's disposition, dominated psychological thinking and had a profound influence on the way many historians approached group conflict. However, by the 1970s, empirical studies revealed so many problems and limitations that the theory was all but abandoned by psychologists.[9] As just two examples: the theory was limited by its inability to address why some groups are targeted but not others,[10] as well as by its complete failure to account for sit-

---

[8] The theory itself can be considered an example of group prejudice, as it is based on German stereotypes and anti-German sentiments that were common in the United States after WWII.

[9] Although largely rejected by contemporary psychologists, the authoritarian personality continues to influence historical texts, including *The War Against the Jews* (Dawidowitzc) and *Hitler's Willing Executioners: Ordinary Germans and the Holocaust* (Goldhagen).

[10] In the X-Universe, for example, mutants are targeted but, for the most part, superheroes who gained their power through other means (e.g., Spider-Man) are not.

uational factors,[11] such as whether other people in the vicinity expressed or denounced the prejudicial attitudes. Subsequent theories of prejudice attempted to address these issues.

REALISTIC GROUP CONFLICT THEORY

The Realistic Conflict Theory attempts to integrate situational and dispositional components. According to this theory, groups compete over scarce resources such as jobs, land, and power. During competition, out-groups are considered enemies in order to justify the attempt to "win," and these enemies are then dehumanized and scapegoated. This theory was first popularized through the classic Robbers Cave study (Sherif) in which the researchers were able to create group prejudice in two randomly assigned groups of twelve-year-old boys by creating group competition (in the form of a tournament) in which the boys competed over prizes, which could only be obtained by being a member of the winning group. Within days, the two groups of boys (none of whom knew each other previously) were on such bad terms that they engaged in fighting and name-calling whenever together and preferred not to eat in the same space (Sherif). Other studies (e.g., Kinder, Runciman), employing very different methodologies, have also supported this theory, as does practically every anti-immigration demonstration, where protestors commonly make (often unverified) claims about the negative impact of immigration on the employment opportunities of "Americans."

As in our reality, there is no shortage of group-level competition over resources in the X-Universe. This is most evident in the form of competition over desirable jobs, especially military, espionage (e.g., S.H.I.E.L.D.),[12] and law enforcement jobs, which are probably most threatened by the presence of mutants with superpowers.[13] However,

---

[11] The profound influence of situational factors was acutely demonstrated by two classic psychological studies: Stanley Milgram's study of obedience and Phil Zimbardo's study of prison roles. Although a detailed description and analysis of these studies is beyond the scope of this essay, taken together, these studies changed our understanding of human behavior, with situational factors taking on a much more prominent role.

[12] S.H.I.E.L.D. originally stood for Supreme Headquarters, International Espionage, Law-Enforcement Division but was changed in 1991 to Strategic Hazard Intervention, Espionage and Logistics Directorate. It is a counterterrorism and intelligence agency in the X-Universe, which deals with superhuman threats (Wikipedia, 2007).

[13] This topic is given a detailed treatment in Alan Moore's critically acclaimed *Watchmen* (DC Comics, 1987).

given the vast array of mutant powers, there are probably few occupations in which humans could truly compete on an equal basis.

Of course, there are other resources to compete for besides jobs, including political representation or, in more general terms, political power. This is one way of understanding why oppressed groups are sometimes at odds with each other rather than presenting a unified front against the dominant group. That is, minority groups are reluctant to work together because each may be afraid that its political, social, and economic interests would be subsumed or even subverted under the umbrella-group's agenda. By the same token, the dominant group is often reluctant to voluntarily include members of minority groups in the political process because of the possibility that these individuals would favor their group interests over those of the majority group.[14] Perhaps this is the real reason for Senator Kelly's campaign against the mutants: He is afraid that, left to their own devices, mutants will eventually acquire political power, which they can then leverage for their own interests that may not coincide with human interests.

Of course, there is more—much more—to prejudice than just competition over resources. Social Identity Theory provides an entirely different perspective.

SOCIAL IDENTITY THEORY

First proposed by Henri Tajfel[15] and John Turner (Taijfel & Turner), Social Identity Theory (SIT) consists of three elements: *categorization*, *identification*, and *comparison*. Categorization consists of people's inclination to put both themselves and others into categories, such as Blacks, gays, feminists, or mutants.[16] Identity (or identification) is then presumed to be determined through an association with those groups that make people feel good about themselves, groups that are seen as good, strong, and positive. However, "good," "strong," and "positive" are relative terms. That is, an in-group is only "good"

---

[14] In this context, it will be interesting to see how Barack Obama fares in the 2008 primary.

[15] Like Eric Leshnerr, Tajfel was a Holocaust survivor.

[16] These categories (especially racial categories) are, for the most part, social constructions. That is, although the variation in people's skin tone and other features is real, we are socialized to give special meaning to "race" that we don't give to other types of human variation, such as eye color or hair color.

if it is better than a relevant out-group, which is where comparison comes in. According to Social Identity Theory, people compare their in-group with other groups, with a strong bias toward viewing their own group positively and the out-group critically.[17] The result of this often-innocent process is out-group prejudice.

Of course, the comparisons are often *not* made innocently, especially by those who push a war agenda. Thus, when the group categories are (1) readily accepted and (2) widely incorporated into people's identity, group comparisons can be used by war hawks on both sides to mobilize their group for conflict. These two criteria are clearly met in the X-Universe, allowing both Magneto and Senator Kelly to appeal to core beliefs (about one's in-group) that are associated with people's willingness to support or engage in group conflict.[18] Senator Kelly appeals is to humanity's sense of vulnerability, cautioning that "We must know who they are, and above all, what they can do" (X-Men), while Magneto makes appeals to several mobilizing beliefs, including vulnerability (e.g., "it's just a matter of time before mutants are herded off to camps"), distrust (e.g., "there is no land of tolerance"), and superiority (e.g., "We are the future, Charles, not them; they no longer matter") (X-Men).

Altogether, the X-Universe's depiction of how anti-mutant prejudice is formed and then manipulated by leaders is psychologically sound. Unfortunately, the creative team's attempt to draw a series of explicit parallels to the Civil Rights Movement is less successful, and it is to this analogy that I now turn.

PARALLELS TO OTHER FORMS OF OPPRESSION

A variety of critics have compared Xavier's (and Magneto's) fight for mutant rights to the U.S. Civil Rights movement of the 1960s. Indeed,

---

[17] This tendency is so strong that individuals even show consistent in-group favoritism in minimal group experiments in which participants are told that they are being assigned to a group based on some meaningless characteristic (e.g., shirt color) and are never given the opportunity to meet or learn anything about either in-group or out-group members. It is worth noting, however, that although minimal groups do yield in-group favoritism, they do not result in out-group derogation. In other words, minimal-group participants may be more likely to describe their in-group in positive terms; they are not more likely to describe out-group members in negative terms.

[18] The five core beliefs are that one's in-group is vulnerable, has experienced injustice, has reason to be distrustful of the out-group, is superior (sometimes expressed as moral superiority), and has the means to win (Eidelson & Eidelson).

there are important parallels, including mob violence and familiar hateful slogans, such as "The only good mutant is a dead mutant." In addition, the X-Universe is populated by a variety of anti-mutant hate groups such as *Friends of Humanity, Humanity's Last Stand, the Church of Humanity*, and *Stryker's Purifiers*, which represent real oppressive forces like the Ku Klux Klan and a variety of other Christian Identity[19] and White Supremacy groups. It is also notable that, like some Blacks in the pre-civil rights South, many mutants keep their status hidden, hoping to blend or "pass" into mainstream society, while others want to actually *be* human so much that they volunteer for a "cure" with unknown risks (*X-Men: The Last Stand*).

However, the mutants' experience of prejudice is in many ways not analogous to the oppression experienced by Blacks and other racial minority groups. To begin with, although many groups experience prejudice, the specific attitudes that people hold and express toward these groups are often very different. This was demonstrated by Susan Fiske et al., who had samples of college students and community members rate twenty-three different out-groups on two dimensions: expressed warmth (i.e., how positively people felt toward out-group members) and perceived competence (i.e., how competent people perceived out-group members to be). Results from both samples (see chart below) revealed three different types of prejudice: *paternalistic prejudice* (high warmth towards group with low perception of group's competence), *contemptuous prejudice* (low warmth towards group with low perception of group's competence), and *envious prejudice* (low warmth towards group with high perception of group's competence). While this study did not include mutants in their list of out-groups (clearly a glaring oversight!), X-Men fans know that mutants tend to be regarded by humans with little warmth but are perceived to be high in competence. This combination would place them squarely into the envious prejudice category, far from most African Americans today and farther still from how Black Americans were perceived during the fight for civil rights in the 1960s.[20]

There are still other problems with the analogy. Although oppressed

---

[19] Christian Identity (CI) is a label applied to a wide variety of loosely affiliated groups and churches with a racialized theology, including Aryan Nations. Many CI believers "justify the use of violence in order to punish violators of God's law," as interpreted by CI ministers and adherents (Wikipedia).

[20] They are similarly far from gay men, another parallel intended by the X-Men creative team.

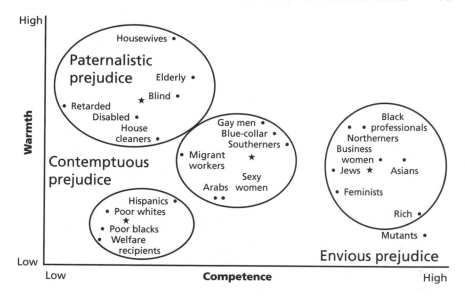

Perception of Out-Groups, from Fiske et al., (2002), JPSP, 82, 878–902.

groups are not necessarily powerless,[21] unlike some mutants, they often lack the physical force or political power to stop their own oppression. Under these circumstances, placing the burden of peace and tolerance on the oppressed group can itself be seen as a subtle form of oppression; for, this expectation blames the victimized for their own victimization. Thus, while it is reasonable to expect super-powered mutants to make accommodations in order to fit into mainstream society, this expectation becomes increasingly less reasonable the less power an oppressed group enjoys *vis-à-vis* mainstream society.[22]

Unfortunately, the tendency to blame the oppressed group for its victimization is not just a fictional or historical phenomenon. Today our society continues to express this mindset in a variety of instantly

---

[21] Oppressed groups have used everything from non-violent resistance, to more physical resistance to more physical resistance like rock and bottle throwing to even more physical resistance like guns and home-made bombs to fight more powerful groups–sometimes successfully, sometimes not.

[22] Taken to an extreme, such a mindset would have blamed Jews in Nazi Germany and Blacks in the antebellum South for their victimization and expected them to make accommodations for the sake of peace, rather than demanding that the society itself become more accepting and less oppressive. In fact, this is what actually occurred as Nazis blamed the Jews for their condition and slave owners rationalized the institution of slavery by arguing that the "uncivilized" Africans needed the firm hand of the slave masters to lead happy and productive lives.

recognizable ways, as when we suggest that a woman who was sexually assaulted should have worn less revealing clothing or imply that a gay man could choose to have a different sexual orientation. On some level, X-Men United (X-2, 2003) understands the folly of this type of thinking. The film even pokes fun of victim-blaming tendencies in its very effective parody (and social critique) of how some families react to a child who "comes out" as gay.[23] Indeed, it is no more possible to will oneself into not being a mutant, as it is to will oneself into not being gay or female or a person of color. Yet, the X-Men creative team fails to take the critique to its logical conclusion, for it accepts the assumption that it is the mutants (and, by extension, gays, lesbians, and people of color) who must somehow make themselves fit into mainstream society, rather than expecting society to become more inclusive.

The portrayal of leaders is yet another serious flaw in the X-Universe's treatment of prejudice. Just as mutants are designed to represent oppressed groups, so are the mutant leaders intended to represent leaders of oppressed groups. More specifically, it is widely accepted by X-Men fans that Charles Xavier and Magneto represent the philosophies of Dr. Martin Luther King, Jr., and Malcolm X, respectively. This argument posits that, like King, Charles Xavier works for better relations between humans and mutants, "dreaming" of peace, acceptance, and integration, while, in contrast, Magneto is a militant "reverse-racist" who, having "lost faith in the unfulfilled 'dream', fights for the liberation of his people 'by any means necessary'"[24] (Morpheus, 2003). It's a provocative argument, and Magneto's use of the phrase "by any means necessary" leaves little doubt that the parallel was intended by the writers. Unfortunately, the analogy is entirely inaccurate. To begin with, despite his contention that "mankind isn't evil, just uninformed" (X-Men, 2000), Xavier starts a school to educate mutants, not humans. His rationale for doing so is that when humans see that the mutants don't constitute a threat, they will have no reason to hate and fear them. The comparable strategy

---

[23] When Bobby (the Iceman) "comes out" (as a mutant) to his family, the disclosure causes his younger brother to turn him in to the authorities, but it is his mother's sugary response that is instructive in this context: "Bobby, have you ever tried not being a mutant?" she asks him gently (X-2, 2003).

[24] Magneto uses this phrase in his conversation with Xavier at the end of X-Men (2000), saying: "The [human-mutant] war is coming, and I intend to fight it by any means necessary."

of educating Blacks on how to work and live better with Whites was, in fact, advocated by some Black leaders in late nineteenth and early twentieth century, particularly by Booker T. Washington.[25] However, this strategy was entirely out of favor by the 1960s, when Malcolm X, King, and other Civil Rights leaders all advocated some sort of resistance. Moreover, Xavier rarely actually agitates, campaigns, or even speaks out for mutant rights, focusing his energy instead on persuading the X-Men to "use their awesome abilities to protect a world that hates and fears them" from other, more malevolent, mutants. This is the equivalent of King shielding the White majority from Malcolm X and the Black Power movement rather than fighting for Black equality and justice. This never happened!

The Magneto/Malcolm X parallel is even more problematic. To be sure, Magneto, like Malcolm X, actually does seem to be genuinely concerned with mutant rights and also at one point adopts a separatist stance. However, despite this concern, as well as his one-time friendship with Xavier, Magneto, for the most part, is more focused on world domination than on mutant rights. Even the name of his organization, Brotherhood of Evil Mutants,[26] is more indicative of fanaticism and terrorism than social activism and racial justice. This supposed representation of Malcolm X is not only historically inaccurate but actually serves to reinforce many White fears and stereotypes about African Americans in general and Black Muslims in particular.

The real Malcolm X was a complex, multi-layered person whose thinking about race and racism evolved over the course of his life. For a period in his life, under the direction of Elijah Muhammad, he loathed all Whites. However, he eventually rejected this racist be-

---

[25] Readers looking for real-world counterparts for Xavier and Magneto should examine the lives and work of Booker T. Washington, and W. E. B. Du Bois, respectively. Like Xavier, Washington stressed the need for the oppressed group (Blacks) to work together with the dominant group (Whites) and saw education (of Blacks) as the primary means toward gaining acceptance and tolerance. Meanwhile, Du Bois started out as Washington's ally but over time grew increasingly critical of Washington for his unwillingness to aggressively confront Whites about Black civil rights. Du Bois called Washington "The Great Accommodator," but the two men continued an ongoing dialogue about segregation and the Black struggle, long after they began to differ on the best way to achieve these rights. Of course, the Magneto/Du Bois parallel is also flawed. Unlike the often-villainous Magneto, Du Bois never advocated violence and, at the end of his life, was sympathetic to the class-less Communist ideology.

[26] The X-Men films removed the word "evil" found in the comics, allowing Magneto to form instead the much more palatable "Brotherhood of Mutants."

lief system,[27] and corresponding adversarial stance, replacing it with a more moderate approach that included working with other Civil Rights activists—White and Black. In the context of the X-Men's appropriation of the "by any means necessary" phrase, it also bears stressing that a close examination of Malcolm X's speeches, autobiography,[28] and private correspondence shows "no evidence that he advocated the use of wanton violence against whites" but rather suggested that Blacks respond to violence with violence when the law fails to protect them (Leader, 1993, p. 174).

CONCLUSION

These are egregious flaws, and their probable harm to readers' thinking about race relations should not be dismissed or minimized. And yet, I cannot bring myself to take an overly critical stance. The X-Men creative teams present an accurate depiction of prejudice and, at times, manage to turn a superhero soap-opera into an opportunity to meaningfully engage readers of all ages with social issues that are all too often ignored by both the mainstream media and mainstream educational institutions. Moreover, even if the X-Men comics and films at times fail to adequately or accurately convey what scholars have learned about prejudice and group relations, they nevertheless open the door for historians and social scientists to enter the discussion and provide their own perspectives. These discussions are sorely needed, if sharing the world is *ever* to be humanity's defining attribute.

---

[27] He later referred to this period of his life as foolishness that cost him twelve lost years (Clarke, 1969).

[28] "I'm not for wanton violence, I'm for justice....And I feel that when the law fails to protect Negroes from whites' attack then those Negroes should use arms, if necessary, to defend themselves....I am speaking against and my fight is against white *racists*. I firmly believe that Negroes have the right to fight against these racists, by any means that are necessary" (Malcolm X and Haley, 1965, 366–367).

Dr. Mikhail Lyubansky is a lecturer in the Department of Psychology at the University of Illinois-Urbana-Champaign, where he teaches *Psychology of Race and Ethnicity* and *Theories of Psychotherapy*. His research interests focus on conditions associated with changes in social identity and beliefs about race, ethnicity, and nationalism, especially in immigrant and minority populations. He recently co-authored a book about Russian-Jewish immigration: *Building a Diaspora: Russian Jews in Israel, Germany, and the United States*. He has no known mutant powers but provides regular Congressional testimony opposing the Mutant Registration Act.

REFERENCES

Clarke, J. H. (Ed.). *Malcolm X: The Man and His Times.* Ontario: The Macmillan Company, 1969.

R. J. Eidelson and J. I. Eidelson, "Dangerous ideas: Five Beliefs that Propel Groups toward Conflict," *American Psychologist 58 (2003):* 182–192.

S. Fiske, A. J. C. Cuddy, P. Glick, and J. Xu. "A Model of (often mixed) Stereotype Content: Competence and Warmth Respectively Follow from Perceived Status and Competition," *Journal of Personality and Social Psychology 82.6 (2002):* 878–902.

Kinder, D.R. "Opinion and Action in the Realm of Politics." In D.T. Gilbert, S.T. Fiske, and G. Lindzey (Eds.), *Handbook of Social Psychology, Vol. 2.* 415–469. New York: McGraw-Hill, 1998.

Kühl, Stephan. *The Nazi Connection: Eugenics, American Racism, and German National Socialism.* New York: Oxford University Press, 1994.

Leader, E. R. *Understanding Malcolm X: The Controversial Changes in his Political Philosophy.* New York: Vantage Press, 1993.

Malcolm X and A Haley. *An Autobiography of Malcolm X. With the Assistance of Alex Haley.* New York: Ballantine Books, 1987.

Morpheus Reloaded. "Beyond Children of the Atom: Black Politics, White Minds and the X-Men." Playahata.com. *28 Feb. 2007.*

Runciman, W. G. *Relative Deprivation and Social Justice: A Study of Attitudes toward Social Inequality in Twentieth Century England.* London: Routledge & Keegan Paul, 1966.
<http://www.playahata.com/pages/morpheus/xmen.htm.>

Sherif, M, Harvey, O.J., White, B.J., Hood, W.R., & Sherif, C.W. (1954/1961). Intergroup Conflict and Cooperation: The Robbers

Cave Experiment. In Classics in the History of Psychology. Retrieved 3-05-07 from http://psychclassics.yorku.ca/Sherif/

Tajfel, H, & Turner, J. C. "An Integrative Theory of Intergroup Conflict," In W. S. Austin & S. Worchel (Eds.). *The Social Psychology of Intergroup Relations* (pp. 33–47). Monterey, CA: Brooks/Cole, 1979.

X-Men. dir. B. Singer. United States: Twentieth Century Fox, 2000.

X2: X-Men United. dir. B. Singer. Lee, United States: Twentieth Century Fox, 2003.

X-Men: The Last Stand. dir. B. Ratner. United States: Twentieth Century Fox, 2006.

Bryan J. Dik, Ph.D.

WHEN I GROW UP
I WANT TO BE A SUPERHERO

For most superheroes, their real job—fighting crime and saving innocent lives—is a calling. It is the logical career path given their abilities
and talents. Most of the time, that calling is fulfilling, despite the sacrifices and hardships. As Dik points out in this essay, we too can become superheroes when each of us works toward the common good;
in doing so, we can find meaning in our work.

SERIOUSLY, WHO AMONG US hasn't imagined what it would be
like to wake up one morning with superpowers? If only we could be
so lucky. One accidental chemical bath and you're stretching your
body into any imaginable form. One newly activated mutant gene
and you're able to manipulate the weather. One brief exposure to
cosmic radiation and you find yourself with superhuman strength,
stamina, and a very helpful resistance to physical injury. Granted, life
as a superhero is not all fun and games—what with having to keep

your superhero identity a secret[1] (what fun would that be?), working odd hours (usually nights), and evil villains constantly trying to harm your loved ones. Regardless of the specific pros and cons, there is at least one advantage granted to superheroes (in addition to their actual superpowers) that mere mortals can envy: ease of career choice. Many people spin their wheels for years trying to figure out the right career for them. But find yourself with a useful superpower, and it isn't a stretch to see that a lifetime of fighting crime is a career choice that just makes good sense.

Despite all our differences, there is much in the lives of superheroes that mirrors the lives of us mortals. (If you've read any of this book, this probably is becoming obvious.) Career development is no exception. Superheroes and mortals approach career choice similarly; we examine the characteristics that make us unique and then look for jobs that best fit our uniqueness. Superheroes and mortals also share similar challenges over the course of their careers (and into retirement); we experience numerous changes we have to adapt to, cycling through predictable stages of adjustment with each change. Finally, superheroes and mortals try to find meaning in their work in more or less the same ways; at our best, we try to connect our work responsibilities to a larger sense of purpose in life, with promotion of the common good as a meaningful, motivating goal. These kinds of similarities point to this conclusion: ultimately—in a sense, at least—all of us are superheroes.

ALL ABOUT FIT: CAREER CHOICE

Peter Parker was the typical insecure teen just trying to survive high school before he received the spider bite that spawned his superpowers. His transformation into Spider-Man was dramatic—from skinny, clumsy (albeit intellectually gifted) teen one day to web-shooting,[2] wall-climbing super-teen the next. Peter immediately knew that his newfound abilities could be put to use to accomplish things he had

---

[1] This characteristic refers to the prototypic superhero. Certainly, there are superheroes whose identities are no secret (e.g., Luke Cage, the Fantastic Four).

[2] Graphic novel purists will note, undoubtedly to their horror, that I describe the movie *Spider-Man* here. For the original comic book Spider-Man, web-shooting was not a natural ability; instead, Peter Parker engineered mechanical web shooters that Spider-Man affixed to his wrists.

never before dreamed possible. His early attempts to capitalize on his uniqueness found him in the wrestling ring and, soon after, pursuing a television career. These career moves started reasonably well, but felt hollow after his Uncle Ben was murdered by a burglar that Peter could earlier have stopped. Fortunately, Peter learned quickly that "with great power comes great responsibility"—and that fighting New York's evil villains was a vocation that fit his strengths extremely well.

Psychologists have been studying how people make decisions about their careers for roughly a century, and in that time have learned some things about what makes for a wise career choice. One of the most critical factors is "person-environment fit." Basically, the idea is that people can be described in ways that make them unique—in terms of things like interests, abilities, personality traits, values, and so forth. Jobs also can be described in ways that make them unique—in terms of things like what needs to get done, what skills are required, what kinds of rewards are offered, and so forth. The challenge faced by the person trying to choose a career involves figuring out what job is the best fit for the kind of person she or he is. This is not a complicated concept. It's not a new concept, either. In fact, Frank Parsons,[3] often called the father of vocational psychology, championed the idea in his classic 1909 book *Choosing a Vocation* (Parsons, 1909).

What makes the phenomenon of late-onset-superheroism so enviable to the chronically career undecided is that it makes assessing fit seem so easy. All of the sudden, there is an ability or skill that is so pronounced, so unique, and so unbelievably cool, any clear-thinking, morally centered person would naturally use it to combat the forces of evil. For the rest of us, identifying what makes us best suited for a particular career is less straightforward. At least in part, this is because mortal abilities—and interests, personality, needs, values, etc.—tend to emerge in subtler ways. Typically, psychologists use the term "traits" to refer to the kinds of characteristics that are most rel-

---

[3] Curiously, Parsons's own vocational path was extremely chaotic. He worked as a civil engineer, then steelworker, then earned a law degree and passed the bar exam before a general breakdown led to his living in the open in New Mexico, after which he taught law part-time at Boston University. Eventually, in 1908, he persuaded a philanthropist to fund the Vocation Bureau of Boston. Parsons died just nine months after this organization was founded; his classic book was published posthumously by friends. Vocational psychologists usually avoid bringing all of this up.

evant for this purpose (see Table 1 for a sampling of work-related human traits). Unlike X-ray vision, invisibility, and freeze powers (see Table 2 for a non-exhaustive list of other superpowers), traits are not all-or-nothing phenomena (i.e., things that either people have in their entirety or don't have at all). Rather, they refer to things that all of us possess, just in different amounts.

Take something like numerical reasoning. Numerical reasoning is a type of ability—specifically, the ability to grasp relationships among numbers and to understand ideas related to numbers. Some people have very high levels of this ability (and are very good at math); some have very low levels, and the rest of us fall somewhere between the extremes. The idea is that all of us can be described by our position on the continuum for this trait. Trait dimensions help describe people in terms of abilities, but also interests, values, personality, and a number of other characteristics. All of us differ from each other on each trait, and each of us has a unique pattern of strengths and weaknesses that might be described using these traits.

To illustrate, imagine if Peter Parker had squashed the offending spider before its fateful bite, never to enjoy the benefits (or endure the drawbacks) of life as Spider-Man. Peter may have wondered, as most of the rest of us did (or do), what kind of job he ought to pursue after high school or college. Given what we know about Peter, he likely would have scored high on trait measures of abilities having to do with science, such as scholastic aptitude, abstract reasoning, and numerical reasoning. He also is likely to have scored high on Investigative and Artistic interests, given his enjoyment of science and photography. Personality characteristics tend to fluctuate until early adulthood, but we might imagine that Peter would be reasonably conscientious and open to experience, characteristics that may have joined with his interests and abilities to reveal graduate school as a viable option. Ultimately, Peter may have expressed values related to autonomy and achievement, which he may have opted to satisfy as, say, a reporter, a research scientist, an engineer, or perhaps a college professor.[4] Ultimately, Peter took advantage of his double-identity by freelancing photographs of Spider-Man that, conveniently, he had a better knack for taking than did any other photographer. This

---

[4] Please forgive any projection of myself onto Peter that may have occurred as I wrote this.

TABLE 1
Four Categories of Work-Relevant Human Traits

Interests[a]

Realistic
Interests in working with one's hands, being outdoors, mechanical activities, athletics, and protective services.

Investigative
Interests in pondering intellectual questions and using the methods of science to investigate those questions.

Artistic
Interests in the arts, broadly defined to include fine arts, writing, drama, music, culinary arts, and general self-expression.

Social
Interests in working alongside people or in roles that directly help people, such as social service or teaching.

Enterprising
Interests in activities involving the use of persuasion, such as sales, management, law, politics, and public speaking.

Conventional
Interests in detail-oriented tasks such as organizing and managing data.

Abilities[b]

Verbal Reasoning
Ability to see relationships between words, understand how words work, and use them effectively.

Numerical Reasoning
Ability to reason with numbers and solve number-based problems.

Abstract Reasoning
Ability to understand and work with visual patterns and to reason without words.

Perceptual Speed and Accuracy
Ability to work quickly on simple visual tasks (e.g., visually scanning two sets of numbers to determine if they are the same) that don't require reasoning.

Mechanical Reasoning
Ability to understand basic mechanicals principles of machinery, tools, and motion.

Space Relations
Ability to comprehend the two-dimensional representation of three-dimensional objects and to think visually of geometric forms.

Spelling
Ability to spell common words correctly and identify misspelled words.

Language Usage
Ability to understand how the language is correctly used, including comprehension and application of grammar.

Scholastic Aptitude
Ability to learn from books and teachers and to perform well in school subjects.

Values[c]

Achievement
Preferences for using one's self-perceived skills and talents, and engaging in tasks that produce a sense of pride and accomplishment.

Comfort
Preferences for tasks requiring sustained levels of energy, completing tasks independently, receiving fair compensation and job security, engaging in a range of possible activities, and working in agreeable physical conditions.

Status
Preferences for having opportunities to advance, receiving recognition readily, having opportunities to exercise authority, and receiving respect and status.

Altruism
Preferences for having supportive relationships with co-workers, for engaging in tasks that promote the welfare of others, and engaging in tasks that are in line with one's moral values.

Safety
Preferences for company policies that are clear and consistent, for supportive supervisors, and for competent and effective supervisors.

Autonomy
Preferences for engaging in tasks that facilitate autonomy and accountability and that are amenable to innovation and creativity.

Personality[d]

Neuroticism
High: prone to distress, nervous, insecure, tense, unstable
Low: relaxed, stable, calm, resilient, secure, content

Extraversion
High: sociable, talkative, assertive, energetic, active, adventurous
Low: reserved, unassertive, self-contained, cautious, prefer intimate relationships

Openness to Experience
High: imaginative, intellectually curious, creative, unconventional
Low: down-to-earth, conventional, practical, content with the familiar

Conscientious
High: responsible, persevering, organized, disciplined, determined
Low: spontaneous, careless, easily distracted, absent-minded, undependable

Agreeableness
High: cooperative, trusting, good-natured, accommodating, unselfish
Low: cynical, irritable, negativistic, headstrong

[a]Holland (1997). [b]Bennett, Seashore, & Wesman (1990). [c]Davis & Lofquist (1984). [d]McCrae & Costa (1997).

TABLE 2
Representative Superpowers and Superhero Examples

Superpower	Superhero Examples
Control of natural elements	Polaris, Storm
Distance energy blast capability	Cyclops, Starfire
Extrasensory perception	Professor X, Saturn Girl
Magic	Dr. Strange, Zatanna
Shape changing	Mister Fantastic, Plastic Man
Size changing	The Atom, Colossal Boy
Superhuman speed	The Flash, Quicksilver
Superhuman strength	The Incredible Hulk, The Thing

job appeared to be a great fit with his interests and abilities, and was a wise move given his uncanny ability for always being in the right place at the right time with the camera. Perhaps photography would have become his day job even if he hadn't become Spider-Man, but we can assume that he would have had to work a lot harder to capture the kind of shots the *Daily Bugle* would have considered newsworthy enough to pay a livable wage for.

Psychologists interested in helping people make informed career decisions generally assume that work-related traits can be measured using psychological tests, and that scores on these tests predict real-life outcomes like career choice or happiness on the job. Research has generally supported these assumptions, which is why scores on such tests can be very useful in career counseling. However, because there are so many human traits relevant for choosing a best-fitting career, because psychologists are still learning about how all these traits interact, and because multiple occupations (not just one) usually are available to satisfy any one person's unique combination of traits, choosing a career remains as much an art as it is a science.

ADAPTING TO CHANGE: CAREER DEVELOPMENT FOR THE LONG HAUL

In *Batman: The Dark Knight Returns* (Miller, Janson, and Varley, 1986), we learn that as Bruce Wayne has entered his middle-age years, his secret identity, Batman, has been retired for a decade. With no caped crusader to deter the crime elements of Gotham City, civil violence has skyrocketed. In a meeting with police commissioner James Gordon, Bruce accepted this toast:

GORDON: To Batman.
WAYNE: It's good that he retired—isn't it?
GORDON: I'm grateful he *survived* retirement.
WAYNE: He didn't. But *Bruce Wayne* is...alive and well.
GORDON: Glad to hear that. You've certainly learned to *drink* (12).

Bruce *was* alive, but didn't, in fact, appear to be well. His penchant for the bottle was raising not only Gordon's eyebrows but also those of Alfred, his longtime butler, who also noted that Bruce wasn't getting out much. Bruce was told, "You just need a woman" (12). Not long before, the possibility of female companionship would not have been considered a stretch; given his good looks, charisma, and millionaire status, Bruce had women available at his beck and call. However, when he was honest with himself, Bruce admitted that he had long ignored the beckoning of another sort: "[I]n my gut the creature writhes and snarls and tells me just what I need" (12). As the news reports about the atrocities committed by the Mutant gang members in crime-riddled Gotham City increased in frequency and intensity, Bruce finally had enough and gave into the urge that had long been welling up inside of him. And thus Batman came out of retirement with a vengeance.

As critical as one's initial career choice often feels, and as much relief as people typically experience once they make that choice, the reality is that career development only begins there. After a period of exploration culminates in the choice of a particular occupational path, most people are left with the daunting task of landing a job, to be followed by the even more daunting future of some forty-plus years of working, with all its joys (so one hopes) and disappointments. Psychologist Mark Savickas (2005) points out that different cultures have different "grand narratives" for how careers typically unfold. In most Western cultures, and certainly in the United States, the prototypic career path generally moves through a series of predictable stages. These stages first were described in the late 1950s by

the aptly named Donald Super (1957), one of the preeminent vocational psychologists of the twentieth century. The stages are as follows:

(1) Growth: In childhood, the individual becomes concerned
about her future career, begins to take control of her work-related activities, forms conceptions about how to make career choices,
and becomes confident in her ability to make and implement those
choices.

(2) Exploration: During adolescence and early adulthood, the individual explores various career options before deciding on a path
to pursue.

(3) Establishment: After landing a job in her chosen field, the individual spends the first part of her career trying to make a name for
herself in that position.

(4) Management or Maintenance: Eventually, the focus shifts to
sustaining what has been established. This requires coping with
changes in the workplace, updating, and innovating.

(5) Disengagement: The individual plans for, and transitions into,
retirement.

Most adults in the United States probably use these stages as an
outline of sorts to help describe for other people what our career
paths have looked like, because the steps still represent a template
that most Americans understand to be typical. It's important to note,
however, that the percentage of people with career paths that conform to this "norm" has decreased considerably since the time Super first articulated these stages. In today's world, career changes are
the rule, not the exception. People move in and out of different careers, and more and more professionals are becoming "free agent"
types who provide services to whichever company is paying, rather than spending their entire careers with one organization. Often,
as soon as people get established in an organization, they leave and
face a transition requiring renewed growth, re-exploration, and re-
establishment. Super identified this phenomenon and increased its
emphasis later in his career, describing the transition as a process of
"recycling" in which people redo the various stages, often repeat-

edly, over the course of their careers (e.g., Super, Savickas, and Super, 1996). For example, leaving the workforce for a time to pursue full-time parenting requires disengagement; re-entering the workforce after time away requires new growth, exploration, and establishment. A layoff forces a very similar process of recycling through the stages, as might a premature retirement.

The aging, restless Bruce Wayne we see in *The Dark Knight Returns* gives us a clear sense of what recycling through career stages can look like for a superhero. Batman hung up his bat-suit after the tragic death of Jason Todd, the second Robin, who was murdered at the hands of the Joker. Not many details are known about Batman's decision to retire, but it seems apparent that the transition was abrupt. Although still haunted by Jason's death, Bruce was haunted to an even greater degree by the decaying state of Gotham and by an inner voice, impossible to silence, that urged the return of Batman. Ultimately Bruce ended Batman's foray into the disengagement stage. Batman entered a period of re-establishment, integrating again into the world of crime fighting, thereby causing the seedy underbelly of Gotham as well as Gordon's police force to rethink their respective strategies and to accommodate the reality that Batman was back on the scene. His return reinvigorated Batman (e.g., "'This should be agony,' he said while hurling himself through the air. 'I should be a mass of aching muscle... but I'm a man of thirty—of twenty again,'" [Miller, Jansen, and Varley, 1986, 34]). Nonetheless, he also felt his age and had to compensate accordingly (e.g., "[I'm] old enough to need my legs to climb a rope," he thought, while doing just that [37]), a kind of adaptation to change typical of the management or maintenance phase.

The heartening part of Batman's story is that even despite the changes that had come with age, he was able to choose a course of action that resonates with his values and then adjust to those changes, working out a way to be successful despite them. Bringing it a bit closer to our own experience is Batman's status as a superhero without actual superpowers (other than his athleticism, specialized training in martial arts, and a utility belt full of gadgets that emulate superpowers). Batman simply utilized his training, past experience, and the resources available to him to adjust well to work-related changes. Doing this requires no superpowers; from accountants and bellhops to youth workers and zoologists, the rest of us have the capacity to do this just as well.

A SUPERHERO'S CALLING

A characteristic shared by many superheroes is the strong desire to help others, even when doing so involves great personal risk. Typically, superheroes are acutely aware of the pervasive social needs that exist in the community in which they live (and sometimes in the global community). Superman stepped in to put a stop to gangsters, lynch mobs, corrupt politicians, and abusive husbands in addition to battling his nemesis, Lex Luther. Wonder Woman was initially charged with the mission of fighting Nazi evils. The Green Arrow fought for the oppressed and underprivileged working class. For many superheroes, knowing that their superpowers are often all that stands between a horde of evil villains and widespread disaster befalling innumerable innocent lives has an unmistakably motivating effect. Essentially, there is a sense of calling—a set of pressing societal needs that compels the superhero, always well-suited for the task, to do all in her or his power to meet those needs.

Psychologists only recently have begun to clarify definitions of calling or vocation and to conduct systematic research on this topic. In my own work, I define calling as having three dimensions: (1) a "transcendent summons" originating beyond the self; (2) an approach to work aimed at connecting activity within the work role to a broader sense of life purpose and meaning; and (3) "other-oriented" values and goals as a key source of motivation (Dik and Duffy, in press). The concept of "transcendent summons" conveys the notion that to be called implies the presence of someone or something issuing the call. This dimension of the concept originated in a religious context, and discerning a calling from God remains a relevant concern for a large percentage of people in today's world. However, the concept is sufficiently broad to include other sources of an external summons as well, such as particular sets of social needs, which arguably serve to summon Superman to fight evils wherever they arise. Superman is prototypic of calling-oriented superheroes (which are many in number). He is among the more principled superheroes; his idealism and belief in justice and humanitarian service clearly are evident in how he manages his job as crime-fighter. This reflects the second dimension of calling in that the activities Superman pursues in his work (e.g., battling villains and rescuing the helpless) are very much in line with his overarching life purpose (e.g., that of promoting justice and humanitarian service). Finally, the third dimension of calling requires the individual to have other-oriented goals for their work; clearly, such goals are central motivators behind Superman's attempts to protect those most in need.

Research on the effects of approaching work as a calling is only now emerging. So far, this research has yielded generally consistent results; people who approach their work as a calling tend to report higher levels of positive characteristics (e.g., life and job satisfaction, work commitment) and lower levels of negative characteristics (e.g., stress and depression) compared to people with other approaches to work (see Dik and Duffy, in press, for a review). This is the case despite the fact that people who approach work as a calling, by definition, are pursuing ends other than their own individual comfort or happiness. In fact, calling-oriented individuals may willingly sacrifice some aspects of job satisfaction (e.g., pay, security) in favor of other aspects more central to their values (e.g., making a difference in society). There are numerous examples of superheroes for which this clearly is the case.

Fortunately, there also are numerous examples of everyday superheroes who approach their work as a calling. Doctors work to restore health to ill people. Teachers help students learn, develop character, and reach their potential. Bus drivers promote safety, reduce traffic and smog, help people save money, and transport riders to places they are needed. Electricians help ensure buildings function the way they are supposed to so that occupants can best accomplish the tasks for which their skills are needed. It may not be difficult to imagine that social workers or community service organization directors can have a positive impact on society through their work, but evidence suggests that any honest area of work can be approached in this way. A student of mine recently described an encounter with a road construction worker whose workday consisted entirely of turning a sign marked "slow" on one side and "stop" on the other. This man enthu-siastically described his work as profoundly meaningful because he was saving lives every day by keeping both his co-workers and ve-hicle inhabitants safe. What may be mind-numbing to one person is the path through which another person can live out his calling.

Imagine a superhero with the powers of untold thousands of peo-ple who choose to work together in our capitalist economy with a sense of purpose toward promoting the well-being of society. Every possible area of expertise that exists is at the disposal of this super-hero; every possible human skill can be utilized and combined with any other, in any combination, to accomplish virtually any human-ly possible task. This vision at least partly represents the view of the good life and the good society that the calling and vocation perspec-tive envisions. Overly optimistic? Of course. An ideal worth striving for anyway? Definitely.

CONCLUSION

In the end, as much as we might try to imagine that our human strengths make us superheroes of sorts, the reality is that the abil-ity to alter your size, move with superhuman speed, or read others' thoughts using extrasensory perception always will trump having good space relations or mechanical reasoning skills when the ques-tion pertains to which abilities are most desirable. Still, it's probably useful to assume that until the day comes when one of your genes mutates to give you a useful superpower, there are ways to use what makes you unique to choose a best-fitting job, adjust to the inevi-table changes that will unfold, and to think about your work—sig-nificant or insignificant as it may be—as a way to contribute to the common good. If all that separates you from a superhero is a super-power, well, there is no shame in that.

Bryan J. Dik, Ph.D., completed his doctoral study at the University of Minnesota and during daylight hours is an assistant professor in the counseling psychology program at Colorado State University. His scholarly interests fall broadly in the domain of vocational psychology and include person-environment fit theories of career development, measurement of vocational interests, and basic and applied research on calling and vocation. He lives with his wife Amy and sons Eli and Silas in Wellington, Colorado.

REFERENCES

Bennett, G. K., Seashore, H. G., and Wesman, A. G. *Differential Aptitude Tests* (5th ed.). San Antonio, TX: Psychological Corporation, 1990.

Dawis, R. V. and Lofquist, L. *A Psychological Theory of Work Adjustment.* Minneapolis, MN: University of Minnesota Press, 1984.

B. J. Dik and R. D. Duffy (in press), "Calling and Vocation at Work: Definitions and Prospects for Research and Practice," *The Counseling Psychologist.*

Holland, J. L. *Making Vocational Choices: A Theory of Vocational Personalities and Work Environments* (3rd ed.). Odessa, FL: Psychological Assessment Resources, 1997.

Parsons, F. *Choosing a Vocation.* Boston: Houghton Mifflin, 1909.

R. R. McCrae and P. T. Costa, Jr., "Personality Trait Structure as a Human Universa," *American Psychologist* 52 509–516.

Miller, F., Janson, K., and Varley, L. *Batman: The Dark Knight Returns 1–4.* New York: DC Comics, 1986.

Savickas, M. L. "The Theory and Practice of Career Construction," In S. D. Brown & R. W. Lent (Eds.), *Career Development and Counseling: Putting Theory and Research to Work* (42–70). Hoboken, NJ: Wiley, 2005.

Super, D. E. *The Psychology of Careers.* New York: Harper and Rowe, 1957.

Super, D.E., Savickas, M. L., and Super, C. M. (1996). The Life-span, Life-space Approach to Careers. In D. Brown, L. Brooks, and associates (Eds.), *Career Choice and Development* (3rd ed., 121–178). San Francisco: Jossey-Bass, 1996.

THE PSYCHOLOGY OF
SUPERHEROES

Peter A. Hancock
and Gabriella M. Hancock

IS THERE A SUPERHERO IN ALL OF US?

What distinguishes superheroes from the rest of us? Hancock and Hancock explore this question, focusing on superheroes' advanced abilities—to see, to hear, to fly, among others—and how these advanced abilities set them apart. But it isn't just these super-*abilities* that make them superheroes. After all, some villains have superpowers too. What, then, distinguishes superhero from super-villain? It is how they *use* their superpowers—the morality that guides their actions.

IN THE BEGINNING

A mighty and powerful father figure sends his only begotten son to serve and redeem the people of one small and backward planet. The son is adopted by a humble but normal human family and grows to manhood in relative obscurity. However, this individual can perform miraculous feats and in so doing he earns a mythical status (Campbell, 1991, 1). He is attacked repeatedly by evil men but in the end he triumphs over all to assure his position as a legend to humankind. But where do these miraculous powers come from? Is he super intelligent as well as possessing other extraordinary abilities? Indeed, what is it like to be such a person? What are the psychological dimensions of this individual's experience and what sort of super reality does he encounter? And perhaps most interesting of all, exactly who is this superhero? To understand the answers to these questions is to begin to understand the superhero in each of us.

UNDERSTANDING SUPER-PERCEPTION AND SUPER-ACTION

Let us begin our quest by looking at the psychological dimensions of these supposed superpowers. We need to start with perception, since perception is the process by which life extracts meaning from the world. As the confluence of sensation and experience, perception underlies all of our reality. As different forms of life each use their own distinct sensory systems, they each create their own individual perceived reality. If perception is the process which extracts meaning from the world then action is the process by which life changes it. Again, different forms of life exert different forms of action to shape the environment in which they live, according to the meaning that they find within it. Perception without action is impotent. Action without perception is purposeless. Perception and action are thus two sides of the same coin so that actions always change perceptions and these new perceptions, in their turn, serve to guide future actions (Gibson 1). So, how does super-perception and super-action create a super-reality beyond that which is experienced by us mere mortals?

The first type of super-perception we need to consider is represented by the highly magnified extensions of our already resident human capabilities. These magnifications are largely a matter of scale and imply a greater level of sensitivity than we regular humans normally possess. So the individual we are considering would possess super-vision and would be able to see things at far distances that would be hidden to the rest of us. They would have enhanced hearing and be able to listen to conversations all over the world at the same time. Similarly, they would have magnified olfactory abilities and would be able to recognize smells that to us are undetectable but to other animals represent a large part of their perceptual world and therefore their reality (Budiansky 1). They would possess super touch—in fact all of the regular human senses would be acutely sensitive. This enhanced level of perception immediately implies the need for a super level of attention, since with these enhanced perceptual powers there would be so much more information available to be sorted, filtered, and processed. For an individual with super perception but only normal attention, the world would just appear to be a "blooming, buzzing confusion" (James 462), which is exactly how William James, one of the fathers of Psychology, described the world of the newborn. Indeed, perhaps this is how we ourselves cognitively mature as individuals—by progressively sorting out meaning from what initially appears to be just an unordered avalanche of stimulation (Tammet 1). But, would a person endowed with these super levels of perception and super levels of attention also have to have an equally enhanced level of intelligence? For if they are not super smart, how do they wield these enhanced powers that they possess? When superpowers are just magnified extensions of normal human capacities, the super-being will still basically experience an enhanced human form of reality—in essence an ultra-reality. Consequently, such a person could walk among us and interact with us in a normal fashion and yet still hide their super abilities—they would be super, but still essentially human.

However, there are super capabilities that are beyond the simple extension of normal human capacities. For example, X-ray vision is not strictly an extension of current human capacities since it accesses a qualitatively different sort of sensation altogether. The capacity to extract information from ranges of the electro-magnetic spectrum normally hidden from human eyes means that the reality created here is not ultra-human, it is trans-human. Now this individual is faced with facets of experience that no unaided human has ever experienced. In this, they would also possess the superior capacities represented in other members of the animal kingdom. For example, they might possess the sonar capacity of dolphins or the radar capacity of bats. Like Dr. Doolittle, they would be able to talk to the animals, or at least communicate in a manner much more understandable to these other species. As a consequence, their reality might be very different from that of a "regular" human being (Nagel 435).

But before we go assuming too much here, remember such sensory displays are actually open to all of us. For example, the Navy uses sonar all of the time and many aircraft (and now even family automobiles) possess their own radar detection systems. What does it matter whether such detection capacities rest within yourself or are simply an ability which is expressed by a machine that you control? If you could make the interaction between yourself and any such technology seamless, would it then not appear that you yourself possessed these powers directly? It has been observed that "any sufficiently advanced technology is indistinguishable from magic" (Clarke 1). What the superhero does with these trans-human powers does appear to be magic. But can we as individuals attain these sorts of powers also? These are the types of questions that face those looking at the future of the so-called symbiosis between humans and machines (Hancock 1).

In general, what applies to perception applies to action also. The magnification of response capabilities would give an individual super-strength, super-speed, and presumably super-linguistic abilities also? However, like perception, we can again conceive of powers that extend well beyond any current human response capacity. For example, heat vision is not just an extension of normal human motor responses; it provides a repertoire of response skills which create a totally new reality. But how would you turn heat vision on and off? Is it a voluntary act or some form of reflex? Indeed, there are some superheroes whose superpowers are turned on only by extremes of emotion which lie largely beyond their voluntary control. Remember there are some heroes who when emotionally perturbed turn large and green and who you "wouldn't like when they are angry." Of course this does not only apply to superheroes. There are many supposedly normal people who you don't want to meet when they are angry either! Emotion can also unleash truly extraordinary responses even in normal, everyday people. There are many reports of individuals under extreme stress performing feats of exceptional strength, such as the popular story of the mother who pulls the vehicle off of her trapped child. There are also accounts of distortions of time perception under stress when normal people exposed to very abnormal conditions appear to be able to achieve extraordinary levels of perception (Hancock and Weaver 193). This then leads us back to our central question—is there already a superhero in all of us?

SUFFICIENTLY ADVANCED TECHNOLOGY CONFERS SUPERPOWERS

With respect to how the future might tease out these abilities, let us first look at technology and the answers anticipated by science fiction writers. In the television program *Star Trek: The Next Generation*, Commander Jordy LaForge cannot see. And yet we know from watching the series, Jordy actually possesses highly complex visual skills and is able to 'see' many aspects of his surrounding environment which are not immediately apparent to his sighted companions. Actually, this harks back to an original *Star Trek* episode when one visitor to the *Enterprise* actually used a crinoline-shaped item of clothing as a technical prosthetic to hide her blindness. Like Jordy, we can use technology to augment and sometimes even replace our normal perception, (e.g. Steve Austin in the television series *The Six-Million Dollar Man*). Another example: no unaided human being can see the vast range of galaxies at the edge of the Universe and yet we have all seen the wonderful pictures of these incredibly distant objects provided by the Hubble Space Telescope. There are also many marvels at the miniscule scale of creation which our eyes alone cannot see, but we now use scanning electron microscopes to look inward to these amazing structures. These instruments expand the spatial range of our normal vision. But we can also use infrared and ultraviolet instruments to stretch our perceptual abilities beyond the visible light spectrum. Although our present access to these levels of super-perception is neither as easy nor as immediate as that of our superhero, there is no logical reason why, in the future, it cannot be. In principle there is no reason why we cannot use technologies such as the World Wide Web to look through these instruments instantly. The limits on this are related to cost alone and not based on any fundamental technical barriers which have yet to be broken. Further, with new augmented reality systems (Goldiez, Ahmad, and Hancock 839), we can look around at our everyday world and see computer-generated overlays which help us further interpret everything we see. Such systems can act as the aid we need to achieve the super-attention required to direct the powers of super-perception and super-action that we are rapidly creating.

There remains, however, skepticism about technologically supported powers. Technology itself is largely free from inherent good or evil (although the act of creation is redolent with moral implications). Primarily, it is the manner in which these tools are wielded that determines their status as either 'good' or 'bad', although hopefully in the future, the design of technology can include a moral dimension (Hancock, 1). In respect of technology and superheroes, the case of Batman, or rather Bruce Wayne, is instructive. He has no superpowers but instead possesses a great deal of money which he uses to finance his crime-fighting career. Remember also in the animated movie *The Incredibles* that the superpowers of the heroes are shown as clear, natural, God-given talents. In contrast, the superpowers of the villain—Syndrome—come not from any inherent abilities but through his mastery of technology. The same principle holds for Superman's arch-enemy—Lex Luthor. This wariness of technology reflects the general fear of science and the specter of uncontrolled forces. Perhaps the epitome of this anxiety is the quintessential transformation shown by the metamorphosis from 'Dr. Jeykll' to 'Mr. Hyde'. Here, the dedicated but misguided scientist unleashes extraordinary powers which, like Frankenstein's creation, threaten everyone. In the original story, Mr. Hyde is represented as an evil monster responsible for killing Sir Danvers Carew. However, in the recent movie *The League of Extraordinary Gentlemen*, Mr. Hyde's manic propensities are tempered somewhat and he is recast in the form of a hero. This is reminiscent of Dr. David Banner and his alter ego the 'Hulk' who despite his uncontrollability, never seems to cause damage to any innocent individual. Behind each of these expressions is a general unease with science and its mixed blessing as both boon and bane of modern society. The theme of science unleashing uncontrolled, or worse, wholly malevolent forces is particularly evident in the work of the character Davros who in the British Science Fiction series *Doctor Who* creates the Daleks as killing machines in a last ditch attempt to win a global conflict. They have been the staple of many British children's nightmares ever since.

In respect of advanced technology then, there is no reason why each of us cannot become a superhero. Indeed, only 500 years ago, just being able to read a line on this page would have made you one of the most able individuals on earth. However, the downside would be that by listening to your iPod and hearing 'voices' in your head you would probably have been burned at the stake! If having super-powers makes you special, such abilities are not granted for free. As we begin to don the mantle of these technologically-supported superpowers, we have to understand, as does Spider-Man's Uncle Ben, that we also assume the responsibility that goes along with the wielding of these awesome forces. But before we face this challenge, is it possible that our assimilation and use of these technologies may actually repeal our humanity?

MORE OR LESS HUMAN

It seems that in order to enhance our abilities to super-human extremes, we risk sacrificing our humanity. There are several dangers in embracing technology this way (to the extent to which it becomes part of us). Those people without superpowers could come to be viewed as sub-human, as in the dystopian society shown in *Gattica* where one's social status and career opportunities are dictated by whether or not one has been genetically engineered. Another danger is that those without these abilities will be seen as non-human altogether. Examples of this viewpoint include Frankenstein's monster, a creature designed to be super-human and able to conquer death. A similar example comes from the Borg of *Star Trek: The Next Generation*. The Borg are species-machine symbiants whose individuality has been suborned to the greater collective. This vision recollects Thomas Hobbes original conception of *Leviathan* which is embodied (literally) in the illustration shown in Figure 1. This shows us a vision which suggests that we might only be able to become super-human at the cost of our own individual humanity.

One of the strongest threats of all is that humanity will become totally eclipsed by the artificial intelligence of modern machines. This frightening vision can be seen in *The Matrix* which presents us with a world where humans have been reduced to nothing more than batteries to energize their mechanical overlords, or in the Terminator series. Some people, however, have a more optimistic view of these, our 'mind's children' (Moravec 1). Here the belief is that our human-conceived artificial beings would be too bored with the parochial concerns of our small planet. Beings with the sorts of capacities we have been discussing would most probably view the whole universe as their playground, perhaps like those who feature in the final scene of *Men in Black*.

SUPER RESPONSIBILITY

Even if we can maintain our humanity, the possession of superpowers would seem to bring with it awesome responsibilities. For example, in a movie featuring perhaps the best known of all superheroes, the hero's girlfriend is trapped in a vehicle during an earthquake, which leads to her death. Our superhero is devastated. So distraught is he, that he flies at super-speed around the earth in order to reverse time. Whether in reality, or indeed super-reality, he could actually accomplish this feat is doubtful indeed, but for the sake of our argument here, let us suppose that he could. Well now, having gone back in time it appears really unpardonably selfish just to save only his girlfriend, does it not? What of the hundreds of equally innocent victims who also died in the same catastrophe? Doesn't any super-being with such powers have a moral obligation to save them as well? And if he has this capacity to reverse time, couldn't he actually do this at any point in time and so save anyone in peril? In fact, wouldn't such a hero constantly have to rescue individuals in the past, as he now does in the present? Well that is one of the conundrums of time, on which this paper has commented elsewhere (Hancock 1). Regardless of the possibility of time-travel, the superhero has to make the same choices in the present moment. Who will he save, who will he let die? These are the moral choices that will face our superhero on a moment by moment basis. Of course, such choices are also faced by regular human beings (e.g. medical

Figure 1. The frontispiece to Thomas Hobbes Leviathan. It shows the battle between the individual and the collective, where Society (the giant figure) is necessarily made up of individuals but always stands in danger of overwhelming that individuality. It further reminds us of the collective of the Borg and indeed the Transformers.

personnel in a war zone, or rescue personnel such as in the recent Kevin Costner movie *The Guardian*). But the never-ending demand on the superhero to decide the fate of a continual stream of people must inevitably, in the end, have a very corrosive effect. How long would it be before someone with such powers began to see them as a curse rather than a blessing?

Our literature has created the fictional world of superheroes. Largely, this vision of superheroes is created for individuals who feel somewhat powerless and weak in the face of the larger natural and social forces that dictate their lives. What we must recognize is that all of us, to some degree, experience these frustrations and limitations and thus the appeal of the 'superhero' solution. The world of the superhero represents our liberation from these oppressive forces. But we must keep our awesome powers under wraps! This is why superheroes must have alter-egos and why many of these alter-egos are 'mild' or shy. Paradoxically, it is the heroes without superpowers such as Bruce Wayne (Batman) and Lance Hunt (Captain Amazing— in *Mystery Men*), who can afford to have flamboyant public personae. But what if we were these superheroes? For how long would we remain the champion of the downtrodden? To such an individual, how would normal people appear? One possible answer is given by Bill in *Kill Bill 2*. In respect of Superman he says "Clark Kent is how Superman views us. And what are the characteristics of Clark Kent? He's weak. . . . He's unsure of himself. . . . He's a coward. Clark Kent *is* Superman's critique on the whole human race." Perhaps the only effectively relevant analogy lies in examining our relationship with some fellow, 'lower' members of the animal kingdom. Yes, it is true we have animal rights groups who champion the cause of other fellow members of the higher animal species. But we have few public groups for insect rights! Thus, it would appear that the degree to which any super-being would champion regular human beings would be in proportion to the degree of their superpowers. It might thus appear that any omnipotent being would be almost supremely indifferent to human affairs. But that is a different story.

THE SUPER HERO IN ALL OF US

Perhaps our need to be superheroes is a goal that we human beings can aim at collectively rather than individually. Instead of having a limited set of especially endowed individuals (Campbell, 1949, 1), perhaps we can achieve some of these extraordinary feats as a species. As we have attempted to show here, the traditional superhero is someone who is characterized most often as possessing magnified human powers of perception and action. If we were writing this chapter four centuries ago, we might have cited the example of a superhero as someone who could fly across the widest ocean in a matter of hours. It would be an undreamed of achievement of the most marvelous kind. Now, we regularly get on trans-oceanic flights and think almost nothing of this feat. Somehow the fact that we need an airliner to do this has blunted our wonder. Perhaps it is the fact that we see technology as made up of objects while we humans are the subjects and it is the object which possesses the power and not we ourselves. But this division is not necessarily a valid one and some would argue that it is the very nature of this splitting between subject and object which leads us into some misdirected thinking (Pirsig 1). Another fact that blunts our wonder is the commonalty of such technically-supported capacities. For, after all, superpowers are always relative and if everyone can do it, then the power itself does not appear to be super by definition. As Gilbert and Sullivan wrote "if everyone is somebody then no-one's anybody," or as Syndrome, the villain of *The Incredibles*, so accurately summarizes "when everyone's super, no one will be." In today's world where crossing the Atlantic Ocean in eight hours is commonplace and open to almost everyone, then superpowers would mean crossing it in eight minutes. This is almost a never ending sequence because when technology supports an eight-minute flight, then the super-individual will have to cross in eight seconds! Eventually, of course, this transport time would drop so low that it would appear to be instantaneous and at that juncture we would evidently appear to have the power of Gods (or at least a Star Trek transporter)! By then, we would have such a marvelous range of super-capacities that we would be engaged in processes which challenge the very nature of what it is to be human. If the technologies which link mind and machine are sufficiently well developed then we might not regard ourselves as individuals at all. By then, the age of wishing to possess extraordinary but secret individual powers will be behind us and the age of exploring our full collective potential will be upon us.

Peter A. Hancock is Provost Distinguished Research Professor in the Department of Psychology and Institute for Simulation and Training at the University of Central Florida in Orlando, Florida. His research focuses on the future of human-machine symbiosis.

Gabriella M. Hancock is his daughter. She is completing a Bachelor of Science Degree in Psychology at the University of Central Florida's Burnett Honors College.

REFERENCES

Budiansky, S. *The Truth about Dogs: An Inquiry into the Ancestry, Social Conventions, Mental Habits and Moral Fiber of Canis Familiaris.* Penguin: New York, 2000.

Campbell, J. *The Power of Myth.* Random House: New York, 1991.

Campbell, J. *The Hero with a Thousand Faces.* Princeton University Press: Princeton, NJ, 1949.

Clarke, A.C. *Profiles of the Future.* Gollancz; London, 1962.

Gibson, J. J. *The Ecological Approach to Visual Perception.* Hillsdale, NJ: Lawrence Erlbaum Associates, 1979.

Goldiez, B., Ahmad, A.M., and Hancock, P.A. Effects of Augmented Reality Display Settings on Human Way-finding Performance. *IEEE Transactions on Systems, Man, and Cybernetics, Part C: Applications and Reviews* 37 (5), (2007): 839–845.

Hancock, P. A. "What Future for Human-machine Symbiosis?" *Ergonomia,* in press, 2007a.

Hancock, P. A. *Mind, Machine and Morality.* Ashgate: *in press,* 2007b.

Hancock, P. A., and Gardner, M. "Time and Time Again: The Muggles Watch, the Wizards Clock. In: *The Psychology of Harry Potter.* BenBella Books, 2007.

Hancock, P. A. and Weaver, J. L., "On Time Distortion Under Stress," *Theoretical Issues in Ergonomics Science* 6 (2005): 193–211.

James, W. *The Principles of Psychology.* New York: Holt, 1980.

Moravec, H. *Mind's Children*. Harvard University Press: Cambridge, MA, 1988.

Nagel, T., "What is it Like to be a Bat?", *The Philosophical Review* 83 (4) (1974): 435–450.

Pirsig, R.M. *Zen and the Art of Motorcycle Maintenance: An Inquiry into Values*. Morrow: New York, 1974.

Tammet, D. *Born on a Blue Day: Inside the Extraordinary Mind of an Autistic Savant*. Free Press: New York, 2006.

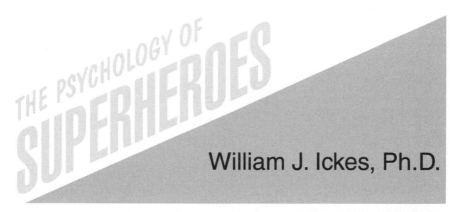

MIND-READING SUPERHEROES:
FICTION AND FACT

Among the various superpowers possessed by superheroes, telepathy is a stealth ability. The superhero with telepathy need not let on that he or she can read the other person's mind. In turn, the person whose mind is being read usually doesn't know that someone else can view his or her mind like a Web page; this ability can exist in secret. But telepathy only exists in fiction—or does it? Are there highly gifted individuals in our world who can read minds? Ickes separates fact and fiction about the type of mind reading that seems to happen among normal humans—everyday mind reading.

WHEN I WAS A KID GROWING UP in Urbandale, Iowa, during the 1950s, the superheroes I read about in the comic books I bought had amazing physical powers. For example, Superman could see through walls with his X-ray vision, fly to outer space, and bend steel with his bare hands. Plastic Man could stretch, contract, and deform his body into virtually any shape imaginable—turning himself into a human trampoline to save the life of a falling child, or stretching himself into a giant rubber band to propel a fleeing criminal back into the arms of the police. And the Flash could run incredible distances at incredible speeds. If he needed to get a package delivered across the country, he didn't have to wait for UPS to airlift it overnight; he could deliver it himself on foot and be back in a flash to collect his own tip!

Things changed in 1963, however, when Marvel Comics introduced its new X-Men series. The X-Men were mutant humans who suddenly seemed to be popping up everywhere, to the unease and consternation of the larger *Homo sapiens* population. One reason the larger population didn't see the mutants coming was that, unlike Superman, whose superpowers were evident early in life (as Superbaby, he amazed his adoptive parents by lifting an automobile off the ground), the X-Men's superpowers were slow to develop, usually not appearing until their teenage years. When their powers did appear, however, it was clear that not all the X-Men were limited to having amazing physical powers. Instead, many of them had amazing mental powers such as telepathy and telekinesis—powers that parapsychologists refer to as *psi* (for psychic or, to use the comic book term, *psionic*) abilities.

The leader of these psychic superheroes, and indeed all of the X-Men, is a charismatic individual named Professor Charles Xavier. Professor X, as he is called, is a dramatic embodiment of the mentalist superhero. Although he has a lean, athletic-looking body, his physical limitations are severe: he is confined to a wheelchair with X-shaped braces on the wheels. As if to emphasize that his power resides primarily in his mind, he has a bald head, a deeply lined face, and a fiercely penetrating gaze.

Recognizing that he and other mutants were at risk of being targeted for extermination by a society that was afraid of their strange powers, Professor X founded Xavier's School for Gifted Youngsters in upstate New York. The school was intended to provide a safe haven in which young mutants could develop their superpowers without fear of persecution. Their goal was to prepare themselves to both protect and attempt to integrate the larger society that would treat them as outcasts.

Using his mentalist superpowers, Professor X reached out with his mind to locate and identify young mutants. Then, by visiting their homes and offering them full scholarships at his school, he was able to persuade their parents to turn their sons and daughters over to him for a few years. During this time, he guided and molded them into mutant superheroes—X-Men!

The X-Men series ushered in the era of mind-reading superheroes— an era that has continued to the present. According to the Wikipedia entry for *Telepaths*, there is a lengthening list of approximately 200 fictional characters who have the uncanny ability to "read" people's minds. And this list suggests that mind-reading ability is an equal-opportunity psychic superpower. Fictional telepaths are both male (Professor X) and female (Jean Grey). Some have Wasp-y sounding names (Emma Frost and Franklin Richards), whereas others have ethnic-sounding names (Anne-Marie Cortez and Raani Jatwinda). There are comic book mind readers (Psimon and Moondragon), science fiction novel mind readers (Tom Bartlett and Charles Wallace Murry), TV series mind readers (Deanna Troi, Matt Parkman), and motion picture mind readers (the Jedi Knights of the Star Wars series). Interestingly, many fictional telepaths have names that begin with the letter M (for example, Mastermind, Mentallo, Mermista, and Mindworm).

Why am I, a research psychologist, interested in mind-reading super-heroes? The reason is simple. To date, I have spent the largest portion of my research career studying what might be called *everyday mind reading*—a phrase that I used as the title of a book I published in 2003. Over the course of the past twenty years, my colleagues and I have examined many different aspects of everyday mind reading.

What is "everyday mind reading"? Let me begin by telling you what it is not. It is not what ESP researchers refer to as *telepathy*, a term that conjures up the image of two people sitting in rooms far removed from each other, with one person attempting to silently transmit thoughts or feelings to the other person in a manner analogous to the invisible transmission of radio or television signals. Instead, everyday mind reading is the product of complex perceptual and psychological processes that occur whenever we interact with another person and attempt to infer the specific content of his or her underlying thoughts and feelings. Everyday mind reading is based on observation combined with educated guesswork; it results in an inference about what the other person is thinking or feeling that may later prove to be right or wrong. To put it simply, everyday mind reading is an activity that lies within the realm of normal, rather than paranormal, psychology.

That doesn't make it any less interesting, however, at least to scientists like me. In the twenty years that my colleagues and I have studied everyday mind reading, we have addressed many fascinating questions in our exploration of this topic, including the following:

- Is it possible to measure people's everyday mind-reading ability?
- Does telepathy play any role in our everyday mind reading?
- If telepathy doesn't play a role in our everyday mind reading, what does?
- On average, are women better mind readers than men?
- Can we improve people's ability to "read" other people's minds?

In the world of fictional mind readers, some of these questions have easy answers. In that made-up world in which nearly everything is possible, there are indeed mind-reading superstars out there, and telepathy does indeed play a role in at least some people's everyday mind reading. But what about the real world, the one we are all forced to live in when we can't escape into the worlds of fantasy, fiction, and dreams? Does everyday mind reading in the real world mirror the telepathic mind reading of the fictional one?

Let's find out. Taking each of the questions in the above list in turn, let's see if we can separate the fiction of telepathic mind reading from the facts about everyday mind reading.

IS IT POSSIBLE TO MEASURE PEOPLE'S EVERYDAY MIND-READING ABILITY?

In order to conduct a scientific study of people's everyday mind-reading ability, it is necessary to devise a way to measure this ability. This is a very basic problem that researchers have to solve, but it is one that comic book writers and screenwriters don't have to concern themselves with. Indeed, in the fictional world of telepathic mind readers, there is no obvious reason to try to measure people's mind-reading ability. On the one hand are those psychic superheroes who can read other people's minds amazingly well. On the other hand are all the rest of us. Although some superhero mind readers have more skill and experience than others, all of them would qualify as mind-reading superstars by our own rather pathetic standards. In short, you've either got it or you don't.

In the real world of our everyday lives, things are more complicated. In the real world, there are also differences in people's everyday mind-reading ability, but they are not nearly as dramatic as they are in the fictional world, where mind-reading superheroes can achieve near-perfect accuracy and everyone else falls far short of that. Imagine a range of everyday mind-reading accuracy that varies from 0 (no accuracy at all) to 100 percent (perfect accuracy). The studies that my colleagues and I have conducted suggest that the *empathic accuracy* of everyday people tends to vary within the more limited range of 0 to 60 percent.

We know this because we have been able to devise a way to measure how accurately one person can infer the specific content of another person's thoughts and feelings. In this procedure, which my colleagues and I developed nearly twenty years ago (Ickes, Stinson, Bissonnette, & Garcia, 1990), we show our research participants videotaped interactions and we pause the videotape at the precise points at which the people who appear in the tape told us that they remembered having had a specific thought or feeling—and exactly what that thought or feeling was.

At each of these tape stops, our research participants get to display their everyday mind-reading skills. Their job is to write down the particular thought or feeling they think the target person had at that point, and to keep on making these empathic inferences throughout the entire videotape. When all of the data have been collected, trained research assistants compare the inferred thoughts and feelings with the actual thoughts and feelings and assign the appropriate number of "accuracy points" to each participant. When the number of accuracy points earned by a given participant is divided by the total number of accuracy points possible, the result is a percentage measure of empathic accuracy that can vary from 0 (zero accuracy) to 100 (perfect accuracy).

Is this a measure of telepathy? No, it's not. Instead, it is a measure of empathic accuracy—a measure of how well, overall, one person can infer the specific content of another person's successive thoughts and feelings.

DOES TELEPATHY PLAY A ROLE IN EVERYDAY MIND READING?

But couldn't our everyday mind reading be based, at least in part, on telepathy? After all, telepathy clearly plays a role in the everyday mind reading of psychic superheroes. They can "read" the unstated thoughts and feelings of people who are standing right in front of them, and they may even be able to learn to "tune into" the thoughts and feelings of people who are physically removed from them. Emma Frost, for example, learned as a college student to isolate the thoughts and feelings of different people she could see down on the quadrangle from her vantage point at the top of a campus building. And Tom Bartlett, one of Robert Heinlein's fictional protagonists, was able to telepathically link his mind to people who were many light years away!

In the fictional world, the upper limit of telepathic accuracy is perfect (100 percent) accuracy. But although we talk as if this level of telepathic accuracy depends upon "reading" other people's thoughts and feelings, in the vast majority of cases our fictional mind readers are "hearing" other people's thoughts and feelings instead. Whether in the X-Men comic books, the TV series *Heroes*, or films such as the Star Wars series, mind-reading superheroes are presented as hearing other people's thoughts and feelings as clearly as if the other person's voice was in the superhero's head. ("Luke, you *must* resist the dark side of the Force!")

In the real world, telepathy is an interesting, but unproven, phenomenon. When I reviewed the research literature on telepathy for the last chapter of my book *Everyday Mind Reading*, I found that it consisted mostly of "case history" anecdotes: brief accounts of instances in which one person purportedly got a psychic, extrasensory message from another person. In these anecdotes, the person who sends the psychic message is usually living, but there are also many examples in which the putative sender is dead (making her, or him, the kind of shadowy presence that likes to whisper back to *The Ghost Whisperer*). Although these anecdotes make great stories, they can't be regarded as established scientific fact.

Only a few scientific studies have been conducted that are relevant to the question of whether telepathy might play a role in our everyday mind reading, and the results of these studies provide no compelling support for the role of telepathy. Two of the better studies (France & Hogan, 1973; Blackmore & Chamberlain, 1993) examined whether twins or non-twin siblings could telepathically "transmit" information to each other. These studies are noteworthy because they both included a control condition in which similarity in the siblings' responses could not be attributed to telepathy, but could be attributed instead to thought concordance based on the use of similar interpretive frames.

Although thought concordance can at times occur by sheer coincidence, it is more likely to occur when two individuals produce the same response to the same stimulus or event because they have interpreted or "framed" that stimulus or event in much the same way. Similar interpretive frames might be especially likely to develop in twins, who are born at the same time and experience many of the same life events at the same points in their development. This similarity in their age and stage of development should give them a similar vantage point on many commonly experienced life events. It should also help to ensure that twins discuss and share their interpretations of such life events more often than non-twin siblings do. For these reasons, twins might develop interpretive frames that are more similar than those of non-twin siblings, whose ages, friendship networks, and current life interests can differ greatly.

To see whether telepathy or thought concordance could be demonstrated in pairs of twins, as opposed to non-twin siblings, Susan Blackmore and Frances Chamberlain conducted the following study (Blackmore & Chamberlain, 1993). The two siblings in each session—twins or non-twins—were randomly assigned to be either the sender or the receiver, swapping these roles halfway through the session. Each sender-receiver pair was given three tasks to perform, and they did each of these tasks twice: once under a condition designed to test for evidence of extrasensory perception, and once under a condition designed to test for evidence of thought concordance. For example, in the first task (Numbers Test):

> The numbers 1–10 were used as targets. In Condition 1 (thought concordance) the sender was asked to write down and concentrate on the first number between 1 and 10 that came to mind. The receiver at the same time tried to pick up what number was being thought about and write it down. This was repeated five times. In Condition 2 (ESP) the procedure was exactly the same except that the experimenter selected the number using random-numbers tables and told the sender which number to concentrate on.

The logic of this procedure was that the siblings might be able to generate a significant proportion of identical responses by means of thought concordance in Condition 1. (Given the freedom to choose their own number, both might tend to think of the same number at a rate exceeding chance.) In contrast, the siblings would have to use ESP in order to generate a significant proportion of identical responses in Condition 2. (Given no freedom to choose their own number, the receivers would have to "read" the senders' minds in order to report the same numbers at a rate exceeding chance.)

Blackmore and Chamberlain's findings, when aggregated across the three tasks, revealed no evidence of telepathy in either the twins or the non-twin siblings. On the other hand, their findings did reveal that the level of thought concordance displayed by the twins (identicals and fraternals combined) was reliably greater than that displayed by the non-twin siblings. These results led Blackmore and Chamberlain to conclude that most, if not all, cases of coincident thoughts and feelings in twins represent nothing more than thought concordance. To the extent that twins are likely to interpret or "frame" their experiences similarly, they will have concordant thoughts and feelings at a rate that noticeably exceeds chance. "This in turn may encourage them to think they have experienced the paranormal or have psychic ability whether they do or not."

Similar findings were obtained in the France and Hogan (1973) study, the details of which need not concern us here. What is important is that, in both studies, the researchers found no evidence for telepathy (a paranormal "psychic" process) but substantial evidence for thought concordance (a psychological process that requires no mystical or paranormal interpretation).

IF TELEPATHY DOESN'T PLAY A ROLE IN OUR EVERYDAY MIND READING, WHAT DOES?

If telepathy does not play a role in our everyday mind reading, as the results of these studies suggest, what processes operate instead, and on what kind(s) of information are they based? This is not an easy question to answer, given the current state of our knowledge. However, as a useful starting point, it is important to distinguish between accuracy in inferring the specific linguistic content of other people's *thoughts*, and accuracy in inferring the specific emotional content of other people's *feelings*.

With regard to inferences about the specific (linguistic) content of other people's thoughts, the results of a study by Randy Gesn and William Ickes suggest that we are most accurate when we listen carefully to what other people say, figure out what interpretive frames they are using, and then use these same interpretive frames to make educated guesses about the content of their underlying thoughts and feelings (Gesn & Ickes, 1999). Accuracy in this case depends heavily on understanding the particular words that other people use and the interpretive frames that those words imply. In effect, we learn to "read between the lines" of what people actually tell us—a process that can easily get derailed when we mistakenly apply one interpretive frame at a point at which a different interpretative frame should have been applied instead (Gesn & Ickes, 1999; Ickes, 2003, chapter 8).

With regard to inferences about the specific (emotional) content of other people's feelings, the results of a study by Judith Hall and Marianne Schmid Mast suggest that although we still rely heavily on what other people say, our accuracy also depends on paying close attention to their nonverbal behavior, including their facial expressions and body movements (Hall & Schmid Mast, 2007). Because other people's emotions can often be seen in their facial expressions, their gestures, and their body postures, nonverbal cues assume a greater importance when we attempt to infer other people's feelings than when we attempt to infer their thoughts.

So far, I have talked about "reading" people from the outside, by listening to their words, observing their nonverbal behavior, and then making appropriate inferences about what they are thinking and feeling. Interestingly, however, there is evidence that our empathic accuracy also depends on "reading" people from the inside, through a kind of physiological and emotional resonance that enables us to feel something of what the other person is currently feeling.

What is the basis of this physiological and emotional resonance? Three interrelated phenomena seem to be involved. At the level closest to our own subjective experience is the phenomenon of *emotional contagion*. At one level down is the phenomenon of *physiological synchrony*. At the lowest, and most basic, level is the operation of what are commonly called *mirror neurons*.

With regard to the first phenomenon, Elaine Hatfield and her colleagues John Cacioppo and Richard Rapson (1994) have called our attention to the considerable body of evidence for *emotional contagion*—the process that occurs when one person, often unconsciously, becomes infused or "infected" with another person's current emotional state. In their book *Emotional Contagion*, Hatfield and her colleagues define emotional contagion as "the tendency to automatically mimic and synchronize [one's own] facial expressions, vocalizations, postures, and movements with those of another person and, consequently, to converge emotionally" with the other. To give you an idea of how this process works, go get a pen to experiment with. Now, see how you feel while holding the pen lengthwise between your teeth (slightly happy?) as opposed to holding the same pen between your pursed lips (slightly concerned?).

With regard to the second phenomenon, psychologists Robert Levenson and Anna Ruef have reviewed the evidence for the process they call *physiological synchrony*—a process that occurs when one person's physiological responses seem to "track" or vary in tandem with those of another person. Here are just some of the documented examples of physiological synchrony that Levenson and Ruef (1997) have cited:

- Many studies have shown that women who are college room-mates or close friends have menstrual cycles that become increasingly synchronized over time.
- One team of researchers found high levels of synchrony in the heart rates of mothers and their infants when they played together.
- Another team of researchers found significant covariations in the skin conductance of discussion group members who reported disliking each other.
- Other researchers have found evidence of synchrony in the heart rates of therapists and their patients during psychotherapy sessions.

With regard to the third phenomenon, Italian researchers Giacomo Rizzolatti, Luciano Fadiga, and Leonardo Fogassi have amassed evidence for the existence of a special class of neurons, called *mirror neurons*, that may provide the basis for the higher-order processes of physiological synchrony and emotional contagion that we have just considered (Rizzolatti, Fadiga, & Fogassi, 2002). Mirror neurons are nerve cells that fire not only when their owner performs a certain action but also when he or she observes someone else performing the same action. Researchers now speculate that mirror neurons are what enable us to unconsciously "mimic" others—that is, to synchronize our physiological responses and our expressive behavior with others in a way that gives us our own sense of what they are currently feeling (and, perhaps in some cases, of what they are currently thinking as well).

As for the claim that psychic superheroes actually "hear" other people's thoughts and feelings as if they had been spoken aloud, I know of no scientific evidence to suggest that everyday people do that too. Although my colleague Randy Gesn and I have found that people's accuracy in inferring other people's thoughts is based more on the words other people use than on the nonverbal behavior they display (Gesn & Ickes, 1999), this finding suggests that you should pay more attention to the words that people are actually voicing than to the words you hear them whispering in your head!

WHAT IS THE UPPER LIMIT OF OUR EVERYDAY MIND-READING ABILITY? ARE THERE ANY MIND-READING SUPERSTARS OUT THERE?

It is important to remember that the various processes and phenomena we have just considered give us only a limited (rather than a perfect) ability to accurately infer the content of other people's thoughts and feelings. As I noted earlier, the upper limit of empathic accuracy—as assessed in our everyday mind-reading research—is about 60 percent of the total number of "accuracy points" possible. On average, strangers can infer each others' thoughts and feelings with about 20 percent accuracy. By comparison, close friends and married couples typically achieve about 30 to 35 percent accuracy. Almost no one ever scores higher than 60 percent. And although stage mentalists purport to be expert mind readers, it is important to remember that they are, fundamentally, illusionists. Their job is to create a convincing illusion that they are expert mind readers, and I know of no hard evidence which reveals them to be actual mind-reading superstars.

The nearest thing to a claim in the research literature that there are exceptionally good mind readers is a claim by psychologists Maureen O'Sullivan and Paul Ekman that they have, over several years, identified twenty-nine "wizards of lie detection" (O'Sullivan & Ekman, 2004). According to O'Sullivan (2007), these people are consistently good at telling when other people are lying or are telling the truth. But psychologists Charles Bond and Ahmet Uysal are skeptical: they argue that of the thousands of people tested in lie detection experiments so far, a number substantially larger than the twenty-nine "wizards" identified by Ekman and O'Sullivan could be expected to occur by chance alone (Bond & Uysal, 2007).

Although O'Sullivan (2007) counter-argues that her wizards are disproportionately likely to come from the ranks of Secret Service agents than from other professions, Bond and Uysal (2007) return fire by noting that Ekman and O'Sullivan allowed at least some of these "wizards" to score and report the results of their own lie detection performance! This debate is likely to continue; the best we can say in the meantime is that Ekman and O'Sullivan's claim for the existence of "wizards of lie detection" has been proffered but not proved. And based on the lack of *any* mind-reading wizards in the hundreds of people we have tested in our own empathic accuracy research during the past twenty years, I remain skeptical.

ON AVERAGE, ARE WOMEN BETTER MIND READERS THAN MEN?

In the world of fiction, superhero mind readers are about as likely to be men as they are to be women. Their mind-reading ability seems to be determined less by their gender than by their innate genetic gifts and by their years of training and experience.

In the real world, there are modest individual differences in empathic accuracy, as I have noted above. However, despite the stereotype of "women's intuition," women again do not have an overall advantage over men in their average level of empathic accuracy. This conclusion may come as a surprise, but it is based on the results of several studies that are reviewed in an article that I published with my colleagues Randy Gesn and Tiffany Graham (Ickes, Gesn, & Graham, 2000).

On the other hand, women do seem to be more easily motivated than men are to try to "read" other people's thoughts and feelings, and this motivational difference often does have an effect. Indeed, we believe that this motivational difference is the basis of the social stereotype regarding the presumed superiority of "women's intuition."

Still, according to the data, it is simply not correct to claim that women, on average, have more empathic ability than men; instead, they just try harder! In fact, a study by University of Oregon psychologists Kristi Klein and Sara Hodges has shown that you can easily close this motivation gap between women and men just by paying the men to be better mind readers! (Klein & Hodges, 2001).

CAN WE IMPROVE PEOPLE'S ABILITY TO "READ" OTHER PEOPLE'S MINDS?

In the fictional world of Xavier's School for Gifted Youngsters, virtually all mutant superpowers, including mind-reading ability, can be trained and enhanced. It's not clear how much this training actually adds, however. When we read the back story of the teenage mutant Emma Frost, for example, we learn that many of her psychic abilities developed naturally and expanded over time, even without Professor X's tutelage. How much his training and instruction added to her naturally developing skills is difficult to assess.

In the real world of laboratory research, Carol Marangoni and her colleagues have shown that people's everyday empathic accuracy can be improved within hours by giving them immediate feedback about whether their empathic inferences were correct or not (Marangoni, Garcia, Ickes, & Teng, 1995). In this study, the researchers asked people to act as amateur therapists by attempting to infer the actual thoughts and feelings that different female clients had reported having had during videotaped sessions with a male psychotherapist.

By random assignment, half of these amateur therapists (those in the feedback condition) got to see the female clients' actual thoughts or feelings immediately after they tried to infer each of them, whereas the other half (those in the no feedback condition) did not. The results showed that although most people's empathic accuracy increased from their very earliest inferences to their final ones, the people in the feedback condition showed a significant additional improvement in their everyday mind-reading skills. These findings suggest that we can indeed train people to be better, more accurate everyday mind readers.

As we near the end of this essay, I would like to note that some people see scientists like me as spoilers. They think we take the wonder out of life by explaining everything in scientific terms. But looking back over the course of my life and my research career, I beg to disagree.

If you enjoy the wonders of life, think about this. Isn't it amazing that we have mirror neurons? (What science fiction writers could have possibly dreamed up that concept, and why didn't they?) Isn't it amazing how our physiological processes—our heart rates, skin conductance, and even (in the case of women) menstrual cycles—become synchronized with those of the people around us? And isn't it amazing that we spontaneously, and largely unconsciously, tend to mimic the facial expressions, vocalizations, postures, and movements of other people (Hatfield, Cacioppo, & Rapson, 1994)? And that all of these elements, acting in concert with our ability to identify and apply other people's interpretive frames (Gesn & Ickes, 1999; Ickes, 2003, chapter 8), enable us to achieve at least limited success in inferring what other people are thinking and feeling?

I hope that my point is clear. For me, science doesn't spoil the wonder of mind reading: it deepens and enhances it. And speaking of life's many wonders, whoever would have thought that the kid who read so many comics about superheroes back in the 1950s would grow up to be The Man Who Measured Mind Reading? I never would have thought it, but the wonder of it all is that *I was that kid!*

William J. Ickes, Ph.D., is Distinguished Professor of Psychology at the University of Texas at Arlington. He is the editor of *Empathic Accuracy* (1997) and the author of *Everyday Mind Reading: Understanding What Other People Think and Feel* (2003). His research on empathic accuracy has been recognized by three international research awards.

REFERENCES

S. J. Blackmore and F. Chamberlain, "ESP and Thought Concordance in Twins: A Method of Comparison," *Journal of the Society for Psychical Research* 59 (1993): 89–96.

C. F. Bond and A. Uysal, "On Lie Detection 'Wizards,'" *Law and Human Behavior* 31 (2007): 109–116.

G. A. France and R. A. Hogan, "Thought Concordance in Twins and Siblings and Associated Personality Variables," *Psychological Reports* 32 (1973): 707–710.

P. R. Gesn and W. Ickes, "The Development of Meaning Contexts for Empathic Accuracy: Channel and Sequence Effects," *Journal of Personality and Social Psychology* 77 (1999): 746–761.

J. A. Hall and M. Schmid Mast, "Sources of Accuracy in the Empathic Accuracy Paradigm," *Emotion* 7 (1997): 438–446.

Hatfield, E., Cacioppo, J. T., & Rapson, R. L. *Emotional Contagion*. New York: Cambridge University Press, 1994.

Ickes, W. *Everyday Mind Reading: Understanding What Other People Think and Feel*. Amherst, NY: Prometheus Books, 2003.

W. Ickes, P. R. Gesn, and T. Graham, T., "Gender Differences in Empathic Accuracy: Differential Ability or Differential Motivation?", *Personal Relationships* 7 (2000) 95–109.

W. Ickes, L. Stinson, V. Bissonnette, and S. Garcia, "Naturalistic Social Cognition: Empathic Accuracy in Mixed-sex Dyads," *Journal of Personality and Social Psychology* 59 (1990): 730–742.

K. J. K. Klein and S. D. Hodges, "Gender Differences, Motivation, and Empathic Accuracy: When it Pays to Understand," *Personality and Social Psychology Bulletin* 27 (2001): 720–730.

Levenson, R.W., & Ruef, A.M. "Physiological Aspects of Emotional Knowledge and Rapport" (pp. 44–72). In W. Ickes (Ed.). *Empathic Accuracy*. New York: Guilford Press, 1997.

C. Marangoni, S. Garcia, W. Ickes, and G. Teng, "Empathic Accuracy in a Clinically Relevant Setting," *Journal of Personality and Social Psychology* 68 (1995): 854–869.

M. O'Sullivan, "Unicorns or Tiger Woods: Are Lie Detection Experts Myths or Rarities?", A response to *On Lie Detection "Wizards"* by Bond and Uysal. *Law and Human Behavior* 31 (2007): 117–123.

Rizzolatti, G., Fadiga, L., & Fogassi, L. "From Mirror Neurons to Imitation: Facts and Speculations," *In A.N. Meltzoff and W. Prinz (Eds.), The Imitative Mind: Development, Evolution, and Brain Bases* (pp. 246–266). New York: Cambridge University Press, 2002.

Chuck Tate, Ph.D.

AN APPETITE FOR DESTRUCTION: AGGRESSION AND THE BATMAN[1]

Not all acts of aggression are alike. As Tate explains in this essay, some acts of aggression are done for the "pleasure" of it; other acts of aggression are a means to an end. Do superheroes act aggressively for the pleasure of it, or is their aggression a means to an end? Tate proposes that, compared to other heroes, Batman's aggression is for the pleasure of it. Tate lays out his argument; you decide whether you agree.

AGGRESSION IS A TOPIC WELL STUDIED in social psychology and well publicized outside psychology. The assertion that portrayals of violence in various media (e.g., television, movies, and video games) are linked to actual violent behavior for children and teen-

---

[1] Many self-described enthusiasts, such as myself, refer to him as "the Batman" rather than just "Batman" based on the original title given him in his first appearance in *Detective Comics* #27 (May, 1939) as "The Bat-Man."

agers (see Anderson & Bushman, 2001) has placed the topic of aggression at the fore of much social discourse. Superheroes have now infiltrated almost every medium (and even radio historically, if not presently) and definitely use aggression. Yet, most social psychologists recognize there is a distinction to be made when studying aggression: Is the aggression *instrumental* or *hostile*? This distinction is roughly whether the aggression is warranted or unwarranted from an ethical standpoint. Beyond ethics, the distinction between the types of aggression points to different psychological processes at work that are worth exploring in their own right. As important as the distinction between the types of aggression is for ethics and psychology, unfortunately, this distinction is rarely made in media reports of studies on aggression or within the research reports themselves (e.g., Bushman & Anderson, 2001). However, as science it behooves the field of psychology to make that distinction for non-scientists and explore how the distinction may be related to discussions of ethics.

Hostile aggression is characterized, psychologically, as actions or intentions to harm someone for the sake of deriving some pleasure from inflicting that harm. In other words, hostile aggression is committed for its own ends; it is not a means to another end. Thus, individuals engaged in hostile aggression are mildly or strongly sadistic, or, at the very least, derive momentary satisfaction from aggressing. We often construe villains in this manner—as those interested in harming others for sadistic reasons. Yet, one need not look to villains alone to find hostile aggression in action. Even the nicest, non-sociopathic individuals sometimes take pleasure in insulting a rival or enemy, and this too is hostile aggression. After all, psychologists agree that aggression can be either physical or non-physical (the latter is technically called *relational*; Crick, Grotpeter, & Bigbee, 2002). Thus, insults and gossip in addition to punches and kicks can be motivated by a desire to hurt someone as the end in itself. *Instrumental aggression*, on the other hand, is, psychologically, a means to achieve a larger goal. People displaying instrumental aggression are considered to use violence or harm only as means to another end, such as helping someone or in pursuit of winning some contest. Thus, police officers, who sometimes use force on suspects (e.g., tackling and/or punching them to subdue them), and sport fighters (e.g., boxers and mixed martial artists), who attempt to knock out or submit each other, engage in instrumental aggression for admittedly different ends. Police use aggression to protect people, while sport fighters use aggression to win prestige and prizes. Yet, despite bad cops and the notorious trash-talk of sport fighters, it is generally believed that neither group as a whole enjoys aggression for its own sake.

Most superheroes engage in instrumental aggression. Superman, Wonder Woman, Spider-Man, Captain America, and the like consistently rush to the rescue of those in need, often doing physical battle with individuals engaged in antisocial behavior designed to hurt others. Superman has no difficulties punching antagonists and rendering them unconscious via choking. Similarly, Wonder Woman does not take pleasure in rendering her foes incapable of fighting. Any satisfaction taken by Superman, Wonder Woman, Spider-Man, or Captain America is almost always in the apprehending criminals, foiling plots that would have caused mass casualties, and knowing that their actions made the world a better place in which to live. In the simplest of analyses, it appears that superheroes and super-villains exemplify the clash of instrumental and hostile aggression. Yet, do all superheroes engage in instrumental aggression? Or, do some superheroes display something much closer to hostile aggression even while they help those targeted by criminals?

Before we consider this question, we need to address two other questions, (a) who fits our definition of a superhero and who is excluded? And (b) which research method should we use to elucidate the answer? Firstly, we need to define what we mean by superhero. Not every protagonist of an illustrated-fiction series[2] should count as a superhero because some of them are merely focal characters, with no implication on the part of the writers that these protagonists should be considered heroic or interested fighting crime or in helping people. Thus, we should exclude protagonists such as Lobo, Swamp Thing, and most of Frank Miller's protagonists when he began illustrating his own novels (e.g. *Sin City*, *300*). These protagonists are excluded because of psychoticism (Lobo), lack of moral

---

[2] I prefer "illustrated fiction" to "comic book" for two reasons. One, Archie and Garfield are "comic," the Batman and Spider-Man are comparatively more serious and are involved in serialized fictional stories, not series of gags. Two, the serialization of the titles makes them less like books and more like magazines.

capacity (Swamp Thing), and the creator's explicit desire to create anti-heroes (most of Frank Miller's work). We need to focus instead on a character who everyone believes is trying to do some good, has a moral capacity (irrespective of the ethical choices made), and who is viewed as a hero. Secondly, we should use one of the methods of the science of psychology to answer this question. While experimentation and systematic observation are well represented in the academe, the better-known method to non-psychologists of the case study is what we shall use. Despite its comparatively infrequent use by academic psychologists, the case study method is still the best method psychologists have for understanding a single individual, fictional or not. Given our first criterion of a suitable hero on whom to conduct the case study, it appears that the Batman would be a good choice. The Batman is considered a hero by most (after all, he is a part of the Justice League of America with the likes of Superman, Wonder Woman, the Green Lantern, and Flash—all paradigmatic superheroes), has a moral capacity as a human being (unlike Swamp Thing, who is sentient but nonhuman), and, while considered a bit eccentric, is not generally considered clinically psychotic or sociopathic.

OUR CASE STUDY: THE BATMAN

Our case study focuses on the Batman and his personal motivations for engaging in aggressive behavior. Within this case study we will not conduct any experiments on him—apologies to those hoping for this. We will, however, build a case-history of him, systematically sample from his past and current behavior, and draw some interesting conclusions from these data about whether his use of aggression is hostile or instrumental. In order to begin our case study, however, we need to acquaint ourselves with the history of the Batman.

The Batman in Brief

A viewing of the 2005 film *Batman Begins* can give the novice a fairly good understanding of who the Batman is. The writers Christopher Nolan (who also directed) and David S. Goyer did a commendable job of staying true to the arc and themes of the original stories while taking some liberties with certain character relationships within the original timeline.[3] Tim Burton's two films about the Batman, 1989's *Batman* and 1992's *Batman Returns* also provide a reasonably good profile of the character. For those who missed these movies (and don't read the series), the Batman's story can be summarized thusly: his parents were killed by a petty thief named Joe Chill when Bruce Wayne (the alter-ego of the Batman—yes, you read correctly) was only six years old. After the death of his parents, Bruce traveled the world, learning escape-arts, illusions, and martial arts, all with the singular purpose of finding and killing Joe Chill. Adding frustration to his anger, when he returned to Gotham City at age twenty-one, he discovered that Joe Chill had been killed some time ago. The object of his revenge now dead, the Batman—his true identity now named—externalized his desire for revenge on Joe Chill to others like Chill, namely criminals. The Batman resorted to intimidation, other fear-inducing tactics, and physical violence to rouse, confuse, and ultimately subdue criminals and continues these practices to the present.

Using an understanding of the Batman that comes from anytime before or after the 1960's Adam West series,[4] we can already start to see quite clearly that the Batman is not an altruistic do-gooder such as Superman or Wonder Woman. He's motivated to get revenge on his parents' killer at first and then transforms his vengeful motivation into something altogether different. Instead of taking solace in the fact that the man who killed his parents was himself killed, the Batman now strove to stop all criminals wherever they might be and make them fear the shadow of the bat, as his first ever appearance on the opening page of *Detective Comics* #27 (May, 1939) indicates "Hurting Criminals *Incidentally* Helps their Victims": The Real Motivation of the Batman. The Batman's desires to intimidate, injure,

---

[3] For example, in the illustrated-fiction series the Batman did not meet Ra's al Ghul until much later in his career. The Batman first appeared in 1939 and Ra's al Ghul was introduced in 1971.

[4] The 1960's Batman television series starring Adam West and the stories in the illustrated fiction series at that time revolved around the Batman using his skills for the advancement of good over evil (with no hint of revenge or animosity toward criminals). However, most Batman-enthusiasts acknowledge this period as incompatible with his true story and resulting from the instantiation of the Comics Code. The Comics Code was designed to respond to the unfounded criticism (by psychologist Dr. Wertham) that Batman was corrupting American youth with his vigilantism (and allegedly homosexual lifestyle). The Adam West series is denounced by Batman-enthusiasts in much the same way that Highlander-enthusiasts reject *Highlander 2: The Quickening* as a part of the *Highlander* mythos—it just never happened! The same goes for the films *Batman Forever* and *Batman and Robin*.

and induce fear in the minds of the criminals he encounters cannot be adequately explained by using instrumental aggression. Superman does not desire to intimidate or physically injure Lex Luthor, no matter how many times his nemesis laces him with Kryptonite and makes him suffer. Similarly, Wonder Woman takes no special pleasure in hurting super-villains even ones who are bent on destroying her. Yet, I submit that the Batman's desire to inflict fear, pain, and even suffering onto "criminality," as the movie *Batman Begins* puts it, is not relieving his own negative feelings about his parents' death or seeing people in similarly traumatic situations. There is a psychological theory called the *negative-state relief hypothesis* (Cialdini, Baumann, & Kenrick, 1981) which proposes that a person feels bad when encountering the plight of the victim and offers help to relieve one's own negative state. However, the Batman focuses almost exclusively on the perpetrators, not the victims, doing all that he can to "strike fear into their hearts," as the 1989 *Batman* film puts it. In fact, he dresses like a giant bat to scare the criminals he ambushes and beats into submission. Furthermore, he derives *pleasure* from the activity of scaring and hurting criminals, a different sort of pleasure than that of knowing that someone was helped. In fact, the Batman appears to care little, if at all, that someone was helped by his actions. He rarely sticks around long enough to be seen, much less thanked, by those he has helped or even by Lieutenant (then later, Commissioner) Gordon. Even in those instances when he saved the first Robin (Dick Grayson; now known as Nightwing) or the third Robin (Tim Drake) from possible death—he sadly could not save the second Robin [Jason Todd] from death at the hands of the Joker—he rarely mentioned these events to his protégés, and remained stoic when thanked by them. In those rare cases when the Batman helps a stranger and does not disappear immediately, he has been known to chastize victims for not taking precautions to avoid becoming targets. Thus, feedback from those helped is largely inconsequential to the Batman's motivations. I therefore submit that the Batman is motivated by self-indulgent aggression, which is another way of referring to hostile aggression while focusing the readers attention on its recurrent nature (i.e., the "self-indulgent" part). Moreover, I contend that the Batman is not focused on helping people at all; instead, helping is simply a consequence of his self-indulgently aggressive behavior.

One might, at this point, object and ask: Is the Batman really helping people? Admittedly, he is often described as a vigilante and an anti-hero, especially by Frank Miller, who, in the late 1980s, helped reintroduce the Batman's earlier (circa 1940s) sharply aggressive and almost sadistic style (e.g., *Batman: The Dark Knight Returns*). But, a psychologist would probably say, "Yes, the Batman is helping people" because being helped is a *consequence*, not a motivation. In social science we separate the outcome from the motivation, which is why, for instance, many social scientists believe that people can behave in racist ways without intending to be racist—the motivation is separate from the outcome. In more technical terms, motivations are used to explain (and generate) the outcomes; consequently, the two have to be separable at some level of analysis. Similarly, the Batman does help people (as an outcome) even if his motivation is not focused on helping them (intention).

I now make the case for my bold statement that the Batman does not intend to help people, but incidentally helps them all the same, and simultaneously shows that he is using hostile, not instrumental, aggression. Here's just one example from a myriad stories in the illustrated-fiction series. In the storyline, "Venom," which appeared in *Batman: Legends of the Dark Knight* #16–20 (1991), and was also published as a collection in 1993, the Batman became addicted to steroids after he failed to lift a 632-pound boulder to save a young girl from drowning in a bombed sewer. He was quite upset with himself for not being strong enough to accomplish this feat and was offered steroids by the girl's father as a way to achieve this and similar feats in the future. At first glance, it might appear that the Batman was upset because the girl died. Yet, a closer reading suggests that the Batman was upset for not anticipating such a possibility (the boulder's weight) and, more importantly, because he could not figure out who put the girl there. The rest of the story showcases the Batman occasionally juxtaposing the memory of the girl's drowning with his own actions of breaking the arms and jaws of suspected kidnappers, but inflicting such grievous bodily injury on suspected criminals is banal for the Batman—even when no one has died. Thus, the girl's death does not make the Batman more violent than usual. However, while on the steroids the Batman does become more sadistic than usual when intimidating criminals and forcing them to talk. At one point he lifted a 220-pound man off the ground by his throat and choked him to the brink of unconsciousness. Yet, the next few panels reveal that the Batman was only concerned with the *excessive pleasure* he derived from injuring people while on the drugs, not the severity of injuries he caused. After he overcame his addiction to steroids, the Batman still broke arms and jaws with his familiar menacing grin; he just took his "appropriate" level of pleasure in so doing.

Likewise, in the early incarnations of the Batman in the 1940s, he sometimes killed people on purpose. A re-released fifteen-episode movie serial (entitled *Batman and Robin: The Complete 1949 Movie Serial Collection* [2004]) includes one scene in which the Batman throws a criminal out the window on one of the upper levels of a ten-story building during a fight. Of course, he could have easily avoided that behavior. He later remarks to Robin in his familiar even-toned manner: "I threw one out the window. He's probably dead." One needs only glance through a current (2007–2008) issue of any *Batman* title to see that in virtually every encounter with a criminal, he either: (a) breaks one of the criminal's limbs (usually the arm), (b) breaks the criminal's jaw, or (c) both. He could easily use nerve gas (which he carries in his utility belt), use aikido (a far less injurious form of self-defense in which he is thoroughly trained), or even avoid the lesser criminals altogether. Instead, he almost always opts to beat the lesser criminals into submission, even when this activity is not necessary to find his true target. *Batman Begins* opens with the Batman mercilessly beating other inmates who tried to intimidate him while all were serving time in jail, and the scene intimates that it is not the first time such a series of events has occurred in the jail. Few conclusions are possible other than the Batman enjoys this violence on a personal level and likes to indulge himself.

Intimidation is another favorite tactic of the Batman. Sometimes instead of (but most often in addition to) causing bodily injury, the Batman purposefully scares his opponents. The movie *Batman Begins* provides a good example when the Batman decides to don the costume of a bat because he wants this image to evoke fear in his enemies. In the 1989 *Batman* film, the first sequence featuring the Batman portrays the protagonist dangling a criminal over the edge of a tall building, threatening to drop him unless he divulges information. While some people might try to justify these behaviors as "harmless" scare tactics (and thus instrumental aggression), like the ones police use when they threaten a suspect with the possibility of physical violence or more jail time, we should remember that police intimidation tactics are not the first or only choice. Real police (and TV police too) often try to get a suspect to cooperate without coercion, only resorting to it if other tactics don't work. In contrast, the Batman isn't choosing from a set of strategies of which coercion is a part; instead, he appears to have only one strategy—the threat of violence either preceded or followed by actual violence. The routine nature of this behavior (with no clear end in sight) leads one to believe that the Batman has very good reasons, in his own mind at least, to intimidate criminals and be violent with them when he could behave otherwise given his extensive training in various martial arts including *aikido* and the combative aspects of *tai chi chuan*, much less violent techniques than his preferred vicious tactics of karate, *wushu*, and *escrima*. As Ra's al Ghul asked him in one of the opening scenes of *Batman Begins*, "Do you hate criminality so much that you lock yourself in with criminals just to fight them?" The answer was a silent "yes," and my final illustration of the Batman's motivation of self-indulgent aggression.

With his indifference to those he helps and his tireless and voracious pursuance of criminals (often neglecting sleep, bathing, and grooming), it becomes difficult to argue any position other than that the Batman is motivated by some very selfish drive from which he derives immense pleasure. Even after he "apprehends" criminals (better, incapacitates them and leaves them bound for the authorities to find), he does not file police reports or make himself available for any adjudication in the legal system. Admittedly, he might want to avoid public attention and the problems of someone figuring out that he has an alter ego (Bruce Wayne), but it could also be that he doesn't really care. The Batman rarely, if ever, complains about the state of the legal or prison systems and the fact that many of his foes regularly escape custody in psychiatric and prison wards. Furthermore, he shows absolutely no interest in the rehabilitation of criminals after he has scared, injured, and defeated them time and again. Maybe the Batman quietly enjoys the opportunity to rough up criminals repeatedly. In fact, the Batman may not complain or work to change the system because it provides him a steady diet of fodder for his apparently insatiable appetite to destroy criminality and derive selfish pleasure from this activity—a pleasure revealed each time he grins as he delivers a ferocious blow to a criminal's body.

Does this mean that the Batman is really a villain? By no means. However, it does illustrate that aggression is a far more complex phenomenon than simply "good guys" using instrumental aggression and "bad guys" using hostile aggression. In the case of the Batman it appears that sometimes "good guys" use the methods associated with the "bad guys," but still end up helping people. Maybe this apparent contradiction explains why Superman and the Batman can't get along. Superman knows that the Batman is closer in behavior and motivations to the villains, and is wary of him because of that association. (It is no coincidence that when both men are present on Justice League ventures, Superman encourages Wonder Woman to keep an eye on the Batman when he cannot.) Likewise, the Batman appears to detest Superman for his ethics—only using violence when it's the last resort and never taking pleasure from it. The Batman's dislike of Superman is so apparent that he carries Kryptonite in his utility belt, just in case he needs to weaken the Man of Steel.[5] Still, the Batman and Superman are two of the most beloved superheroes, and have been for nearly seventy years, despite being on opposite sides of the aggression continuum.

> Chuck Tate, Ph.D., is an assistant professor of psychology at California State University, Bakersfield. Like the Batman, he has a rarely seen alter ego who is gregarious and witty but in reality Dr. Tate is obsessed with research and spends much of his time in his cave-like office plotting his next set of studies.

---

[5] It is worth noting that the Batman trusts none of the members of the Justice League. In fact, he knows the weaknesses of all the members and stocks his utility belt accordingly.

REFERENCES

C. A. Anderson and B. J. Bushman, "Effects of Violent Video Games on Aggressive Behavior, Aggressive Cognition, Aggressive Affect, Physiological Arousal, and Pro-social Behavior: A Meta-analytic Review of Scientific Literature," *Psychological Science* 12 (2001): 353–359.

B. J. Bushman and C. A. Anderson, "Media Violence and the American Public: Scientific Facts versus Media Misinformation," *American Psychologist* 56 (2001): 477–489.

R. B. Cialdini, D. J. Baumann, and D. J. Kenrick, "Insights from Sadness: A Three-step Model of the Development of Altruism as Hedonism," *Developmental Review* 1 (2001): 207–223.

N. R. Crick, J. K. Grotpeter, and M. A. Bigbee, M. A. "Relationally and Physically Aggressive Children's Intent Attributions and Feelings of Distress for Relational and Instrumental Peer Provocations," *Child Development* 73 (2002): 1134–1142.

Kane, B. (writer) & Finger, B. (1939, May). "The Bat-Man." *Detective Comics, 27. Batman and Robin: The Complete 1949 Movie Serial Collection.* Dir. S. Bennet. United States: Columbia Pictures, 1949/2004. *Batman Begins.* Dir. C. Nolan. United States: Warner Bros, 2005. *Batman.* Dir. Tim Burton. United States: Warner Bros, 1989. *Batman Returns.* Dir. Tim Burton. United States: Warner Bros, 1992.

O'Neil, D. (w.), von Eeden, T. (l.), Braun, R. (p.), García-López, J. L. (i.), Schubert, W. (l.), Oliff, S. (c.). *Batman: Venom.* New York: DC Comics. 1993.

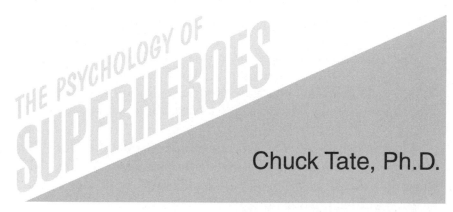

THE PSYCHOLOGY OF SUPERHEROES

Chuck Tate, Ph.D.

THE STEREOTYPICAL (WONDER) WOMAN

Wonder Woman has unique powers and abilities and grew up in an all-female society. In what ways has her unusual upbringing shaped who she is and how she relates to the rest of the world? Tate provides a history of Wonder Woman—both of her own history and that of her creators—and explores issues of gender stereotypes as they relate to Wonder Woman. He reveals how psychological research illuminates her view of herself in the world and how others see her.

WONDER WOMAN first appeared in December 1941 and has become one of the best known superheroes. The popularity of Wonder Woman may lie in the fact that unlike her female hero predecessors, she was gender atypical in many ways.[1] Her creator Dr. Wil-

---

[1] Wonder Woman is not the oldest female superhero. Olga Mesmer, the Girl with X-Ray Eyes, appeared in one issue of *Spicy Mystery Stories* (October 1938) and is arguably the oldest superhero (pre-dating Superman by one year). Wonder Woman was also preceded by Invisible Scarlet O'Neil, the ghost-like maiden who saved children from fires and the like.

liam Moulton Marston (who wrote the stories under the pseudonym "Charles Moulton") was clear about the social purpose of Wonder Woman from the outset. In a 1943 article in *The American Scholar* Marston wrote:

> Not even girls want to be girls so long as our feminine archetype lacks force, strength, and power. Not wanting to be girls, they don't want to be tender, submissive, peace-loving as good women are. Women's strong qualities have become despised because of their weakness. The obvious remedy is to create a feminine character with all the strength of Superman plus all the allure of a good and beautiful woman.

Marston was a psychologist trained under the famous Hugo Münsterberg and used his training to diagnose a social problem and attempt a remedy in the popular (though not critically regarded) medium of illustrated fiction.[2] Thusly, Suprema, the Wonder Woman (shortened to "Wonder Woman" before publication) was created. Yet, contained in Marston's quote is the almost invisible struggle that Marston and the subsequent writers of *Wonder Woman* have endured—a struggle between U.S. gender stereotypes and the origin of Wonder Woman, which runs counter to these stereotypes; a kind of "gender stereotype balancing act."

As a psychologist, Marston would likely appreciate a revaluation of Wonder Woman with current psychological theories. Marston used many then-current theories of the 1920s and '30s to develop the storylines for Wonder Woman and advance his social philosophy. Future writers took the ideas further, but what they all had in common was they portrayed a Wonder Woman driven more by U.S. societal stereotypes than the logic of Wonder Woman's nature and upbringing.

WONDER WOMAN'S PSYCHE FROM A SOCIAL STRUCTURE ANALYSIS

Social structure theory is an attempt to explain differences (and similarities) between men and women in any society (Eagly, 1987; Eagly

---

[2] I prefer the term "illustrated fiction" to "comic books" because the stories of superheroes are illustrated and fictional and usually not funny. The common name comes from the same publication format as *Archie Comics*, which were funny.

& Wood, 1999; Wood & Eagly, 2002). This theory proposes a mechanism for how gender stereotypes get their content; that is, how people in the United States, for example, expect women to be passive and men to be aggressive.

The theory is complex but its core can be stated succinctly. Social structure theory proposes that men and women evince differences *on average* because of how societies are structured (Wood & Eagly, 2002). In more basic terms, people learn these social differences; they are not innate or natural. Social structuralists do not deny that women and men have physiological, organic, and genetic differences; however, these biological differences do not cause social and psychological differences.[3] Instead, some differences, such as women being the group who can gestate and birth offspring, may result in social behavior differences, which may later be turned into expectations for genders (Eagly & Wood, 1999).

A concrete example might aid understanding. Let's imagine ancestors living in a small society hundreds of thousands of years ago trying to figure out who in the community should hunt. An obvious set of candidates are young adults because they possess the right combination of strength and skill. Yet, this age group also contains women who can become pregnant, and when pregnant, the dangers of hunting could kill their eventual offspring. As a result, young males make the most reliable corps of hunters. Over time, this society may create a social expectation that men are hunters and women are not (because women could be pulled from the hunting force during pregnancy for safety). Notice that young men are not naturally better hunters; rather, by virtue of never becoming pregnant they represent a reliable group for this task. Hunting is therefore neither inherently nor even appropriately "man's work"—men do it because it works within the social structure. Of course, social structuralists do not deny that men *on average* may have some natural abilities based on testosterone and its relationship to muscle mass that are helpful for hunting. In point of empirical fact, the only two large and meaningful differences between men and women on motor measures are in throwing distance and throwing velocity (Hyde, 2005). These differences might

---

[3] Some evolutionary psychologists (e.g., Buss, 1995) argue the differences between men and women are innate and result from different selective pressures on males and females.

help with spear-hunting for game, yet some anthropological studies suggest that most human food gathering was undifferentiated until late in human evolution (Leibowitz, 1983), with evidence that both women and men cooperated (in the past and still do today in some societies) in net-hunting (see Fouts & Lamb, 2005), which does not require throwing strength or velocity to accomplish. Additionally, the gender division of labor in terms of hunting is not universal (see Eagly & Wood, 2002). In a small number of societies women are the primary hunters (Noss & Hewlett, 2001).

The detailed example and factual evidence above also showcases the flexibility that social structure theory allows. If a society disallowed women from having heterosexual intercourse between the ages of twelve and eighteen, these women could easily be hunters like their twelve to eighteen-year-old male counterparts (because the safety issue no longer applies). In this case, men and women should have similar qualities, such as aggressiveness, because the activity of hunting cultivates the quality of aggression (or vice versa), and whoever engages in the activity will develop the trait. Accordingly, we only have the stereotypes in the U.S. of men being self-reliant and independent and women being interdependent because we encourage them to engage in activities promoting one but not the other (Eagly & Wood, 1999; Wood & Eagly, 2002). In this way, people learn and then accept (or reject) their society's gender stereotypes.[4]

Lending additional support to the social structural account by showing how flexible it is, women are commonly credited in various cultures as being great warriors and sometimes even as the progenitors of certain martial arts systems. The most famous example of a strong female warrior to Western readers might be Joan of Arc, well known for her strategy and prowess with a sword. However, in addition to Joan, there are other famous real life examples, such as Boudica, the Celtic Queen of the Iceni people who almost successfully drove the Romans out of Britain. She too was known as a brilliant military strategist and fierce one-on-one warrior. Much less well known to Western readers are the great female warriors of Japan and China. In Japan, there was a female samurai known as To-

---

[4] The approach is also flexible because it allows gender stereotypes to change over time as the social structure changes (cf. Eagly, 1987).

moe Gozen[5] who was quite feared for her prowess with the *katana* (the sword, a traditionally male weapon; women traditionally used the *naginata* or longspear). In one historical account it is mentioned of Tomoe "as a swordsman she was a warrior worth a thousand [warriors]" (McCullough, 1998, p. 291). Finally, the most famous kung fu style (by name at least), Wing chun—the one Bruce Lee learned before developing his own style—is credited to a nun named Ng Mui according to the legend of how the style developed. The legend goes that she developed the style to save her monastery from consistent raids by marauders. She passed the style on to another woman, Yim Wing Chun, who further refined it to its widely disseminated form (cf. Chu, Ritchie, & Wu, 1998), and several movies have been made about Yim Wing Chun including one entitled *Wing Chun* in 1994 (starring Michelle Yeoh in the lead role). Thus, the most popular martial system in southern China and one of the most effective systems in the world was developed by a woman. A friend of mine is fond of saying that martial arts were developed as a way for the little person to defeat the bigger one, so it is little wonder that some women (on average smaller in physique than men) would be in the fore of developing the martial arts. Furthermore, these historical examples of exceptional female warriors illustrate the social structuralist point—women can be just as effective as men, if given the opportunities. Additionally, the fact that Boudica, Tomoe, and Ng are not well-known names when considering great warriors may illustrate another aspect of social structure theory—that expectations of men being warriors relegate women who are warriors into a background position.

From a social structure standpoint, one can theorize about Wonder Woman's personality based on her origin story as a denizen of an all-female society.[6] In this Amazonian society, women engage in all the social roles; they are the politicians, the warriors, the educators, the childcare providers, the artists, and the scientists. From the social structure analysis, the qualities associated with these roles are distributed across the women in that society. Thus, some women in

---

[5] "Gozen" is an honorific title, roughly translated as "Lady," not her family name.

[6] This statement is true for the Marston-era accounts of her mythos. Later Wonder Woman's home was dominated by women (with a few men around as laborers or in minor social roles).

the society will have qualities that we in the U.S. associate with the **woman** gender stereotype (e.g., passivity, interdependence) while other women (e.g., the warriors) will have many of the qualities that we in the U.S. associate with the **man** gender stereotype (e.g., aggressiveness, independence) because the traits are derived from certain roles, no matter which sex fills those roles.

"Wonder Woman" is actually a title donated to Diana (her American name) by the society's governing body for being the best warrior in the land and a diplomat to the rest of the world. Accordingly, Diana would have all the confidence and self-reliance that comes with being the best of the best (as a warrior) and the shrewdness and even-tempered judgment of a trained delegate. Three major psychological attributes follow from her two roles: swagger, cultural perspective, and warrior-mentality.

Swagger. Given her cultural upbringing, Diana should have the swagger that goes along with being the very best and knowing it. Even Michael Jordan was never completely humble; and why not, he was considered by many to be the best basketball player of all time while he was still playing. Similarly, while often soft-spoken and kind, Bruce Lee had a swagger in real life (not just in his movie roles) based on developing the best fighting system to date in his mind. Likewise, Wonder Woman is the best warrior of her time so one might expect her to have the swagger befitting a warrior-champion who has defeated many opponents (and who, in the later incarnations, held her own against Superman and Darkseid—the two most powerful characters in that universe [in addition to Wonder Woman]).

A Different Cultural Perspective. As a diplomat for her homeland of Themyscira,[7] she would be well aware of the gender asymmetry that exists in the United States (not na ve about it as one writer, George Pérez, made her to be). Accordingly, the problem of her being "a woman in a man's world" (as Pérez put it) would actually be much different in her mind. She would likely think of herself as "an enlightened person in a backward world." Based on her experience in her own culture, she knows that women are capable of far more than they are allowed in the United States. Additionally, because the

---

[7] Writer George Pérez's name for what Marston called Paradise Island.

U.S. is not her origin-culture, she may feel sympathy toward U.S. women but feel no special obligation toward them. As a warrior, she may be sworn to protect and help everyone, but as with any warrior class in actual history, she would probably maintain a certain distance for objectivity (as soldiers in this culture do today). Finally, Wonder Woman would probably be less than impressed with the fact that a number of U.S. women appear complicit in their own lack of equality. In this case, U.S. women would appear to her as ambivalent in terms of a struggle for equality.[8]

A Warrior (Not Sport Fighter). Based on her experiences in her own culture, she would probably wear more clothes, if only for the armor value. True warriors understand the importance of not exposing themselves via movements or clothing. Full armor has historically been employed by both male and female warriors in China, Japan, and Europe for protection and item-storage. Even present-day soldiers wear full fatigues in battle, not half-shirts and short-shorts— where are they going to store anything?! Even the scantly clad Greek warriors used full-body shields for protection and item-storage. A sport fighter is different than a warrior but the two are oft-confused in U.S. culture. Sport fighters, from ancient gladiators to modern-day boxers and mixed-martial-artists, reveal skin on purpose for both sex appeal and so that clothing cannot be used against them based on the rules of their sport.[9] As a *warrior*, Wonder Woman would be all too clear about these differences. Warriors don't adhere to sport-fighting rules—how could they? It would be difficult to tell an assailant, "we can't hit each other here or there and we must take breaks every few minutes"—and even a thin layer of full-coverage clothing provides a first line of defense against attacks. Thus, if Wonder Woman ever did wear her familiar, revealing outfit, it would be when competing in some sport-fighting exhibition, not saving the world.

Integrating the psychological attributes above, a solid picture of Wonder Woman as the prototypical "stranger in a strange land"

---

[8] The reader is encouraged to examine Joan Jacob Brumberg's *The Body Project: An Intimate History of American Girls* (1997) or the Naomi Wolf's *Beauty Myth: How Images of Beauty Are Used Against Women* (1991) to understand how women can be considered complicit, to varying degrees, in their own inequality, largely by accepting and instantiating gender stereotypes. See also Rudman and Heppen's (2003) research article on the "glass slipper effect."

[9] They also oil their bodies to literally be too slippery for an opponent's attacks and avoid cuts and incidental scraps.

emerges. Undoubtedly, Wonder Woman would find the United States to be a circus in many ways. It would be entertaining at times, sometimes upsetting, but mostly a very different cultural experience. And, even if all the problems the U.S. society evinces upset her, she could take comfort in the fact that Themyscira is always there.[10] Thus, all the stories of Wonder Woman struggling with her own place in a man's world are inconsistent with her origin understood from a social structural account; Wonder Woman is an interested *observer* of U.S. culture, not an American woman. This misstep is understandable, though, when one considers the power, pervasiveness, and endurance of gender stereotypes at all levels of U.S. culture, right down to Wonder Woman's creators and writers.

GENDER STEREOTYPES

All cultures have stereotypes about gender groups. In the United States, the stereotypes are familiar and accessible enough simply from watching television or flipping through a magazine. Male stereotypes include being powerful, both mentally and physically, and initiators in sexual and non-sexual situations. Female stereotypes, in contrast, include being weaker than men, both mentally and physically, and being followers (viz. passive) in sexual and non-sexual situations.

Two conclusions become apparent from the content of stereotypes. One, there is an oppositionality (or some might claim complementarity) between the stereotype sets—what men have, women lack and what women have, men lack. Two, there is some expectation that the majority of men and women possess the stereotyped qualities.[11] Of course, it is easy enough to find exceptions to the stereotypes. Yet, what makes the theory of stereotypes useful is that it predicts that exceptions are not integrated into the stereotype (e.g., Fiske, 1993).

[10] It is noteworthy, because Wonder Woman enthusiasts know as much, that Themyscira was destroyed once by the God of War, Mars, but was rebuilt and successfully defended itself from numerous attacks by aliens such as the feared warlord Darkseid (whom even Superman has trouble defeating).

[11] A third, less apparent, conclusion is that these gender stereotypes describe heterosexually identified men and women. Because U. S. society is *heteronormative*—presuming that everyone is heterosexual—sexual orientation is often unstated. Nevertheless, the same gender stereotypes are present in the perception of homosexually identified individuals (e.g., "butch" [masculine] and "femme" [feminine] lesbians as well as "queens" [feminine] and "butch" [masculine] for gay males).

Instead *subtyping* takes place; in effect, a special place in the mind is made for exceptions (Brewer, Dull, & Lui, 1981; Taylor, 1981). In this case, exceptions to stereotypes are thought of as a "special" category. Many empirical studies support this claim by showing that confirming instances are recalled better and used more in our dealings with people based on disconfirming instances (Hewstone, Macrae, Griffiths, & Milne, 1994; Johnston & Hewstone, 1992; Maurer, Park, & Rothbart, 1995; Kunda & Oleson, 1995; Plaks, Stroessner, Dweck, & Sherman, 2001). The lesson is that gender stereotypes powerfully organize people's experiences and that disconfirming cases are often marginalized (Ruble & Stangor, 1986). (That's why it's hard to remember Joan of Arc, Boudica, Tomoe, and Wing Chun as great warriors.)

What happens when a person is repeatedly presented with an individual who is gender atypical? This question is very pertinent to any discussion of Wonder Woman because her character violates certain gender expectations in the U.S. In response to the question, two outcomes are possible. One outcome is further subtyping ("women are still expected to conform to the stereotype, but Wonder Woman is an exception") and even denigration of the individuals in question (Rudman, 1998; Rudman & Fairchild, 2004; Rudman & Glick, 1999). Denigration can be seen in the treatment of female bodybuilders who are often said to be "not real women" or denigrated as "looking like a man" or otherwise thought of as ugly by both men and women. The other outcome is an attempt to "balance" a kind of gender stereotype equation. In this case, a person looks for instances wherein the atypical individuals confirm the gender stereotype then includes these instances in the representation of those individuals (cf. Rudman & Glick, 1999). The popularity of female action heroes such as Sydney from *Alias*, Lara Croft from *Tomb Raider*, and Kate from *LOST* are good examples of how physically strong and very aggressive women are "balanced" as sexy (e.g., an emphasis on their breasts or nudity) and usually deferring to men in romantic relationships. With the "feminine" side represented, these characters are not viewed (by the creators or the audience) as severely violating expectations of the gender category **woman**, and thereby avoid denigration. In less formal terms, if women are too "masculine" (e.g., strong) then they *must be* "feminine" (e.g., sexy) to "balance out" the gender stereotype. I argue that Wonder Woman is (unfortunately) no exception to this "balancing."

USE OF GENDER STEREOTYPES IN THE WONDER WOMAN SERIES (1941–1998)

The Marston/Peter Era (1941–1947)

Marston (as Charles Moulton) wrote the series from 1941 to 1947 and described the character as including the best qualities: strength and submission (to peace, restraint, and good judgment). Marston's "submission" is not passivity. Submission as a psychological concept in the 1920s to1940s was viewed as we might view "moderation" or "restraint" today—as good qualities for everyone to possess (see Marston, 1928/1999). Thus, Wonder Woman's personal qualities do not reflect this struggle to "balance" gender stereotypes; in fact, they are either gender atypical or gender neutral, such as her intrepidness and zeal for justice. Marston and artist Harry Peter's choice of Wonder Woman's appearance is the crux of the gender stereotype struggle. Peter designed the familiar high-heeled boots, strapless bustier top, and star-spangled shorts for which Wonder Woman is so well known based on Marston's notes (Daniels, 2000). While this outfit is uninteresting today, imagine how it was received in the 1940s, when women were still wearing skirts past the knee (as any page of the Wonder Woman series at that time depicts) and when racy outfits (strapless tops and tight shorts) were found in so-called "bad-girl art" and illustrated erotica of the time. In fact, Dorothy Roubicek, a hired advisor on the stories, argued that Wonder Woman should wear a modified Greek tunic to make the character "feminine and yet not objectionable...as those short tight panties she wears might be" (Daniels, 2000, p. 62). Additionally, on Paradise Island (Wonder Woman's home) scantily clad women bound each other as a training technique for self-restraint. The sexual overtones of these scenes were known to Marston and Peter even while Marston argued that the bondage was not sexual in nature but a depiction of the concept (Daniels, 2000). The sex appeal that Marston knew Wonder Woman conveyed was likely an illustration of the "female beauty" Marston wanted her to possess. The foregoing argument is strengthened by the fact that Marston and Peter were very willing to portray women in a wide range of dress styles, including drag. For instance, Dr. Poison and Hypnota, two of Wonder Woman's more insidious foes, dressed and presented themselves as men even though they were women. It is no coincidence that Marston believed men to be more violent and devious than women *by nature* and therefore probably chose to attire these heartless female enemies as men while making sure that everyone knew Wonder Woman was decidedly a woman (by accentuating her curves) as she pulled Nazi warplanes out of the sky and stopped moving trains (a la Superman).

Kanigher Era (1948–1968)

The next major writer was Robert Kanigher (1948–1968).[12] His Wonder Woman was campy and completely stripped of her self-reliance and intrepidness. Wonder Woman was now quite interested in fashion and marriage (to her rather uninteresting sidekick U.S. army officer Steve Trevor) and did little more than occupy her time with these thoughts and fight the occasional human-sized dinosaur. Wonder Woman was now carried around by Steve Trevor as the cover to *Sensation Comics* #94 (November–December, 1949) depicts—even though she was orders of magnitude stronger than him—and also became a babysitter (to a baby dinosaur and others) in *Wonder Woman* #90 (May, 1957). Kanigher even helped make Wonder Woman the secretary of the Justice Society (later, Justice League of America) even though she was as powerful as Superman and thus a natural second-in-command.[13]

O'Neil/Conway Era (1968–1986)

Dennis O'Neil (who would later become a notable Batman writer) assumed writing duties and with artist Mike Sedowsky created a new Wonder Woman who was stripped of her powers and her old costume. O'Neil claimed that rendering her an ordinary woman would showcase her independence. Yet, it was later revealed in *Wonder Woman* #178 (September–October, 1968) that she gave up her pow-

---

[12] Marston died in 1947.

[13] Wonder Woman was and remains the only female member of the Justice League.

ers for the love of Steve Trevor![14] Moreover, O'Neil's new Wonder Woman had an epiphany about her own attractiveness, commenting about how gorgeous she was before starting a shopping spree in the first few panels of the same issue. To O'Neil's credit, Wonder Woman did learn martial arts from the master I-Ching and became a crime fighter (like the Batman), but still made time for shopping on the side. Notably, in 1972, Gloria Steinem placed Marston's version of Wonder Woman on the debut cover of *Ms.* magazine with the text "Wonder Woman for President," apparently using the older version as a symbol for women's liberation, while inside Joanne Edgar decried O'Neil's stripping of Wonder Woman's power as making her submissive (in the negative sense), not independent. Also during the 1970s, the campy Wonder Woman television series starring Lynda Carter debuted.[15] Gerry Conway began writing and Wonder Woman was still chasing campy adventures and considering marriage to Steve Trevor. They finally wed in 1986 (*Wonder Woman* #329, February), ending *Wonder Woman*'s forty-five-year consecutive run, and cementing her in many minds as decidedly gender typical.

Pérez era (1987–1992)

George Pérez took over writer/penciller duties in the reboot of Wonder Woman after the "Crisis on Infinite Earths" story closed. *Wonder Woman* vol. 2, #1 appeared in March 1987 with Pérez as penciller. Six issues later, he was plotting the issues; and sixteen issues later he was writing dialogue too. As Pérez puts it, he "was pleased... to get in touch with his feminine side" (Daniels, 2000, p. 168) and wanted to get the input of women for the stories, including Gloria Steinem. By his own admission, Pérez wanted to make Wonder Woman nice and peace-loving and sacrificed story action to convey these points (Daniels, 2000). Interestingly, Superman is nice and peace-loving but his stories are never at a loss for action. Pérez developed the idea of Man's World (his label for "patriarchal society") and Won-

---

[14] Thankfully Steve Trevor was put out of his misery (and ours) when he died two issues later in *Wonder Woman* #180.

[15] Years after the television series ended even Lynda Carter expressed the gender stereotype balancing act when she described the character thusly: "[Wonder Woman] represents everything good in a woman: strength, beauty, intelligence, and compassion" (Daniels, 2000, p. 148). It is good that "strength" comes first, but interestingly "beauty" comes before both "intelligence" and "compassion."

der Woman's struggle within it. Pérez's Wonder Woman also became friends with Professor Julia Kapatelis and her teenage daughter Vanessa. Much time for this trio was spent discussing teen romances, hot flashes, as well as engaging in copious amounts of hugging and weeping (Daniels, 2000)—an interesting departure from the Marston/Peter days.

Kupperberg/Messner-Loebs/Deadato Era (1992–1995)

In 1992 Paul Kupperberg took over as editor with William Messner-Loebs as writer. Possibly as a response to Pérez's self-styled feminist approach, Kupperberg wanted to make Wonder Woman sexier (Daniels, 2000) and hired artist Mike Deadato to accomplish this task. Deadato's Wonder Woman was extremely buxom with a thin waist and high-cut star-spangled panties to show off her long, shapely legs. Her poses were often sexualized and drawn at angles implying nudity when she flew. Her fight sequences were sexualized as well, often resulting in clothing covering female characters' nipples but not much else.

Byrne Era (1995–1998)

In 1995 artist-writer John Byrne, who was already well established in the industry, tried his talents at plotting and penciling Wonder Woman's adventures with *Wonder Woman* #101 and tried to avoid the extremes of both Pérez and Deadato (Daniels, 2000). Interestingly, he did maintain the bustier-and-panties outfit, probably because of his confession that he appreciated seeing Lynda Carter as Wonder Woman running in slow motion (Daniels, 2000, p. 193). His Wonder Woman was decidedly more powerful than any incarnation since Marston's. Byrne's Wonder Woman hurled army tanks and fought Darkseid (an alien warlord whom even Superman feared). Although she retained the familiar outfit, she was drawn with more muscles than curves (which some readers decried; see Daniels, 2000—illustrating the readership's struggle with gender stereotypes). Notably, in his final issue, Byrne made Wonder Woman immortal and thereby invincible, but maintained that Wonder Woman was a heterosexual virgin (Daniels, 2000).

DISCUSSION OF THE SERIES

Despite the range of writers and passing of decades, Wonder Woman's portrayal always had more to do with stereotypical views of women than with the logic of her upbringing, which suggest a much different Wonder Woman than any of these writers envisioned. All the *Wonder Woman* writers from 1941 to 1998 were engaged in a kind of gender stereotype "balancing act" with the character (admittedly, to varying degrees) and this situation has not changed ten years later.

Using the psychological perspectives presented here, hopefully one day soon Wonder Woman can assume her status alongside Superman, as her creator Marston had hoped, as one of the true juggernauts of illustrated fiction. With powers beyond imagination and an interesting character psyche that keeps her readers intrigued, a fully clothed Wonder Woman could be showered with the adoration of millions. She may even exude an undeniable attractiveness that flows from her swagger, analogous to the attractiveness Superman exudes based on his strong moral character. Yet, this attractiveness would always be secondary to her personality, as it is with Superman. Maybe then, someone can write an essay titled "How Wonder Woman Overcame Gender Stereotypes in the United States."

Chuck Tate, Ph.D., is an assistant professor of psychology at California State University, Bakersfield. His research interests include how people define and use broad social categories like gender, sexual orientation, and 'race' in various aspects of person perception, including self-concepts and prejudice. Writing this chapter has given him new respect for Wonder Woman and the struggles that the character has endured. A definite sympathizer in the past, he is now a zealot for establishing Wonder Woman's pre-eminence in illustrated fiction and popular culture!

REFERENCES

M. B. Brewer, V. Dull, and L. Lui, "Perceptions of the Elderly: Stereotypes as Prototypes," *Journal of Personality and Social Psychology* 41 (1981): 656–670.

Brumberg, J. J. *The Body Project: An Intimate Hhistory of American Girls.* New York: Random House, 1997.

D. M. Buss, "Psychological Sex Differences: Origins through Sexual Selection," *American Psychologist* 50 (1995): 164–168.

Chu, R., Ritchie, R., & Wu, Y. *Complete Wing Chin: The Definitive Guide to Wing Chun's History and Traditions.* Boston: Tuttle, 1998.

Daniels, L. *Wonder Woman: The Complete History.* San Francisco, CA: Chronicle, 2000.

Eagly, A. H. *Sex Differences in Social Behavior: A Social Role Interpretation.* Hillsdale, NJ: Erlbaum, 1987.

A. H. Eagly and W. Wood, "The Origins of Sex Differences in Human Behavior: Evolved Behaviors versus Social Roles," *American Psychologist* 54 (1999): 408–423.

S. T. Fiske, "Social Cognition and Social Perception," *Annual Review of Psychology* 44 (1993): 155–194.

M. Hewstone, C. N. Macrae, R. Griffiths, and A. B. Milne, "Cognitive Models of Stereotype Change: Measurement, Development, and Consequences of Subtyping," *Journal of Experimental Social Psychology* 30 (1994): 505–526.

J. S. Hyde, "The Gender Similarities Hypothesis," *American Psychologist* 60 (1994): 581–592.

L. Johnston, and M. Hewstone, "Cognitive Models of Stereotype Change: Subtyping and the Perceived Typicality of Disconfirming Ggroup Members," *Journal of Experimental Social Psychology* 28 (1992): 360–386.

Z. Kunda and K. C. Oleson, "Maintaining Stereotypes in the Face of Disconfirmation: Constructing Grounds for Subtyping Deviants," *Journal of Personality and Social Psychology* 68 (1995): 565–579.

Leibowitz, L. "Origins of the Sexual Division of Labor." In M. Lowe & R. Hubbard (Eds.), *Women's Nature: Rationalization of Inequality* (pp. 123–147). New York: Pergammon, 1983.

Marston, W. M. *Emotions of Normal People.* New York: Routledge, 1928/1999.

K. L. Maurer, B. Park, and M. Rothbart, "Subtyping versus Subgrouping Processes in Stereotype Representation," *Journal of Personality and Social Psychology* 69 (1995): 812–824.

McCullough, H. C. (trans). *Heike Monogatari* [The Tale of Heike]. Palo Alto, CA: Stanford University Press, 1998.

A. J. Noss and B. S. Hewlett, "The Contexts of Female Hunting in Central Africa," *American Anthropologist* 103 (2001): 1024–1040.

J. E. Plaks, S. J. Stroessner, C. S. Dweck, and J. W. Sherman, "Person Theories and Attention Allocation: Preferences for Stereotypic versus Counterstereotypic Information," *Journal of Personality and Social Psychology* 80 (2001): 876–893.

D. N. Ruble and C. Stangor, "Stalking the Elusive Schema: Insights from Developmental and Social-psychological Analyses of Gender Schemas," *Social Cognition* 4 (1986): 227–261.

L. A. Rudman, "Self-promotion as a Risk Factor for Women: The Costs and Benefits of Counterstereotypical Impression Management," *Journal of Personality and Social Psychology* 74 (1998) 629–645.

L. A. Rudman and K. Fairchild, "Reactions to Counterstereotypic Behavior: The Role of Backlash in Cultural Stereotype Maintenance," *Journal of Personality and Social Psychology* 87 (2004): 157–176.

L. A. Rudman and P. Glick, "Feminized Management and Backlash toward Agentic Women: The Hidden Costs to Women of a Kinder, Gentler Image of Middle Managers," *Journal of Personality and Social Psychology* 77 (1999): 1004–1010.

L. A. Rudman and P. Glick, "Prescriptive Gender Stereotypes and Backlash toward Agentic Women," *Journal of Social Issues* 57 (2001): 743–762.

L. A. Rudman and J. B. Heppen, "Implicit Romantic Fantasies and Women's Interest in Personal Power: A Glass Slipper Effect?" *Personality and Social Psychology Bulletin* 29 (2003): 1357–1370.

Taylor, S. E. "A Categorization Approach to Stereotyping." In D. L. Hamilton (Ed.), *Cognitive Processes in Stereotyping and Intergroup Behavior* (pp. 145–182). Hillsdale, NJ: Erlbaum, 1981.

Wolf, N. *The Beauty Myth: How Images of Beauty are Used against Women*. New York: Morrow, 1991.

W. Wood and A. H. Eagly, "A Ccross-cultural Analysis of the Behavior of Men and Women: Implications for the Origins of Sex Differences," *Psychological Bulletin* 128 (2002): 699–727.

THE PSYCHOLOGY OF SUPERHEROES

Andrew R. Getzfeld, Ph.D.

WHAT WOULD FREUD SAY? PSYCHOPATHOLOGY AND THE PUNISHER

The Punisher (a.k.a. Frank Castle) is a complex character—he seems like a villain, but his targets are the bad guys. To criminals that he targets, he becomes their judge, jury, and executioner. What's the matter with him that he's so ruthless? In this essay, Getzfeld grapples with the question of whether the Punisher is a criminal, is mentally ill, or both. Getzfeld walks us through the Punisher's history and then explains how psychologists might diagnose and treat him.

FRANK CASTLE IS THE PUNISHER. He is as famous as a "superhero," known to the world through comics, movies, and DVDs. But did you ever consider that the background and behavior of the "typical" superhero may well fit the criteria for a psychiatric diagnosis?

As a psychologist, it has always been a challenge to accurately diagnose an individual, especially since in most cases psychologists cannot perform definitive tests the same way that medical doctors can. Sometimes we even make "mistakes," which can lead to dire consequences. I grew up reading DC and Marvel comics, but I was always fascinated by the field of Psychology. At times I have wondered: *What would it be like to have Frank Castle lying on the proverbial couch? What types of psychopathologies does The Punisher demonstrate?* This chapter will attempt to accurately diagnose Frank Castle and give him a prognosis. A prognosis here means that we will be "guesstimating" how successful he would be in therapy; in addition, we will guess his long-term outlook once he has completed treatment. Mr. Castle, please lie down on our comfortable couch.

THE PUNISHER: A CASE OF ANTISOCIAL PERSONALITY DISORDER, OR SOMETHING ELSE?

Frank Castle (or Castiglione) is an interesting individual, since he is one of the relatively few superheroes that has no superpowers and in fact acts like an anti-hero. In addition he has no secret identity and is widely known among friend and foe. At the least we can safely say that he is comfortable being The Punisher, since he has no reason to hide his true identity (and no real reason to fear retaliation since it is known who he is). Unlike Spider-Man, Batman, and other superheroes, Frank Castle murders without remorse and without impunity. However, it needs to be noted that his victims are all criminals (or appear to be). This makes Castle stand out, since if (or when) a superhero kills a villian, it is generally by accident. If it does occur deliberately, it makes news in the comics world, and often will be mentioned by the media. How did Castle get so inured to killing, and how would we diagnose and treat him if he appeared in a psychologist's office?

Frank Castle is a former U.S. Marine who served in Vietnam; he also qualified to be a Navy S.E.A.L. Before Frank joined the Marines, he was studying to become a Catholic priest, but changed his mind because he was unable to forgive those who committed evil acts. Prior to his enlistment, he married his wife Maria, who was already pregnant with their first child. Thus you have an individual who wanted to help others through prayer and reflection but ended up being a cold-blooded killing machine, out to eliminate crime.

What sent Castle off the deep end and changed him so much? Frank Castle, Maria, and their children were in New York's Central Park for an afternoon picnic when they witnessed a Mafia gangland execution that caused the Costa crime family to murder Castle's family on the spot. Castle survived his wounds, and he was able to identify all of the murderers but because the police were deeply involved with the Costa family, they didn't help him find the murderers. Because of his tremendous grief and outrage over police corruption, Castle decided that the only punishment criminals deserve is total destruction. From that point on he became The Punisher and waged his one-man war on crime while he extracted his revenge.

DEFINING ABNORMAL BEHAVIOR

Before we continue, we need to define abnormal behavior so we can distinguish it from unusual or eccentric behavior (Eccentrics have odd or unusual habits but are not mentally ill [Weeks and James, 1995]). It can often be quite difficult to clearly define abnormal behavior, as many factors are involved. The field of psychology uses three perspectives to define abnormal behavior.

The Statistical Frequency Perspective considers behavior to be abnormal if it occurs rarely or infrequently in relation to the behavior of the general population. The Social Norms Perspective considers behavior to be abnormal if the individual's behavior deviates greatly from accepted social standards, values, or norms. (Norms are spoken and unspoken rules for proper conduct.) These social standards, values, or norms are established by a society over time and are naturally subject to changes over time. The Maladaptive Perspective views behavior as abnormal if the said behavior(s) interferes with the individual's ability to function in life or in society. By this we mean: Is the individual able to work, take care of him/herself, and have normal social interactions?

There are several other features that psychologists and other helping professionals use to define abnormal behavior. First, is the individual's behavior causing danger to him/herself or to other people?

If these individuals are dangerous, it is more likely that they pose a threat to themselves and not to others. Second, is the individual's behavior causing him or her distress? In many cases the individual's family or loved ones are more distressed than the individual themselves. (For example, family members of an alcohol-dependent individual are often more stressed than the dependent individual him/herself.) Finally, we also look for the duration of the behaviors, the age when the behaviors first began, and the intensity of the behavior(s). Therefore, are Castle's behaviors eccentric, criminal, or psychopathological? Let us examine Castle's behaviors in more detail.

DIAGNOSING FRANK CASTLE

If Castle was to come into our office and we were to diagnose him, we would first consider the presence of a Personality Disorder, specifically Antisocial Personality Disorder (ASPD). ASPD is one form of psychopathology or mental illness according to the *Diagnostic and Statistical Manual of Mental Disorders-4th Edition-Text Revision* (*DSM-IV-TR*) (American Psychiatric Association [APA], 2000). According to the *DSM-IV-TR*, a personality disorder is "an enduring pattern of inner experience and behavior that deviates markedly from the expectations of the individual's culture, is pervasive and inflexible, has an onset in adolescence or early adulthood, is stable over time, and leads to distress or impairment.... The clinician should assess the stability of personality traits over time and across different situations" (685–6). Personality disorders affect about 15 million adults in the United States and are coded on Axis II of the *DSM-IV-TR*. Axis II diagnoses represent long-standing, deeply rooted problems (in this case personality traits) that are very difficult to treat successfully and/or modify. These disorders are also viewed as producing personality features that are maladaptive and inflexible and often cause adjustment problems or personal distress. Personality disorders are not diagnosed in individuals under eighteen years old (APA, 2000).

Personality Disorders are grouped into three clusters, based on the similarities among each disorder in the cluster. Cluster A includes disorders where the individual is viewed as being odd or eccentric. Cluster B includes disorders where the individual is viewed as being overly emotional or erratic in his or her behavior. Their behavior tends to be impulsive and may have antisocial features. Individuals with Cluster B disorders are more likely to come in contact with mental health professionals, but not by choice in many instances. Cluster C includes disorders where the individual appears anxious or fearful (APA, 2000).

According to the *DSM-IV-TR* (APA, 2000), individuals with Antisocial Personality Disorder need to have at least three of the following seven diagnostic criteria in order to receive the ASPD diagnosis: First, the individual needs to violate the rights of others through deceit, repeated lies, or aggression, usually to profit somehow or to get pleasure. These violated rights can be personal (lying to someone) or legal (assault). However, neither deceit nor aggression is absolutely necessary for the diagnosis, since this is only one of seven diagnostic criteria. Castle certainly violates the "rights" of criminals since they are innocent until proven guilty. However, he sees them as having no rights since they are criminals and therefore he is extremely aggressive towards them. Does he get pleasure by violating their rights and by being aggressive towards them? Second, the individual needs to have repeatedly performed behaviors that are considered as grounds for arrest. The use of illegal weapons and assaulting and killing people, even if they are criminals, satisfies this criterion for Castle. The *DSM-IV-TR* notes that these behaviors must not adhere to social norms, and Castle's actions clearly violate them. Third, the individual will demonstrate impulsivity or the inability to plan for the future, a related sign of impulsivity. Castle certainly seems to be impulsive, since at times he acts towards the supposed criminals before checking out the evidence; however, he does seem able to plan for the future. For Castle, the future means the elimination of all criminals and thus the elimination of crime, and he will not stop until he is stopped—dead.

Fourth, the individual will be repeatedly aggressive by getting involved with numerous physical fights and assaults; this needs no further explanation. Fifth, the individual will demonstrate a reckless disregard for the safety of others. Additionally, the individual will also demonstrate a lack of regard for his/her own safety. Castle does not care about criminals' safety, and he wants to eliminate all of them. He does his best to not involve innocents in his war on crime but of course when you use extreme violence, innocents can and do get hurt. He does not want to get hurt (and miraculously he rarely does), but his actions put him in a position to get hurt or killed no matter how well trained he might be.

Sixth, the individual will be consistently irresponsible. This is demonstrated by repeatedly failing to hold down a job consistently, or the repeated reneging on financial obligations. Castle has no regular job and there is scant evidence that he reneges on any financial obligations. He uses the money gained from his executions to further fund his war on crime and his safe houses, so he really does not need a regular job. Finally, the individual will demonstrate a lack of remorse. This is indicated by the individual being indifferent to, or rationalizing, having hurt, mistreated, or stolen from another individual (APA, 2000).

How important is the lack of remorse criterion? First, recall that it is not necessary for someone with ASPD to have a lack of remorse, although it is commonly seen in these individuals. The question arises, however: Is the lack of remorse a premorbid indicator of ASPD, or is it a natural occurrence for everyone who experiences tragedy such as Castle? Castle was trained by the United States government to kill as an elite soldier. The government ideally wants individuals who feel little when they kill; "They are just following orders." However, does the constant exposure to violence, death, and destruction lead to a lack of remorse?

Robins (1978) notes that ASPD may begin early on in a child's life. According to Robins (1978), the greater the number of antisocial behaviors the child demonstrates in his or her childhood, the more likely that child will develop ASPD later on. Robins states that this criterion is the single best predictor of developing ASPD. In addition, Robins also notes that the earlier these symptoms are demonstrated, the greater the likelihood of developing ASPD (1978; 1991). Therefore, we will hypothesize that premorbid symptoms of ASPD occur early in a child's life and that the lack of remorse begins to develop then.

Certainly Castle is aggressive in his use of excessive force since his goal is to commit murder, although he sees murder as the only way to accomplish his goal of destroying all criminals. Castle makes himself judge, jury, and executioner; he carries out his own death sentences without the criminals having the benefit of a fair trial. In his mind he is doing the police and the law-abiding citizens a favor by saving taxpayers time and money, and he is gaining revenge at the same time. In essence, his perspective on who should be exterminated as a criminal is correct regardless of the evidence.

Some people would probably say that people like Castle have no soul. He enjoys (in the sense that it is satisfying to him) killing for revenge but not for actual "bloodsport." How do we know this? Castle himself says so! In Castle's first appearance in *Amazing Spider-Man* #129 (February, 1974), he makes the declaration, "I kill only those who deserve killing and Spider-Man deserves to die!" Castle wrongly believed Spider-Man murdered Gwen Stacy and Norman Osborn (the Green Goblin). More to the point, Castle tells Spider-Man during one of their encounters about his goal of executing all criminals, "Not something I like doing. . . . Simply something that has to be done. . . . And I've got nothing to lose by risking what's left of my life wiping out your kind of parasite" (*Amazing Spider-Man* #129, 1974). Therefore, is this normal behavior, even for someone as traumatized as Castle is? In addition, does he really believe that he can kill Spider-Man, a hero with significant superpowers? Finally, does this make him an individual demonstrating psychopathological views by stating that this is his role, wiping out "parasites"?

There is a slight problem with diagnosing Castle: We need to know quite a bit about his childhood years and we do not have that information. There is a reason for this: The *DSM-IV-TRs* definition of Antisocial Personality Disorders (ASPD) states that some symptoms of Conduct Disorder must have been present before the age of fifteen. Some symptoms of Conduct Disorder are frequent lying, truancy, running away from home, theft, arson, aggression towards animals and other people, and destruction of property (graffiti for example). We do not know whether these symptoms were present in Castle's childhood, but we can surmise that they probably were not, especially since he wanted to become a Catholic priest (Although some individuals wishing to enter the priesthood could be diagnosed with Conduct Disorder). Two qualifiers are also included: The ASPD behaviors must have been occurring since the age of fifteen; the individual must also be at least eighteen before an ASPD diagnosis can be made (APA, 2000).

Is Frank Castle a psychopath? In the past individuals with Antisocial Personality Disorder were called psychopaths. The term psychopath implies that something is pathological with the individual's mind or with their psychological makeup. ASPD individuals and psychopaths are usually involved with breaking laws, but there are some significant differences between the two categories. Hervey Cleckley (1982) came up with sixteen key characteristics of psychopathic individuals. We will review some of the most important criteria. First, the individual possesses considerable superficial charm and average or above average intelligence, a criterion that fits Castle. Next, the individual lacks delusions and other signs of irrational thinking. Castle's thinking may not be totally rational but he does not appear to be delusional (false beliefs that individuals insist are true, regardless of overwhelming evidence against them). Third, the individual lacks anxiety. Fourth, the individual demonstrates deceit and insincerity. Certainly Castle has to lie to accomplish his goals, but he can rationalize this by saying that he must lie in order to lure criminals to their doom. He is sincere in his mission to the point where this has become his life and defined who he is. Fifth, the individual demonstrates antisocial behavior which is inadequately motivated and poorly planned, seeming to stem from an inexplicable impulsiveness. Is Castle impulsive? He appeared to be in his first appearance (*Amazing Spider-Man* #129, 1974), when he was ready to eliminate Spider-Man, who he thought killed Gwen Stacy and the Green Goblin, even though there was no solid evidence to support this. In addition, the Goblin was a master supervillian, so why would Castle kill Spider-Man when he in fact did Castle's job? Castle's behavior is of course antisocial but it is well-motivated and well-planned. We can also conclude that it is too impulsive at times leading to innocent deaths. Sixth, the individual demonstrates poor judgment and fails to learn from experience. Castle is an excellent student. Any time he makes mistakes he makes sure never to repeat them. For Castle, a mistake might lead to his death. Seventh, the individual demonstrates pathological egocentricity, is self-centered, and is incapable of demonstrating (or feeling) real love and experiencing attachment. Castle was able to demonstrate interpersonal attachment in the past, but I suspect that this ability has now been lost. He is attached to his mission, nothing more. Eighth, the individual lacks any true insight and is unable to see him/herself as others do. We believe that this fits Castle, since he cannot realize that while many applaud his actions, many more are repulsed by his methods and beliefs. Many of the superheroes are against his methods and motives and try to apprehend him. He sees everyone who disagrees with his mission as wrong and only sees his point of view, similar to a small child who only believes that his/her perspective is right. Next, there is no history of genuine suicide attempts. We know of none mentioned in the comics and it would go against the character's personality to attempt suicide. However, his mission is a form of eventual suicide, as at some point he will probably get killed. Tenth, the individual has a poor sex life. We recall no evidence of Castle having sex once he became The Punisher. Our view: It would compromise his mission to get involved with these activities. Finally, the individual will not have a life plan and will not live in any ordered way, unless it promotes self-defeat. The last thing Castle wants to do is to get hurt or to die, as that would conclude his mission. His life is now totally planned out with his one goal in mind and he demonstrates no self-defeating behaviors, perhaps with the exception of not having a secret identity (Cleckley, 1982).

Research has demonstrated that there are two dimensions (clusters or factors) of psychopathic behaviors. The first refers to emotional detachment and includes traits such as a lack of remorse and callousness, and basically describes an individual who has inflated self-esteem and who exploits other people. Castle certainly exploits other people (including other superheroes) to accomplish his goal of destroying criminals. The second factor characterizes an antisocial lifestyle and the traits reflect the individual's behaviors: antisocial, socially deviant, irresponsible, and impulsive (Hart & Hare, 1997). Hart and Hare note that this second dimension is more closely related to the *DSM-IV-TR*s diagnosis of ASPD than is the first dimension. A concomitant problem is the criterion of having a lack of remorse. This is a key criterion of psychopathy, yet it is only one of seven criteria for the *DSM-IV-TR* definition of ASPD. Thus, it is possible to receive an ASPD diagnosis while not having the lack of remorse critical to a psychopathy diagnosis.

Therefore, is Castle a psychopath? Castle demonstrates a lack of empathy, inflated and arrogant self-appraisal, and glib and superficial charm. We can safely state that he lacks empathy for those he hurts and/or kills and we can also state that he probably lacks feelings, or that his true feelings are so deeply repressed that he rarely (if ever) is able to access them. Psychopaths do not experience anxiety about their behaviors; therefore, they cannot learn from their mistakes and thus they continue to hurt or harm others. Castle does learn from his mistakes although he does not feel anxious when he kills criminals, "Four dead, and my pulse is still under 80. Not bad for a warm up." (*Punisher War Journal* #7, 1989).

According to Hare (1996) psychopaths cannot be understood in terms of poor upbringing or developmental problems. They are viewed as morally depraved individuals whose violence is planned, purposeful, and emotionless, similar to a serial killer and perhaps similar to Castle, although we do not think so. Hare notes that it is difficult to understand their motivations, as their history generally shows no emotional bonding with others, not the case with Castle. Psychopaths tend to be grandiose, entitled, and sadistic. Castle is grandiose but appears to be realistic in that he knows his limitations. Finally, psychopaths tend to be career criminals; Castle is not doing this to make money or to get sadistic thrills.

Our conclusion: Castle is a vigilante, or perhaps a bounty hunter, but we do not see him as a psychopath. Instead, we see him as an individual who has Antisocial Personality Disorder. Castle had a normal family life before he became The Punisher, and we will presume that he had a somewhat normal childhood. Finally, he is not a career criminal and is not involved in random senseless violence.

TREATING FRANK CASTLE

Since we presume that Castle has Antisocial Personality Disorder (ASPD), how would we treat him? Treatment of patients with ASPD is very difficult due to their lack of insight (Andreasen & Black, 1995). In addition, ASPD individuals rarely come into treatment voluntarily since they do not see anything wrong with their behavior. These individuals often present with much charm, making it easier for them to be extremely manipulative with their therapists. Thus it is not surprising that many clinicians do not predict successful treatment for an individual with ASPD. Some well-known researchers have stated that it is a fruitless endeavor to make any attempt to either treat or try to alter the behavior of a patient with ASPD (See for example Cleckley, 1982). ASPD patients also tend to be recidivists, i.e., they are well known to jails, prisons, and to mental-health clinics and hospitals. For them, all of these institutions have revolving doors and they are always going in, staying for a short period of time while experiencing no changes, and then leaving, either because they were discharged or because they were sent back to jail or prison. These patients also have a tremendous tendency to relapse shortly after treatment has concluded.

Castle would probably manipulate his way through therapy, pretending to work hard and trying to gain insight, while all he wants is to feign success so treatment will end. ASPD patients—similar to Castle—are generally unable to benefit from therapy because of their symptoms, such as being unable to form a trusting relationship with the therapist (or anyone for that matter), lying without really knowing they are lying, only living in the present and not planning or foreseeing the future, and seeing nothing wrong with their behaviors even though they are crimes. It is logical that Castle cannot form trusting relationships with anyone. His family was murdered before his eyes, and he was trained by the U.S. government to kill. To be honest, if remorse exists it would be rather miraculous.

Thus, do we attempt to treat Castle? Unequivocally, we have to make an honest and complete attempt to treat him, even if all seems hopeless. Perhaps he will gain some insight into his tremendous pain and anger, and direct it in a positive fashion instead of using it negatively. If nothing else, Castle has a tremendous amount of energy to continue his vigilantism all these years. His prognosis for successful treatment, and for not having a "relapse," is poor.

Andrew R. Getzfeld, Ph.D., received his B.A. in psychology from Vassar College, his MSSW from the University of Wisconsin, and his Ph.D. in school psychology from the University of Tennessee. An associate professor in psychology at New Jersey City University and an adjunct associate professor at New York University, Andrew's areas of interest include eating disorders and the addictions, abnormal psychology, and psychopharmacology. He has written two books: *Abnormal Psychology Casebook: A New Perspective* (Pearson Prentice-Hall, 2004), and *Essentials of Abnormal Psychology* (Wiley, 2006). Andrew loves international travel, writing, and grew up with Spider-Man and Superman, often wishing he too could bend steel with his bare hands.

REFERENCES

American Psychiatric Association. *Diagnostic and Statistical Manual of Mental Disorders* (4th *ed.-text revision*). Washington, DC, 2000.

Andreasen, N. C., & Black, D. W. *Introductory Textbook of Psychiatry* (2nd *ed.*) Washington, DC: American Psychiatric Press, 1995.

Cleckley, H. M. *The Mask of Sanity* (6th *ed.*). St. Louis: Mosby, 1982.

R. Hare, "Psychopathy: A Clinical Construct Whose Time has Come," *Criminal Justice and Behavior* 23 (1996): 25–54.

Hart, S. D., & Hare, R. D. "Psychopathy: Assessment and Association with Criminal Conduct." In D.M. Stoff, J.Breiling, & J.D. Maser (Eds.), *Handbook of Antisocial Behavior*, (pp. 22–35). New York: John Wiley, 1997.

Robins, L. N. "Aetiological Implications in Studies of Childhood Histories Relating to Antisocial Personality." In R.D. Hare & D. Schalling (Eds.), *Psychopathic Behavior: Approaches to Research* (pp. 255–271). Chichester, England: John Wiley, 1978.

L. N. Robins, "Conduct Disorder," *Journal of Child Psychology and Psychiatry* 32 (1991): 193–212.

Weeks, D., & James, J. *Eccentrics: A Study of Sanity and Strangeness.* New York: Villard, 1995.

THE PSYCHOLOGY OF SUPERHEROES

Siamak Tundra Naficy

COMING TO TERMS WITH BIZARRO

In this essay, Naficy provides a brief history of costumed heroes and secret identities, and focuses on some of the unique elements of Superman's story. Unlike most other superheroes, there was no event, no turning point where he went from human to super-being. This essay also examines what Naficy calls Superman's "other alter ego"—Bizarro—and the general link between identity and culture.

SUPERMAN IS PERHAPS THE MOST RECOGNIZED costumed superhero ever. As such, it is not surprising that he has been interpreted, deconstructed, and discussed in a myriad of forms throughout the years. The character's status as the first costumed *super*hero has allowed him to be used in many mediums and various studies discussing and referencing the genre, from Jerry Seinfeld to Umberto Eco, the latter noting that "he can be seen as the representative of all his similars" (Eco). Created during the Depression, he is the epitome of visible invisibility: he is a normal human (Clark Kent) and he is not (Superman). Superman's dual identity is a necessary part of his heroism in order to be uniquely American: half where he came from, half where he is now. In this way, he is the ultimate American since he is a resident, a blue-and-red-wearing icon, but also an immigrant. He thus becomes the ultimate and ideal immigrant, especially evocative of the era and concept of "the American" at the same time of Superman's creation (1930s).

It's interesting and perhaps provocative to note how his more public persona, Clark Kent, is the more American of his identities, while the defender of the United States and the American Way is the alien Kryptonian one. Superman does wear the red and blue. However, when Superman is in his own private home, his Fortress of Solitude, it can be argued that his immigrant self is better expressed.

It's also important to note that Superman's role, during the real-life reign of Al Capone in the 1930s, was to fight crime and uphold the law. In this way, perhaps, he mirrors the perceived needs of society from a superhero: if the police can't uphold the law, Superman can. Is it a wonder then that in the next decade Superman fought Nazis and sold war bonds, while anthropologists have argued that during the 1950s he was a placeholder for our feelings on the Cold War?

In his book, *The Great Comic Book Heroes* (2003), the Pulitzer-winning American cartoonist, editor, and author, Jules Feiffer, argues that Superman's real innovation lies in the creation of the Clark Kent persona, noting that what "made Superman extraordinary was his point of origin: Clark Kent." Feiffer develops the theme to establish Superman's popularity in simple wish fulfillment, a position Superman creators Jerry Siegel and Joel Shuster support. Siegel commented that "If you're interested in what made Superman what it is, here's one of the keys to what made it universally acceptable. Joe and I had certain inhibitions...which led to wish-fulfillment which we expressed through our interest in science fiction and our comic strip. That's where the dual-identity concept came from."

This essay is concerned with the question of Superman's dual identities, both in how they are formed but also in essence, a deconstruction of a singular identity. That is, first, I'll look at the ways in which Superman's identity shifts to meet the needs of the various eras he exists in, much in the same way historical epics and films (like the films *M*A*S*H* or *300*) are often more telling of the political polemics they were created in than actual history. For this reason, it is useful to track Superman on the American psyche in relation to history, culture, politics, and popular references to these things in media and entertainment. Moreover, as I discuss further below, Superman's identity formation mirrors how our own identities may be shaped by what is required and expected from us by others.

Second, to further strengthen the discussion of identity, I'll look at various dual-identities of Superman himself—not as much in the Clark Kent/Superman personas (and I'll discuss why below), but in the dichotomous divide between Superman and Bizarro Superman, the twisted and bizarre version of the Man of Steel. To help, I'll briefly consider some contributions from the fields of psychology and anthropology. In this way, I'll also look at what identity, itself, may be and consider what to make of certain cross-cultural variations in the perceptions of it. However, before we get into the social sciences, let's take a closer look at the origin of the general superhero identity, as a starting point.

CAPED CRUSADERS AND COSTUMED PERVERTS

The origin of costumed heroes can perhaps be first found in Baroness Orczy's hero, the Scarlet Pimpernel, written in 1903; itself an inspiration for Johnston McCulley's *Zorro* (1919). Both are independently wealthy men with secret identities they maintain by the use of fantastic costumes, while publically appearing as politically irrelevant dandies, only to draw away unwanted attention. In their hero disguises, both characters endeavor with superior fighting prowess and reasoning for justice and fairness in a field in which the state is too incompetent to act. But Superman, first created in 1932 (but not published until 1939), is the first of these "costumed perverts" (to steal a line from noted blogger, journalist, and science fiction writer, Cory Doctorow) that transcends his depiction in comic books, TV series, radio shows, film, and video games to become a fable. In this way, Superman goes beyond authorial reference to become public property. He is ours now. He has transcended to become myth.

As myth, Superman certainly holds a unique place among the legions of superheroes. Much of Marvel's X-Men costumed superheroes are about marginalized minorities and the loss of connection inherent in our shift towards an urbanized, increasingly anonymous society. Other superheroes typically reflect our own fears and misgivings about advancing technology. Some superheroes, such as Marvel's Captain America, Wolverine, and Sabretooth, among others are part of the Super-Soldier program byproducts of Cold War nuclear horrors, playing out a Derridean deconstruction of the uncertain nature of the new science: nuclear power and genetic engineering. These heroes inhabit worlds that are decidedly chaotic and inherently dangerous. In contrast, Superman's world seems rather ordered. The government is uncorrupted and the newspapers are filled with hard-working journalists dedicated to the truth, so Superman's role is seemingly about maintaining that order. He is the maintenance manager. Where Batman is similar to the hardened beat cop, Superman is more like a hall monitor or Boy Scout. He protects us from the occasional failed dam or impending earthquake, and perhaps more provocatively, from the rare non-conformist who cannot or will not fit in. This is a role that is perhaps most appropriate for him during the horrors of war in the 1940s and at the height of the Cold War in the '50s—when the enemy was "the other," either the German Nazis or the Soviet Communists.[1]

Neil Gaiman, who has written much on the nature of heroes and myth, took on "The Myth of Superman" with Adam Rogers in a May 2006 issue of *Wired* magazine. Gaiman and Rogers tracked the appeal and mythic quality of Superman to the "internal war between Superman's moral obligation to do good and his longing to be an average Joe"—a tug-of-war between doing the right thing and playing along, embodied respectively in Superman and his milquetoast alter ego, Clark Kent. This is also echoed in Quentin Tarantino's *Kill Bill Vol. II* (2004), and while I'm not sure if Tarantino is the source of this idea, it is, as is typical of Tarantino, an insightful and memorable piece of dialogue:

---

[1] As an aside, this kind of fiction may be less relevant in a world where the enemy is not obvious, and in a world without an obvious external enemy, perhaps fiction changes and becomes more about the conflict with the psyche.

BILL: As you know, I'm quite keen on comic books. Especially the ones about superheroes. I find the whole mythology surrounding superheroes fascinating. Take my favorite superhero, Superman. Not a great comic book. Not particularly well-drawn. But the mythology.... The mythology is not only great, it's unique. Now a staple of the superhero mythology is, there's the superhero and there's the alter ego. Batman is actually Bruce Wayne, Spider-Man is actually Peter Parker. When that character wakes up in the morning, he's Peter Parker. He has to put on a costume to become Spider-Man. And it is in that characteristic Superman stands alone. Superman didn't become Superman. Superman was born Superman. When Superman wakes up in the morning, he's Superman. His alter ego is Clark Kent. His outfit with the big red "S", that's the blanket he was wrapped in as a baby when the Kents found him. Those are his clothes. What Kent wears—the glasses, the business suit—that's the costume. That's the costume Superman wears to blend in with us. Clark Kent is how Superman views us. And what are the characteristics of Clark Kent. He's weak...he's unsure of himself...he's a coward. Clark Kent is Superman's critique on the whole human race.

As interesting an idea as this is, especially with regard to the darker analysis of Superman's paternalistic and condescending attitude towards those he helps and protects, I'm not sure I agree with its thesis. What sets Superman apart from most superheroes is not, I think, his connection with his *supposed* alter ego in Clark Kent but, rather, the nature of his own *super*ness. Other superheroes became what they are, whereas Superman's *super*ness is part of his natural and inherent make-up. He didn't need victimized parents to inspire and drive him to fight crime, he didn't need a super-serum to give him his muscles or a radioactive spider to give him his abilities. He *is* Superman. Likewise, it's important to note that while villains like The Joker taunt Batman with the darker aspects of his own personality, or Peter Parker oft wrestles with his burden/power, Superman's weakness just seems to be Kryptonite—an accident of his natural superlative. This is what Lex Luthor and other villains use to attack him. In this,

Superman is more like a god than a prophet. Indeed a trailer from the recent Superman film, *Superman Returns*, hinted at his divinity with messianic overtones: "Krypton's last son sent to protect us." There seems to be a theme in Superman that one can also find in Pixar's *The Incredibles*: being special is a birthright, not something that can be attained by one's own efforts. One of the more memorable quotes from *The Incredibles* is, "If everyone is special, then nobody is special."

Indeed, in listing (by comparison to other superheroes) Superman's rather bland arch-enemies—villains like Luthor and Brainiac—we shouldn't miss perhaps the greatest and most underrated super-villain in Superman's world—Superman himself. Or, rather, the negative potential inherent in anyone so far removed from the ordinary human realm, embodied by Superman's *other* alter ego, and arguably his *truer* alter ego: Bizarro Superman. It is in battling Bizarro and not, say, bald blandly human Lex Luthor, that Superman struggles with his own darkness. By establishing Superman's real nemesis, his alter ego in Bizarro, we can now start getting into Superman's identity.

(BIZARRO) CULTURE AND (BIZARRO) IDENTITY

British-born but Americanized anthropologist Gregory Bateson first coined the word *schismogenesis* in the 1920s when studying the *Iatmul*, a group of indigenous people of New Guinea. Bateson wanted to understand the process by which individuals take on a personal identity in a larger social dynamic. He observed that when one of the Iatmul men showed off (which was apparently often), other Iatmul men would, too. At the same time, there was an inverse correlation with regard to the behavior of Iatmul women—the more boastful and loud Iatmul men became, the more serene and watchful the Iatmul women became.

Bateson, who knew nobody reached a conclusion without first jumping to it (to steal from Tim Park's wonderful book, *A Season with Verona*), quickly argued that any behavioral action would provoke either a parallel or a complementary reaction in others and that this would generate a schismatic process, with individuals taking on either one identity or the other—but always in relation to each other. Soon after, other anthropologists began talking about schismogenesis in all sorts of rituals, from the dynamic of the family to mythology, politics, etc.

Bateson himself, however, was clever enough to understand that there must be more than just schismogenesis going on. For the business of action and reaction, whether competitive or complementary, is not a process that could go on forever. If my behavior continuously arouses the same or opposite behavior in you, then at some point this cycle can and will lead to dangerous excesses. And also, if behavior was made in this way alone, then our personal range of experience would be almost binary (in a way) and very limited indeed.

So, Bateson did not name his work on the Iatmul, "schismogenesis." He called it *Naven*. Naven is the name of a set of Iatmul rituals practiced at regular intervals. What's significant is that within the boundaries of the rituals of Naven, the normal patterns of appropriate behavior are reversed! Iatmul men must dress up as women and Iatmul women must dress as men. Likewise, Iatmul women take on aggressive postures, becoming loud and boastful while Iatmul men take on submissive, passive demeanors, even submitting to simulated anal rape. For our purposes, it is this ritual that is significant and Bateson suspected that it was this release of pent up aggression and frustration through role reversals—both on the part of women *and* men—in safe, controlled, and predictable conditions that allowed the normal strict roles to stay in place.

It is all too easy to see something of the same thing going on in Superman/Bizarro. Superman *needs* Bizarro Superman, or more precisely (since he is a fictional character), we need to release his frustrations, or to at least see them released. The reader needs Bizarro to better deal with the demigod-hood and goody goody-ness of Superman. Systems of order are often reversed in play and comic books. After all, all have more than an incidental element of play.

Bizarro, the most extreme opposite of Superman's "enemies" (he sometimes tries to ally with Superman!) first appeared in the Superman comics in 1959. Created by Lex Luthor's flawed replicator ray, Bizarro is Superman's monstrous imitation, having all the superpowers of Superman, but at the same time lacking the character that makes Superman a superhero. In this way, Bizarro's flaws highlight Superman's strengths. But Bizarro also highlights darker and, yes, foreign aspects of the Man of Steel. For example, Bizarro has poor immigrant grammar, saying things like "Me am Bizarro," while Superman speaks in fully articulated sentences as is expected of a native-English speaker. Superman is handsome whereas Bizarro is, well, bizarre-looking. While Superman has a seemingly year-round tan, Bizarro is depicted as having very pale flesh and black hair, stereotypical of Eastern European immigrants. It may be significant to point out here that "Eastern European" is often used as a euphemism and the creators of Superman are both of Jewish descent.

The most significant Bizarro characteristic, however, must be his backwards sensibility. Perhaps Bizarro's problems are in part due to his inhabiting the alien planet called *Htrae* (Earth backwards) where everyone behaves backwards (and foreign?). So, on Htrae, people congratulate each other for their ugliness, children are rewarded for misbehaving, and popular films are terrible and boring (*The Slowest Gun in the West*). However, Bizarro did get the upper hand on his own alter ego in that he consummated his relationship with Bizarro Lois. Bizarro Lois was created when Bizarro kidnapped the real, or better yet, the original (?) Lois Lane for himself, and this Lois focused the replicator gun on herself, creating Bizarro Lois *for* Bizarro. In comparison, our poor Superman, like a saint, may never spoil his virginity, not even for the love of his life.

ME AM BIZARRO

In 1897, W. E. B. Du Bois, writing for an article in the *Atlantic Monthly*, first used the term "double consciousness" (first discussed by American transcendentalists such as Emerson) in a new way—an idea he'd later expand on in his 1903 collection of essays *The Souls of Black Folk*. The concept of Du Boisian double consciousness describes how the self is understood through the eyes of others, specifically with regard to the plight of African Americans.

Double consciousness is the awareness of one's self as well as an awareness of how others perceive that self or person. The danger of double consciousness, Du Bois wrote, is in conforming and or changing one's identity to that of how others perceive the person.

A few years later, in 1899 (though postdated to 1900 by the publisher), Sigmund Freud published his *Interpretation of Dreams*. This work introduces the *Ego*, describes Freud's theory of the *unconscious*, and goes on to argue that the "self" is in fact often in conflict with it-*self*. Though much of Freud's original work is no longer in scientific fashion, his insight into the divided "selves," or how we may be driven by motives that are not always entirely clear to ourselves, is considered by some to be the crown jewel in modern psychology.

These and other sociological studies lead to a body of thought devoted to the duality of the self. It is after this era, but against this backdrop, that Jerry Siegel and Joe Shuster created the legend of Superman. Again, when seen in this light, Bizarro becomes simply the other side, the darker side, of Superman's identity. This may be the more authentic id side to Superman's super-ego, and not Clark Kent. Seen in this way, Kent is more of a ruse, a sham—Bizarro is out of his control and thus more real.

In 1971, a team of researchers led by Philip Zimbardo of Stanford University conducted the now infamous "Stanford prison experiment," designed to be a psychological study of the human response to captivity, specifically with regard to the effects of imposed social roles on behavior. In this experiment, undergraduate volunteers were asked to take on the roles of either prison guards or prisoners and live in an *ersatz* prison in the bowels of the Stanford psychology building.

As the official Web site of the experiment (!) (http://www.prison-exp.org) illustrates, the problem was that "guards" as well as "prisoners" quickly came to identify with their randomly assigned roles, going well beyond what had been asked of them. This soon led to dangerous and psychologically damaging situations in which a full 1/3 of guards exhibited "genuine" sadistic tendencies, to the point that the experiment was quickly terminated.

Psychologists have proposed the idea of *situationism*—the idea that our identities may be significantly directed by what is needed of us, what we believe society expects from our role in it fits well within the superhero genre and especially Superman (for a discussion of situationism, see Krahe). A forefather of modern sociology, Emile Durkheim suggested that different specializations in social roles created dependencies that bound people to one another, since people could no longer fill in all of the needs by themselves. In a sense then, our social roles, our identities may be like specific employment opportunities we are required to complete. We get hired to fill in required jobs in a complex and multifaceted division of labor that is human civilization. Similarly, in the M. Night Shyamalan's 2000 work, *Unbreakable*, the author and director demonstrate a world in which the villain's identity, "Mr. Glass," is formed by his relationship to the hero with the super-abilities: "David Dunn."

Likewise, in Mark Millar's 2003 graphic novel, *Superman: Red Son*, Millar asks the question, what would have happened to Superman had the rocket ship carrying his infant body crashed, not in the U.S., but in the Soviet Union? Of course, the "red" Superman is a champion of the Soviet state and perhaps, just as importantly, we find that without Superman's influence on Lex Luthor, Luthor grows up to become a successful American scientist and the husband of Lois Lane.

The point, ladies and gentlemen, is this: these ideas of "situationism" and "double consciousness" are fully compatible. When I am teaching my class, for example, my identity as *instructor* is not the same as my identity as a son to my mother. My role as teacher, or son, is determined in part by what I think a teacher or son is, but also by what I believe my audience expects from a teacher or my mother expects from a son. I am *and* I am not the same person in both those contexts.

Alexis C. Bunten, currently a post-doctorate at the University of California at Berkeley, has observed indigenous tourism practices, focusing on the conventional and innovative ways in which Southeast Alaska Native people reincorporate commercial art objects (originally intended for non-Native consumption) into their everyday and ceremonial lives. Her work turns the idea of what or who is authentic on its head. Authenticity in this way is seen in a dynamic and at least, dyadic way. It is interdependent.

In the end, identity itself may be best thought of as a construct. It is something that you have, but importantly, it is a plurality. You are different people *to* different people. You are different people in different contexts. The "real you" is up to you. Take the recent surge in online gaming—games like *Everquest* or *World of Warcraft* have legions of admirers. *World of Warcraft*, with just more than 8 million subscribers (according to the administrators of ibold.net) can boast of a population larger than some countries! Many of these millions of people identify with their online personas *more* so than their mundane real-life ones. It's like the old song by *Loverboy*, "Everybody's Working for the Weekend," where the lyrics describe a nation of grudging workers, going about boring and unexciting tasks, just so they can have the ritual of the weekend, a time they can be free to be themselves.

Moreover, there's evidence that the construct of "identity" even varies across cultures. The term *fundamental attribution error* (also known as correspondence bias or overattribution effect) was first coined by Lee Ross after experiments in 1967 by Edward E. Jones and Victor Harris. It describes the tendency for people to over-emphasize dispositional—or personality-based—explanations for behaviors observed in others while under-emphasizing situational explanations for their behavior. In plainer English, it demonstrates that many people have an unjustifiable bias to presume that a person's behavioral actions depend on the kind of person one is rather than on the social and environmental forces that influence the person. However, psychologist Geoffrey Miller, from the University of New Mexico has demonstrated evidence to support the contention that cultures that tend to emphasize the individual over the group (Western "individualistic" cultures) tend to make more dispositional attributions than do the "collectivist" (Eastern) cultures. So, in a very general way, Western cultures tend to assume that identity and behavioral actions are driven by content (a quality of "self")—that a kind of homunculi exists in us that tells us what to do and that when this content is different, we see different actions—whereas many Eastern cultures may do the opposite and assume that identity and behavioral actions are driven by context (social and economic pressures, etc.).

So, is Superman a hero? Of course he is, he is a *super*hero, but importantly, just like real people, just like you and me, he is a plurality—he is Superman, Bizarro, Clark Kent, and even a Soviet Super-Soldier, depending on the circumstances. He is different things in different places *and* different persons to different people.

Documentary evidence for the life of **Siamak Tundra Naficy** proves frustrating. Immigration records show him in these United States since 1978 and tax records exist in the files of government bureaucracy, undoubtedly, but don't set him apart from contemporaries. His interests were apparently broad and he appears to have been enrolled in an Anthropology Ph.D. program at UCLA, since a thesis has been filed with the university since 1999. Further biographical information that dates from 2003 appears in the form of documents that suggest he somehow obtained access to dogs, cats, and wolves for research into inter- and intra-species communicative intelligence.

REFERENCES

Adminstrators, "World of Warcraft's Population Exceeds Most Small Nations" *Ibold.net*, 12 Jan. 2007. <http://www.ibold.net/2007/01/12/world-of-warcrafts-population-exceeds-most-small-nations/>

Bateson, G. *Naven: A Survey of the Problems Suggested by a Composite Picture of the Culture of a New Guinea Tribe Drawn from Three Points of View*. Stanford University Press (2nd edition), 1958.

The Incredibles. Dir. B. Bird. Walt Disney Home Entertainment, 2004

Doctorow, C. "Marvel Comics: Stealing Our Language" *Boing Boing* 18 March 2006. <http://www.boingboing.net/2006/03/18/marvel_comics_steali.html>

Du Bois, W. E. B. *The Souls of Black Folk*. New York: Penguin Classics, 1903, 1989.

Eco, U. In Jeet Heer & Kent Worcester: *Arguing Comics*. [1962]. (2004) University Press of Mississippi. <http://en.wikipedia.org/wiki/Umberto_Eco">

Feiffer, J. *The Great Comic Book Heroes*. Seattle: Fantagraphics Books, 2003.

Freud, S. *The Interpretation of Dreams*. Barnes & Noble Books, 1900, 1994.

Gaiman, N. and Rogers, A. "The Myth of Superman," *Wired* May 2006. <http://www.wired.com/wired/archive/14.06/myth.html>

Millar, M. *Superman: Red Son (Elseworlds)*: DC Comics, 2004.

J. G. Miller, "Culture and the Development of Everyday Social Explanation," *Journal of Personality and Social Psychology* 46 (1984): 961–978.

Unbreakable Night. dir. M. Shyamalan. Walt Disney Video, 2000.

Kill Bill, Vol. II. dir. Q. Tarantino. Miramax Home Entertainment, 2004.

The official Web site of the Stanford Prison Experiment: <http://www.prisonexp.org/>

Stephanie R. deLusé, Ph.D.

COPING WITH STRESS...
THE SUPERHERO WAY

Part of the appeal of superheroes is that through them we can live out
our dreams and fantasies. But the life of a superhero is fraught with
stress: Saving the city (or planet) from the nefarious plots of evil-do-
ers; and the hassles of daily life, such as finding a convenient spot to
change into the superhero costume, or juggling being the host of a
charity fundraiser while simultaneously taking out the bad guys who
crash the event. Like superheroes, we humans are also confronted
with stress. As deLusé points out in her essay, we can learn from our
superheroes how to cope effectively with stress.

"The man who doesn't relax and hoot a few hoots voluntarily, now and
then, is in great danger of hooting hoots and standing on his head for
the edification of the pathologist and trained nurse, a little later on."

—ELBERT HUBBARD, AMERICAN PHILOSOPHER AND WRITER

WE LIVE IN STRESSFUL TIMES. We don't need the news, with its stories of natural disasters and various political or military skirmishes, to remind us of how stressful life is as all of us are dealing with our own major life events (divorce, death, job loss, etc.) and challenges with family and work, health and money, and a myriad of daily hassles. With all we have going on we may wish a superhero would rescue us from the mundane or dramatic stresses of our lives! But while all our wishing may not materialize a caped crusader to save us, we can still learn to cope like a superhero and, ultimately, save ourselves. Indeed, it's worth considering what lessons we can learn from superheroes as few individuals face more stress than those who must constantly protect the world from crime and destruction. If they can survive that, we can certainly survive our lives.

STRESS

Stress can be difficult to define. What's stressful to me might be exciting to you. What's too much for you to handle may be a walk in the park for me. Some stress is good in that it might, for example, facilitate productivity or help prepare you to engage in something you've been anticipating. This is sometimes referred to as "eustress" ("eu" as in euphoria). Some stress is bad or "distress" ("dis" as in disease, displeasure). But stress in general is how your body (and mind) respond to a demand to step up. The response is now commonly referred to as the "fight or flight" response when our ancestors, for instance, might have had to suddenly decide to run from the saber-tooth tiger or battle it. Once the saber-tooth tiger was either evaded or conquered, their systems would return to a balanced state. For modern humans, the choice isn't always that simple. It would be simple if our primary stressors were undeniably physically present (like tigers), but many of our stressors are subtler and tied up with how we *perceive* the situation (again, why some activities are stressful to me, but not to you). We may not have the option (or desire) to fight or run from our stressors and what we have to deal with doesn't always go away. Yes, we may still have acute (sudden) stressors, like when Batman sees the Bat-Signal light up over Gotham City, and must decide whether to swing into action *now* (fight) or hide (flight). But much of what we deal with seems to be chronic (sustained) stressors that can wear and tear at our bodies, minds, and spirits over time. So if we can't (or don't want to) fight or flee, what might help us cope?

COPING WITH STRESS

You may be thinking there isn't anything special we can do about stress, that there are no special weapons to employ because the ability to cope, or not, generates from within. You may believe it is a matter of character, constitution, or personality that predicts if, or how, we cope with stress. Well, to some degree you'd be correct. It does help to have certain global personality traits that have been found to help with resiliency (that ability to bounce back when pressed). Two such traits that come to mind are dispositional optimism and locus of control. Dispositional optimism relates to a general expectancy that good things will happen in one's life. Peter Parker is an excellent example of a typically optimistic personality. Taken aback by his spider changes at first, he soon realizes the potential in it and remains ever hopeful that some of the successful experiences he has in the public domain of kicking evil's fanny will, at some point, in some way, positively affect his personal life—that some of the confidence he demonstrates as Spider-Man may eventually allow him similar confidence in dealing with the challenges that face him at home, school, and work. Locus of control refers to a generalized expectancy of whether one feels a sense, or lack, of power over the events that happen in one's life. If we perceive events as unrelated to our own behavior (beyond control) we fall on the "external" side of the control continuum. If we perceive events to be under our control we fall on the "internal" side. The funny thing is that sometimes, no matter what our dispositional leaning is, we may be wrong when we are assessing where to place "blame" for an event. So the coping strategies we're about to cover will help regardless of our typical locus of control tendency, if we allow ourselves to be flexible in our appraisal of and reaction to events.

Regardless of personality, there are a myriad of ways to cope with stress that we'll divide into three major categories: problem-focused coping (silver bullets), emotion-focused coping (invisible shields), and proactive coping (gadgets and other resources). And, as we'll see, social support (supporting cast) is an important buffer to stress and is especially key to proactive coping.

1. PROBLEM-FOCUSED COPING—SILVER BULLETS

Problem-focused coping involves direct efforts to confront stressors head-on rather than to deny them. They are like silver bullets in the sense that you find a specific tool to handle a specific job. This would include planning specific steps to minimize, modify, or avoid the stressor through taking specific action. These strategies are generally more active than some others and usually work well in situations where we actually have an opportunity to make a change or exercise some control. The actions aren't always of the in-your-face BAM, POW, BONK variety like Batman might use to beat a person or problem into submission. We might have a gentler touch. We might emulate a set of Batman's skills, like his strategic, detective-like thinking and ability to get straight to the heart of the problem to choose our problem-focused strategies. We might, for example, in focusing on the problem of traffic, arrange to arrive to and leave from work on a schedule that avoids traffic, listen to a book-on-tape (to help the traffic time pass more pleasantly), or arrange to telecommute. Or, taking a tip from the Pulitzer-Prize winning Metropolis reporter, Clark Kent, we might thoroughly research the issue via information gathering when, say, we must deal with a medical diagnosis or problem in ourselves or family members. We read books, search the Web, talk with counselors, mentors, or those who've dealt with something similar before. You can see how the information-gathering form of coping can be a precursor to more specifically focused actions by, for instance, leading one person to, say, deal with depression through the use of pharmaceuticals, another to divorce their abusive spouse, and yet another to engage in regular exercise—often a powerful antidote to depression.

And, while holding positive expectations is helpful coping in itself, we must remember not to be too disappointed if perfection doesn't result the first time out or immediate results don't ensue. Sometimes coping is an iterative process: sometimes things we try work well from the gate; other times, in the style of a Peter Parker, we may fumble our way through a number of well-intentioned, integrity-based attempts that ultimately lead to success. A key here is to not get lost in information-gathering but use it as a tool and learning process to forward healthy coping and, hopefully, resolution to the stress. Another problem-focused strategy is, paradoxically, practicing restraint, as it allows us to observe the situation in order to assess it, gives us time to see if the issue might lessen or pass, or permits strategically waiting for the right time to act or bring something up. Yes, a sequential or multi-pronged approach to problem-focused coping is not unusual and may prove more effective.

Some of these strategies may work like a charm, but active, problem-focused strategies sometimes won't work as well when, for instance, something is just outside our control or isn't worth the effort. When trying to control or confront something directly requires more vigilance and energy than we can muster, or when it overwhelms our sense of personal responsibility (or simply *isn't* our responsibility), these strategies may not be the best choice. Likewise, if it would contribute to an already over-controlling type personality (the classic "Type A"), it may be worthwhile to try a different approach. In short, being able to discern when we do have some control and when we don't, what we can handle and what we can't, is an important skill that can be challenging at times but can be improved with practice. (Consider it a way of building an aspect of your own version of Spidey-Sense, which, if you are a normal mortal, we consider the sum total of our individual experience and intuition.) In the world of superheroes facing super-evil, more often than not the evils are easily identified and dispatched head-on or with minimal strategy. So much of the coping superheroes do would be considered very problem-focused as the enemy is often the immediate stressor. But once we get into a hero's back-story or personal life, we see how there are times when situations are out of their control—like the loss of parents or other loved ones, or discovering they're different and having powers develop. So let's consider another set of particularly useful strategies to help in these cases.

2. EMOTION-FOCUSED COPING—INVISIBLE SHIELDS

When we can't do anything much about a problem directly we always have emotion-focused coping strategies that we can use. Emotion-focused coping strategies are like invisible shields because, unlike bullets, folks might not necessarily know you are using the technique or employing a shield (since they tend to be quiet and transparent) and they help us with things we can't really do much else about. These strategies, as the name implies, help us regulate the emotional response to the stress of life events (like death or divorce) or, for instance, chronic health situations—and we know "mutation" and the accidents that cause superhero powers are chronic! Emotion-focused coping techniques are also useful as short-term strategies to help us cope if there is a problem or stressor we *can* actually do something about but the timing is off for some reason.

One approach is to reframe or reinterpret the issues to see what good can come of it. For example, turning into Spider-Man is pretty freaky and could have sent Peter into withdrawal, self-loathing, or a hissy fit, but he kept an open mind to what good could come out of it. But many things just strike us as bad all around...there may be no silver-lining to see via reframing or we just aren't ready for that. In that case, one emotion-focused strategy to try might include distracting one's self in some healthy way. "Healthy" would be something challenging like digging into your work, exercising, or engaging in some hobby like gardening or reading—not smoking, drinking, shopping, or food binging for, as we know, vices, debt, and low self-esteem can create villains more often than heroes. Indeed, remember that two of Spider-Man's enemies developed, in part, from what some would consider low self-esteem issues as both Eddie Brock (who turned into Venom) and Harry Osborn (who turned into the Green Goblin II) had fathers who were cold and disapproving of their sons. But clearly allowing pain, jealousy, or anger into our mind and letting them motivate "evil" deeds toward self or others is a less heroic choice than finding a healthy distraction. Peter had the stress of losing his beloved uncle and was still coping with his physical changes into Spider-Man, but he distracted himself with doing what he could do (experimenting with his powers, trying to woo Mary

Jane, etc.) instead of getting lost in his problems or indulging in distractions that could cause new problems.

Similarly, "shutting down" for awhile by temporarily suppressing unwanted thoughts or feelings around a specifically painful topic or trauma can be useful, as sometimes our minds and hearts need a little space and time to process before we can talk about or deal with something more directly. Think of it as going into your Batcave for a good think, or maybe a good nap or some journaling time. Whatever you do, the key is to not let that "down time" go on for too long or feed on itself to the exclusion of using some other coping techniques. Though we may all do it a little bit, wallowing isn't the goal here as much as simply "re-grouping," if you will. Related to this is simple relaxation and deep-breathing, which can be helpful coping strategies that reduce our immediate arousal and let us get our thoughts and feelings straight which, in turn, helps us make better decisions about how to handle problems. (Maybe that's what Superman is up to, in part, when he inhales deeply and exhales with a gale-force wind.)

Instead of a shield, sometimes we need a mirror to help us cope. That is, we can look at ourselves and confront our own "demons" by talking or writing about the stressors, and our various reactions to them in a safe place. These can be excellent ways to process our grief, anger, disappointments, and fears, allowing a path to release some of the energy that is bottled up in us about an issue or event. It can be a temporarily challenging emotional and physiological stress in itself to do that—to talk it or write it out—but once you've told your story it is often as if you can *see* what you've been feeling or thinking instead of it feeling such a jumble inside. That has a way of helping many folks feel, or at least start to feel, better. This sort of processing can be a precursor to accepting in a peaceful way (with or without the help of a spiritual belief system) whatever happened and simply learning to live with it. Indeed, as simple as it sounds, choosing to "let it go" is often a most powerful option as few things release stress and return peace and power back to us faster than truly letting something lift from our minds and our shoulders.

3. PROACTIVE COPING—SPIDEY-SENSE, STOCKPILES, AND A SUPPORTING CAST

The problem- and emotion-focused coping strategies we just covered assume something has occurred and you are responding to it—you are dealing with stressors that are present or have already happened. Ah, but there is so much more to coping than just reacting! A wise person will start to build their Spidey-Sense to ward off stressful events, or at least minimize them, before they even happen. If we are pro-actively coping (what Spider-Sense is all about!) instead of just reacting to life's big or little onslaughts we try to prevent them. For instance, if you sense change in the wind at work about lay-offs or reorganization, you might start networking or sending out résumés. Then you're a little ahead of the game by buying yourself some space and time, a head start to the job hunt, if you need it. So if Spidey-Sense is a resource in itself, so is the space and time it can buy us, and the building up of various resources are key to proactive coping. Think of it in terms of Batman or other gadgeteer heroes building up a stock of weapons or gadgets so they know they are ready in advance. That's pro-active coping. Even Batman's other identity is pro-active in that Bruce Wayne certainly has a nice stock of money (and probably various forms of health and property insurance). So financial-related resources or planning can also buffer us from some stresses as we know the lack, or mismanagement, of finances causes great woes. And even our costume, er, I mean our clothes can be a resource if we think pro-actively. We may not have or need the special cool clothes that Batman has but we can still be preventive in our attire. That is, superheroes would certainly think to wear SPF 30 fabric if they'd be hiking in the sun (or had skin cancer in the family), dress for success for a date or an interview, and button up their overcoat when the wind is free. So space, time, tools, clothes, and money are all important resources that we can think of as we develop our Spidey-Sense or gadgeteer's tool belt. But there are resources that lay within us, or within those around us, that are as, or more, valuable.

Possibly one of the most important resources for coping—whether for pro-active coping or for after-the-stressor coping—is social support. Social support is, in short, making and keeping good friends.

We don't have to have a lot of them as the key here is quality...we need folks to whom we can talk, who will listen to us talk, and, whether they know it or not, offer us some form of comfort. Even an animal companion, or a Wookie, can be an important source of support with their quiet, loyal company. Self-awareness is another important internal resource we can build with time. Being willing to know ourselves through introspection and getting feedback from trusted others is helpful in acknowledging our hot buttons and weaknesses. Once we learn, and are really willing to acknowledge, what things act like Kryptonite to us we can then avoid them or plan how to handle them. That's pro-active coping at its best.

Related to self-awareness and social support is an interesting personal resource, of sorts, in the form of role diversity. By role diversity, I mean consciously realizing and observing the different roles we inhabit in our life that make up our identity. For instance, we may be a child, a parent, a sibling, a manager, an employee, a co-worker, a hiker, a member of the bowling team, a volunteer at a civic organization, etc. When we remember that we are more than any *one* of our roles, we are better able to cope with disappointment or trauma in any one area (or cope with distress in general), assuming most of our other roles are positive experiences. Think of this as similar to the warning not to "put all your eggs in one basket." If we do—if we have very few roles, or only one—it may be quite a bit more stressing when something goes wrong in that one area as we wouldn't have the good stuff in the other roles/areas of our lives to help balance it out. Yes, of course, there is a balance to be had. Logic would dictate that *too* many roles, or too many that we perceive as negative, over-demanding, or unrewarding, could cause role-overload. But if we have developed our Spidey-Sense, in this case an honest sense for what is stressful for *us, as individuals*, we can each then decide if there is a diminishing return in taking on a new role, or keeping hold of versus letting go of an old one.

Superheroes, it's true, may not have the same range of roles that we do as their primary role is often so all-encompassing. But their non-hero identities or love interests provide some role diversity and it is hard to argue against the benefits that Batman gets from having Robin as a sidekick, or what Peter Parker or Clark Kent get from their personal lives. Peter, for instance, seems to enjoy his role being mild-mannered and helpful to his aunt, Mary Jane, and others in his birth identity. That doesn't keep him from being a kick-ass wisecracker as Spider-Man. He learns a lot from his various roles and grows through the honorable decisions he makes in regard to the family and friends that help anchor him. Yes, not being a total loner introduces some stress as he is aware that his loved ones are at risk if his enemies learn his true identity, but keeping the people in his life, and keeping his secret, is worth it as these loved ones—through providing him general social support, tips to help him be more self-aware, and adding to his role diversity in a healthy way—also help him combat stress.

Along the same lines of being self aware about the role of identity and social support, we can learn from superheroes about the stress of feeling alone in the world. Consider that some of the most popular superheroes were orphaned and some notable villains had a mean or unloving parent. Indeed, these situations that involved feeling isolated, alone, or misunderstood in the back-stories of many comic book superheroes or villains help us relate to them. We may relate because it resonates with how alone *we* feel at times (whether it is during stressful times or not), how isolated or different or alien(ated) we may sometimes feel from those around us (especially when some of our "mutant" characteristics start surfacing). The positive coping that superheroes demonstrate (compared to super-villains) helps us appreciate what our culture values in rugged individualism and pulling ourselves up by our own bootstraps—something we have to do all too often, yes? Still, while superheroes often have the loss of loved ones in their past or present, and often have to go it alone for awhile (or in some ways), they find ways to take strength from that and, really, aren't so alone as they may think. (And neither are we). Superheroes seem to have the love of their real or surrogate families and/or have joined a new family, in some sense of the word. For instance, they might create their own "family" with other superheroes who come together by virtue of similar levels of excellence in their mission, like with the Justice League band of super superheroes. Or they might come together due to a similar sense of being misunderstood or persecuted minority mutants, like with the X-Men in which

Professor Xavier and Magneto both play father-like roles for their bands of marvelous mutants who support each other in their respective missions. With the Fantastic Four, they were friends and relatives before they suffered a similar transformational fate and, thus, continued to value sharing the ups and downs of life together afterward. Even Buffy the Vampire Slayer who, like previous slayers, was *supposed* to work alone in order to keep her focus and not risk innocents, found that she became a much better (and longer-lived) slayer by having her friends work with her and, in the end, finding a way to share her power with many others. These heroes are just like you and me in that we have our biological family of origin, we have families or groups we are more or less thrown into, and still other "families" we choose or create. Good coping often includes finding or making a place that feels good with people who like us for who we are and will help us grow to be the best we can be. (Or, I suppose, in the case of the villains who band together, help us on the way to being the worst we can be.) Our comic book comrades, like us, find ways to meet our apparent need to belong. Interestingly, perhaps you have partially met that need by being a superhero fan, yes? That is, when specific groups of fans develop that follow a certain hero, we sometimes—without even trying—suddenly belong to a group of folks who understand certain universes of being that many others do not. So, if, perchance, we felt like an outsider before then we aren't anymore—we've become an insider. We've found a clutch of social support, we've found another role.

With social support being as important as it is, you can imagine that the flip-side is equally important—we need to, like any superhero would, dispatch without delay any people who are *not* supportive or, worse, who do us wrong. While open communication and forgiveness may be appropriate in some circumstances, it isn't always. When encountering an "anti-supporter," a super-villain (a toxic person who is damaging to us mentally, emotionally, physically, or spiritually) or a symbiote (someone who sucks the life out of us like an energy-vampire with their neediness), we need to take decisive, definitive action. Indeed, no matter how much we think we can take someone's toxin and no matter what little boost of ego we may get from being needed or "rescuing" someone, it isn't worth the risk. A wise superhero would banish them quickly to The Vault (the maximum security prison for super-villains in the Marvel universe) or The Void (that has housed mutant bad guys in a video game version of the X-Men universe). Whatever you want to call it, the key is to vanquish, in one way or another, the people in our life who treat us poorly, don't appreciate us, or who neglect or actively work against our enjoyment or fulfillment of our life goals and dreams. Modern day heroes like us—of the ordinary, human variety—really don't have the resources and time for drawn out interactions with these enemies, no matter how subtle their poison.

YOU ARE HEROIC

Many of us admire superheroes because we want to be like them somehow—they often deal so well with the major stressors they encounter as they protect the planet, fight crime, and rescue the innocent, or go to war for some vengeful reason (if you're into the darker hero sorts). For us mortals, our lives may not be so much about dealing with the dire and dramatic, but our modern stresses can compare to the roughest rogue's gallery of any superhero. The thugs across the street, the goons at work, and the criminals in traffic; we deal with our own version of stresses. When Superman saves the day, the crowds cheer. But many a superhero's good deeds are not publicly displayed; many occur unobserved by anyone other than the criminal he's bested and the person he's protected. These deeds occur just because they are the right thing to do and not for the accolades they may garner. Beyond issues of "right" or "wrong," the deed could occur as a random act of kindness, something a hero does "just because."

That's how it is for us most of the time, isn't it? We do many little things, like kindly let people ahead of us in lines or in traffic. Or, we probably "save the day" more often than we get credit for. Big or small, our heroic deeds often go unnoticed when we really do deserve a cheer or a pat on the back—even if we provide it for our selves. Indeed, being our own cheerleader is one more way we can buffer stress and it is important to acknowledge our minor triumphs, the small hurdles, and subtle victories that accumulate to equal our happiness, our success, and our well-being. And often what we admire in superheroes is their sense of purpose, powerful passion, or clear mission. For some of us, our purpose may be hazy at times and we may not know what something in our life means until, like a movie, we finish the scene or have seen the final ending. (Truly, it's sometimes hard to know from just one frame of film how to contextualize an experience.) For others, we may have a purpose that underpins our entire lives or one that shifts as we mature and encounter different challenges and opportunities. For still others, we may at times feel our life is either a painfully dull rut or a stressful cauldron void of meaning. Even then, a heroic coper will remember that we have a choice; we can choose to find or make meaning in each minute, or each episode, even if it is just to enjoy, learn, or survive—if not become a hero crusading against, or protecting others from, the evil that caused the rut or temporary void of meaning.

Yes, staying alert to meaning, finding a moment to remember all we've accomplished, and being grateful for what we have can be some of the best coping strategies of all. After all, think about it: while you may not be a force to be reckoned with on the scale of a comic book superhero, you *are* a success and have been a hero in your own life (and, no doubt, in the lives of many others) in great and small ways. Remember that and remind yourself of all you've seen, learned, done, and overcome. Hold yourself in the same positive regard in which you hold your favorite superhero. Imagine yourself as the hero in your *own* comic book. Therein lies the seed to seeing your own personal greatness and claiming inner peace, if we just take the time to notice.

Dr. Stephanie R. deLusé, psychologist, researcher, author, and teacher, is also Associate Faculty Director of the Bachelor of Interdisciplinary Studies (BIS) program at Arizona State University. Her graduate training focused on social and personal issues that affect most of us at one time or another—issues around individual/group interactions, family support and divorce, and health and wellness. Her most recent academic efforts have earned her recognition for her teaching, including selection as one of ASU's Featured Faculty in 2006 and an Outstanding Faculty Award in 2005. In her sparse free time she communes with nature most frequently in the guise of her cat, her trees, and her herb garden replete with insect life and lizards.

ACKNOWLEDGMENTS

Many thanks to my friends and colleagues Dr. Stanley Parkinson, Dr. Linda Luecken, Tracy Perkins, Fred Lloyd, and James Kretz for talking about this topic with me or commenting on drafts of this work. I appreciate each of them in unique ways and appreciate their social support—they are among the personal heroes in my life (and Stanley has risen to superhero status for all his help).

Bradley J. Daniels

ARKHAM ASYLUM: FORENSIC PSYCHOLOGY AND GOTHAM'S (NOT SO) "SERIOUS HOUSE"

Did you ever notice how many of Batman's worst enemies—such as the Joker—keep breaking out of Gotham City's Arkham Asylum? What's up with that? In this essay, Daniels focuses on Arkham Asylum, treating us to a history of the asylum and explaining how criminals are likely to end up at Arkham (for the criminally insane) rather than Blackgate Penitentiary (for criminals who, in theory, are not insane). Daniels also explains the ways in which Arkham, and the treatment it provides, is similar to and different from actual institutions for the criminally insane.

IN THE DC COMICS UNIVERSE, whenever the Dark Knight captures a member of his rogue's gallery or some other deranged criminal, they are almost always inevitably committed to the Elizabeth

Arkham Asylum for the Criminally Insane, commonly referred to as Arkham Asylum. When writing a serial comic book that relies on its readers' continued subscription, it is a smart idea to keep most of the villains Batman faces from issue to issue recognizable, and Arkham Asylum provides a perfect vehicle for just that to occur, as security at the facility appears to be (insert sarcasm here) somewhat less than airtight. Arkham Asylum has been bombed on multiple occasions, leading to numerous mass breakouts. In addition, employees of the facility are often corrupt and sometimes mentally ill themselves (Harley Quinn, anyone?). Members of Batman's rogue's gallery appear to be able to escape from the facility pretty much at will, no one villain more indicative of this fact than the Joker. Now, not to pass judgment on the citizens of Gotham City, but if a similar institution such as Arkham existed in the real world and had experienced the same amount of escapes, attacks, and general corruption, you'd think a call for the facilities' closing and/or a massive change in policy would be in order!

How exactly is it, though, that these criminals get committed to Arkham in the first place? How is it that the Gotham judicial system determines which criminals get referred to Arkham versus which ones simply get sentenced to nearby Blackgate Penitentiary? Throughout this essay, I will attempt to answer these questions, as well as provide you with insight into how these questions are addressed in the real world through a brief introduction into the field of forensic psychology. Before we get to that, however, let us first go back to the beginning, so that we may bear witness to the "birth" of Arkham Asylum.

ARKHAM: A HISTORY

Though Arkham Asylum is shown in a great number of Batman comics, one particular portrayal stands out. In Grant Morrison's 1989 Graphic Novel *Arkham Asylum: A Serious House on Serious Earth*, the Asylum and its sordid history take center stage. In the story, the inmates at Arkham, led by the Joker, take over the facility and, in their demands for the release of hostages, insist that Batman be sent in to join them in the facility. Though Batman does appear peripherally throughout the story, the history of the facility itself is the primary focus. Psychologist Amadeus Arkham, following the death of his mentally ill mother, Elizabeth, decides to turn her home (which he inherited) into a facility for the treatment of mental illness. Prior to the facilities opening, Martin "Mad Dog" Hawkins, a former patient of Arkham's, brutally murders Arkham's wife and daughter, cutting them into pieces and going so far as to place his daughter's head inside a doll house. Understandably, following this event, Arkham himself suffers a mental breakdown. He does, however, continue with the facilities opening and one of the first residents of Arkham Asylum is the recently recaptured "Mad Dog" Hawkins, who Arkham insists on personally treating. On the one-year anniversary of his wife and daughter's death, Arkham straps "Mad Dog" into a chair and proceeds to deliver electroconvulsive therapy (ECT) until he dies. Although obvious to those in the field, it warrants mentioning that psychologists and other mental health professionals are bound by a very strict code of ethics, the most notable of which being the 2002 edition of the *Ethical Principles of Psychologists and Code of Conduct* (American Psychological Association). Listed in this code are very specific rules that state that it is unethical for a psychologist to perform therapy on a patient when a "dual role" or multiple relationships are present, meaning that the psychologist would know the person in both a professional and personal role. Specifically, section 3.05 of the code states:

> A psychologist refrains from entering into a multiple relationship if the multiple relationship could reasonably be expected to impair the psychologist's objectivity, competence, or effectiveness in performing his or her functions as a psychologist, or otherwise risks exploitation or harm to the person with whom the professional relationship exists (American Psychological Association 1065).

Clearly, any reasonably ethical psychologist, even if given the option to, would refrain from treating the murderer of his wife and daughter, as there is simply no way that personal feelings and bias could not affect the psychologist's ability to properly treat the patient.

As the novel progresses, Arkham eventually suffers another mental breakdown and becomes a resident of the asylum. Though somewhat different than a typical foray into the Bat-verse, writer Grant Morrison and illustrator Dave McKean have provided readers with one of the most psychologically profound and visually arresting graphic novels to date. One notable fact involving the psychological symbolism presented within the novels' pages is the influence of the works of Swiss Psychiatrist Carl Jung, who was a colleague of Sigmund Freud's. Much like Freud, Jung is associated with the early days of psychoanalysis and was also a big proponent of the ideas of the unconscious; however, he and Freud had somewhat different ideas about what the unconscious was, with Jung taking a slightly more spiritual/mystic outlook on the phenomenon (compared to Freud's primarily sexual outlook) and positing the ideas of a collective unconscious and the presence of archetypes (1968), a concept that is briefly referenced by Dr. Jonathan Crane and attributed to Jung in the 2005 film *Batman Begins*. These differences in opinion, as well as other factors, led to a rift between the two psychiatrists (Wikipedia.org). It's worth noting that Morrison's Arkham Asylum was so heavily influenced by Jung's work that the likeness of Jung is once drawn inside the pages of the comic itself.

ARKHAM ASYLUM VS. BLACKGATE PENITENTIARY

Now that we are familiar with the history of how Arkham Asylum came to be, let us consider how the facility gets populated. In an overwhelming majority of the Batman comics, Batman spends the bulk of the comic solving a mystery and tracking down the criminal responsible. Usually this criminal is some sort of a costumed super-villain, more often than not a member of Batman's rogue's gallery (e.g., Joker, Penguin, Poison Ivy, Two-Face, The Riddler, Mr. Freeze, etc.). Towards the end of the comic, Batman inevitably will face off against the particular criminal and emerge victorious. One page later, the criminal is shown safely tucked away in their cell at Arkham, with no further detail given as to the process with which they went through to get there after being apprehended.

Batman doesn't always face off against the criminally insane, however, and some of Batman's more "normal" foes are often sent to Blackgate Penitentiary rather than Arkham Asylum. As very little is ever shown in the comics about how exactly it's determined which criminal goes where and when, much of this information has to be inferred after the fact. Based on the current authors' experience with the Batman comics, it appears that the decision to refer to Arkham rather than Blackgate is based on the answers to a few simple questions:

> **Question 1**: Did the defendant wear a costume when committing the crime? (*If yes, move on to Question 2.*)
>
> **Question 2**: Were the crimes the defendant committed centered around some sort of compulsion or theme, such as the number two (Two-Face), birds (Penguin), plants (Poison Ivy), or riddles (The Riddler)? (*If yes, refer to Arkham.*)
>
> **Question 3**: Were the crimes the defendant is charged with something reasonably normal? In other words, could you easily imagine this type of criminal living in and committing this type of crime in the real world? (*If yes, refer to Blackgate.*)

In general, the answers to these three questions seem to best predict the final destination for a criminal caught by Batman more so than whether or not they are, in fact, insane. For example, Mr. Freeze is generally considered to be a sane individual, but a number of factors place him at Arkham rather than Blackgate. For starters, he has to wear a special "costume" for life support in order to keep his body temperature low. In addition, his crimes are generally themed around cold, or ice. Lastly, for a reason that (to the best of my knowledge) has never been adequately explained, Arkham Asylum is properly equipped with a refrigerated cell, whereas Blackgate is not.

MALINGERING AND FORENSIC PSYCHOLOGY

On occasion, other sane criminals will be transferred to Arkham under the false pretenses of being mentally ill or insane. In the 2004 graphic novel *Arkham Asylum: Living Hell*, by Slott et al., financial genius Warren "The Great White Shark" White successfully uses insanity as his defense for perpetrating the greatest act of stock fraud in American history, when he is in fact clearly sane. He utilizes this defense in order to keep himself out of prison, not realizing at the time that the judge would remand him to Arkham, the consequences of which would eventually lead to his disfigurement (to look more like a shark of course) and actual insanity. Another example of persons using this tactic is Carmine Falcone (and most of his goons) in the film *Batman Begins* (2005). This phenomenon is known as malingering. Malingering is defined by the American Psychiatric Association in the *Diagnostic and Statistical Manual of Mental Disorders, 4th edition text revision* (a.k.a. DSM-IV-TR) as the "intentional production of false or greatly exaggerated symptoms for the purpose of attaining some identifiable external reward" (1994, 739). In other words, mental illness or some other deficit is faked for some sort of secondary gain. As is the case in these examples from the Batman comics, the identifiable external reward or secondary gain involved is the avoidance of prison, a reward in and of itself. Malingering is also a phenomenon found in civil legal cases as well, where persons purposely fake an illness or deficit. An example that easily comes to mind of this phenomenon would be someone falling at work and hitting their head, sustaining only minor injuries, yet later pretending to have sustained so severe a head injury or deficit that they can no longer work again in order to obtain a large financial settlement.

Luckily for us in the real world, there is an entire subfield of clinical psychology known as forensic psychology[1] that specializes in conducting psychological practice while working side-by-side with the legal system. These individuals often have advanced specialized training in dealing with the unique questions that arise when the two fields meet, and have over time become particularly adept at detecting malingering in both criminal and civil cases. In both instances, the tools used to assess malingering are rooted heavily in the scientific method, and are developed only after years of research. For malingerers faking mental illness while facing criminal charges, detecting their malingering is usually as simple as showing that these "fakers" endorse experiencing symptoms of mental illness so bizarre, rare, or inconsistent that even individuals with the most severe forms of

---

[1] If you are interested in learning more about just how psychology and the legal system interact, I recommend *Psychological Evaluations for the Courts: A Handbook for Mental Health Professionals and Lawyers, Second Edition* by Melton, Petrila, Poythress, and Slobogin (1997).

psychopathology do not have them. For malingerers faking injury in the civil domain, such as our person who slipped and fell at work mentioned above, detecting malingering usually involves a comprehensive neuropsychological evaluation conducted by a forensic neuropsychologist,[2] who attempts to show that the person's pattern of performance across a wide range of neuropsychological tests is indicative of either inadequate effort or is clearly inconsistent with all commonly known patterns of brain functioning.

ARKHAM IN THE REAL WORLD

Before we go any further, let me say that it I am fairly confident that there is no actual place in the real world like Arkham. Yes, there are State forensic hospitals and other institutions that house mentally ill individuals involved in the legal system; however, it is unlikely that any of these facilities could possibly be as corrupt (or as easy to escape from) as Arkham. However, these facilities do exist, so the remainder of this essay will address how a person in the real world charged with a crime might be sent to a forensic hospital rather than jail or prison.

In general, there are two primary routes in which this might occur. The first route involves a person being charged with a crime, and then a legal question being brought up of whether, either due to mental illness or some other deficit, they are (at the present time) Incompetent to Proceed to Trial (ITP). Criteria for competency vary from state to state; however, they remain mostly consistent. As an example, consider Florida's criteria, listed in Chapter 916.12 of the Florida Statutes. In considering an issue of competence to proceed, a formal assessment conducted by a forensic psychologist should examine and report upon a defendants' capacity in the following six areas, listed in the table below:

After a competency evaluation is conducted, a forensic psychologist will write up a report with their findings, which will be considered by the judge. If the court deems the defendant incompetent to proceed to trial, they are typically then sent to a State forensic hos-

---

[2] For an excellent look into this highly specialized and fascinating subfield, see Glenn Larrabee's *Forensic Neuropsychology: A Scientific Approach* (2005).

COMPETENCY CRITERIA UNDER CHAPTER 916.12 OF THE FLORIDA STATUTES	EXAMPLE QUESTIONS A FORENSIC PSYCHOLOGIST MIGHT ASK
1. Appreciate the charges or allegations against the defendant	What are you charged with?
	What are they accusing you of doing?
	Is that a felony or a misdemeanor?
	Is that a first-, second-, or third-degree offense?
2. Appreciate the range and nature of possible penalties, if applicable, that may be imposed in the proceedings against the defendant	If convicted, what are the minimum and maximum sentences you may be facing?
	What is probation?
	Is probation a possibility in your case?
3. Understand the adversarial nature of the legal process	What does a prosecutor/public defender/judge/jury do?
	If you testify on your own behalf, and the prosecutor asks you questions, what is he trying to do?
	What are the four types of pleas?
4. Disclose to counsel facts pertinent to the proceedings at issue	Who is your attorney?
	Do you feel your attorney has your best interests in mind?
	Are you willing to work with him to plan your defense?
	If your attorney recommended you plead guilty to a lesser offense, would you?
5. Manifest appropriate courtroom behavior	What would happen if you stood up and walked around during court?
	What is contempt?
	If someone is on the stand testifying against you, and they tell a lie, what would you do?
	When are you allowed to speak in the courtroom?
6. Testify relevantly	Can you tell me a little about what happened on the day of the alleged offense?
	What do you remember?
	Were you under the influence of alcohol or drugs at the time of the alleged offense?
	Were you experiencing any delusions or hallucinations at the time of the alleged offense?

pital, where they undergo treatment. During their treatment, they attend therapy sessions, are provided (if necessary) with pharmacological treatment such as an antipsychotic, and attend regular competency classes, where they are educated on the nature of the court system so that they can be restored to competency. Regular follow-up evaluations are conducted and, if a person is found after undergoing treatment to now be competent, they are then referred to the appropriate facility (usually jail) where they will wait to stand trial. Although I cannot claim to have read every Batman comic, I am fairly well-versed in the material. As such, although I have seen various portrayals of residents at Arkham undergoing individual therapy and receiving various medications, I do not believe I have ever seen any of Arkham's residents portrayed attending legal competency classes, and therefore must assume that most of the residents found their way there through the other route, which I will now discuss.

INCOMPETENCY VS. INSANITY

It is important to note that not every mentally ill person charged with a crime is automatically deemed incompetent. In fact, a person can be severely mentally ill, actively psychotic, and yet still be competent to stand trial. For those mentally ill individuals who do go to trial, the option of pleading Not Guilty by Reason of Insanity (NGRI) remains. The first "modern" formal definition of insanity used in the legal system was formulated in England in 1843, and is commonly known as the M'Naughten test of insanity. It states:

> "To establish a defense on the ground of insanity, it must be clearly proved that, at the time of the committing of the act, the party accused was laboring under such a defect of reason, from disease of the mind, as not to know the nature and quality of the act he was doing; or, if he did know it, that he did not know what he was doing was wrong."

Although there have been many changes and revisions to this definition of insanity by the American legal system, about half of the States in the U.S. still abide by its definition.

There are a number of common misconceptions about the insanity plea in the United States. For starters, most people dramatically overestimate how often it is used. According to Melton et al., a study conducted in Wyoming between 1970 and 1972 found that the average person estimated that the insanity plea was used in 43 percent of criminal cases. In actuality, fewer than half of 1 percent of all criminal defendants raise the plea.

Truth be told, pleading insanity is the easy part. After a defendant has pled insanity, the burden of proof during the trial switches from the prosecution to the defense, and the defense must now prove that the defendant is either insane or that the defendant's Mental State at the time of Offense (MSO) was that of an insane person, even if they are currently no longer insane. Steadman et al. have estimated in their research that this defense strategy only works in approximately 25 percent of the cases in which it is raised (401). To reiterate how small this number is, we're talking about one quarter of one half of one percent of individuals who are actually deemed Not Guilty by Reason of Insanity. Some famous defendants who were unsuccessful in proving their insanity pleas include Ted Bundy, John Wayne Gacy, David Berkowitz, Sirhan Sirhan, Ted Kaczynski, Jeffrey Dahmer, and Charles Manson.

Even if a person is found to be Not Guilty by Reason of Insanity, that does not mean they are simply free to walk out of the courtroom and right back into the community. In most cases, these individuals are sent to a State forensic hospital for treatment. This is how most of the member's of Batman's rogue's gallery likely ended up at Arkham. Only after a substantial amount of time in treatment and numerous risk assessments to ensure that they were no longer a threat to themselves or others would an individual found Not Guilty by Reason of Insanity be transferred to a less restrictive civil psychiatric hospital or released back into the community. Luckily for us, for people who have perpetrated violent crimes like murder, this is likely to be a very, very long time. That is, unless of course, there is a mass breakout like there is at Arkham every two weeks. Luckily for them, they've got the Dark Knight ready to round them all back up.

Bradley J. Daniels, M.S., (Brad, for short) earned his B.A. (*summa cum laude*) in psychology from the University of Central Florida. He began attending the University of Florida in 2003, and completed his M.S. in psychology in 2005. He is currently a doctoral candidate working on a Ph.D. in clinical and health psychology, with a specialization in clinical neuropsychology (and a particular interest in forensic neuropsychology). He also teaches as an Adjunct Assistant Professor at Santa Fe Community College. He is an avid film and pop culture enthusiast, and regularly uses these media in the classroom as a tool to enhance the teaching of psychology. He has also published a previous essay in BenBella's *Psychology of Joss Whedon* anthology.

ACKNOWLEDGMENTS

I would like to thank Frank Miller, Jeph Loeb, Alan Moore, Grant Morrison, Tim Sale, Dave McKean, Lynn Varley, Jim Lee, David Goyer, and Christopher Nolan, for their personal contributions to the Batman mythos, and for helping to shape just who "my" Batman is. Lastly, I would like to thank my wife, Tiffany Leigh Daniels, for her constant love and support and willingness to marry someone so geeky that they actually have a personalized idea of who "their" Batman is.

REFERENCES

American Psychiatric Association. *Diagnostic and Statistical Manual of Mental Disorders Fourth Edition, Text Revision.* American Psychiatric Association. Washington, D.C., 2000.

American Psychological Association. Ethical Principles of Psychologists and Code of Conduct. 2002. <http://www.apa.org/ethics/code2002.html>

Batman Begins. dir. Christopher Nolan. Perf. Christian Bale, Michael Caine, Liam Neeson, Katie Holmes, Morgan Freeman. Warner Bros., 2005.

Jung, C.G. *The Archetypes and The Collective Unconscious.* London: Routledge, 1968.

Larrabee, G. *Forensic Neuropsychology: A Scientific Approach.* New York: Oxford, 2005.

M'Naghten's Case, 10 Cl. F. 200, 8 Eng. Rep. 718 (H. L. 1843).

Melton, G., Petrila, J, Poythress, N., and Slobogin, G. *Psychological Evaluations for the Courts: A Handbook for Mental Health Professionals and Lawyers, Second Edition.* New York: The Guilford Press, 1997.

Morrison, G., and McKean, D. *Batman: Arkham Asylum: 15th Anniversary Edition.* New York: DC Comics, 2004.

Slott, D., Sook, R., Von Grawbadger, W., and Royal, J. *Arkham Asylum: Living Hell.* New York: DC Comics, 2004.

H. Steadman, "Factors Associated with a Successful Insanity Plea," *American Journal of Psychiatry* 140 (1983): 401.

The 2007 Florida Statutes: Chapter 916.12. 31 Aug 2007. <http://www.flsenate.gov/Statutes/index.cfm?App_mode=Display_Statute&Search_String=&URL=Ch0916/SEC12.HTM&Title=-%3E2007-%3ECh0916-%3ESection%2012#0916.12>

Wikipedia.org. "Jung and Freud." 31 Aug. 2007. <http://en.wikipedia.org/wiki/Jung#Jung_and_Freud>

Christopher J. Patrick, Ph.D., and Sarah K. Patrick

THE INCREDIBLE HULK: ORIGINS OF RAGE

When the Hulk gets angry, he becomes like a toddler having a temper tantrum, except because of his strength, his rage destroys people and things around him. As explained in this essay, the Hulk is an unusual superhero—he doesn't set out to fight crime and save innocent lives. The heroic aspects of his behavior are byproducts of what happens when he's enraged. In this essay Patrick and Patrick examine anger and aggression in detail—its components and factors that contribute to them—and then apply this knowledge to offer insights about the Hulk and his alter ego, Bruce Banner.

> "I'm as mad as hell and I'm not going to take this anymore!"
>
> —HOWARD BEALE

> "Anger is only one letter short of danger."
>
> —ELEANOR ROOSEVELT

WHAT ARE THE ORIGINS OF ANGER and rage reactions in humans? Is anger fundamentally irrational, or does it serve some important adaptive function? Why do some people react to annoying or frustrating events in sensible and constructive ways, whereas others lose their temper and respond in erratic, destructive ways? Why do some individuals commit acts of extreme violence that seem to strike to the very heart of society? Can such individuals be recognized before their violent acts are unleashed? In this essay, we consider the topics of anger and aggression with reference to the saga of the Incredible Hulk. Our basic thesis is that the capacity for angry emotion exists in all human beings as a function of our evolutionary heritage, but that individual differences in proneness to extreme anger and aggressive action arise as a function of constitutional factors (i.e., genetic inheritance) operating in conjunction with experiential influences (i.e., learning history). The intersection of relevant constitutional and environmental influences can be seen as important to the origins of the fictional Hulk—as well as to the emergence of individuals in real-life society who perpetrate acts of extreme violence.

Anger is one of the most basic and powerful of the human emotions. In its most extreme form, we call it *rage*. A variety of colloquial expressions exist for this emotional state, including: "exploding," "blowing your top," "flying off the handle," "losing it," "freaking out," "flipping out," "going haywire," "going berserk," and "going ape." These expressions highlight some notable features of rage as an affective state. It entails irrationality ("craziness") and a loss of control over one's actions. It is marked by intense bodily arousal that can give way to explosive behavioral reactions. In extreme states of anger, otherwise sensible people can act "like animals" ("go ape"). People are scary when they get really mad because we can't predict what they will do and we fear the worst from them.

The emotion of anger is central to the story of the Incredible Hulk because intense emotional arousal (including anger) serves as the catalyst for the periodic transformations of scientist Bruce Banner into the Hulk. When Banner is threatened or strongly provoked, the towering figure of the Hulk emerges to take charge of the situation and eradicate the provocation or danger. Rage is also the state in which the Hulk spends much of his time; as the feelings of rage subside, the Hulk persona recedes and gives way once more to the rational, controlled persona of Banner.

The Hulk differs from most contemporary superheroes in that he is not a rational, prosocial being. Even superheroes with a "dark side" (such as Batman) show a willful dedication to protecting the welfare of society and possess a conscious identity that remains consistent across crime-fighting episodes and everyday life. But in contrast with his human counterpart Bruce Banner, the Hulk is an atavistic beast, driven by instincts for self-preservation. Outcomes that are beneficial to society arise as a byproduct of his efforts to combat assailants or oppressors rather as a direct product of his efforts to do good.

Nonetheless, among contemporary comic heroes, the Hulk represents a uniquely sympathetic and intriguing figure. This is in part due to the character of his alter ego, Bruce Banner—who is admirable for his scientific genius, personal sensitivity, and inner psychological complexity. But it is also attributable to the nature of the Hulk himself—explosive and destructive in his actions, yet childlike in his perceptions and emotional reactions. The angry feelings that drive the Hulk arise from circumstances we can readily relate to because of similar situations we have experienced in our own lives. Each of us has felt the rush of anger that arises when we are intimidated, criticized, or blocked from something we want, and some of us (like the Hulk) have experienced episodes of "blind rage" in which we acted in ways we later regretted—or that we at least recognized as irrational. And many of us who have not experienced blind rage ourselves have witnessed it in others—including people we know and care about—at one time or another. We sympathize with the experience of anger because we have felt it ourselves, and we are intrigued by exhibitions of extreme anger (i.e., rage) because such reactions can transform seemingly normal individuals into "monsters."

BRUCE BANNER A.K.A. THE HULK: KEY STORY ELEMENTS

The Hulk's counterpart, Bruce Banner, experienced a difficult and painful childhood that foreshadowed the problems with anger and aggression he would evidence so dramatically in his later life. Bruce's father, atomic scientist Dr. Brian Banner, was physically and psychologically abused by his own father while growing up—causing him to develop a hostile, paranoid view of the world. Although successful in his career as a scientist, Brian Banner was nevertheless plagued by emotional instability and alcoholism throughout his adult life.

One fateful day, before his son Bruce was born, Brian arrived drunk at the atomic research center where he worked. In his intoxicated state he committed an error in operating one of the nuclear devices, causing it to overload. Although stationed behind a protective shield at the time, Brian was convinced his body had absorbed a toxic dose of radiation. Despite subsequent medical evaluations to the contrary, Brian held fast to this belief and vowed never to have children for fear he would pass his supposed mutant genes along to his offspring. However, within a year after the accident, Brian's wife Rebecca became pregnant.

Brian and Rebecca Banner had always maintained a positive relationship with one another, but Brian hated his son Bruce from the day he was born. Because of his paranoid thought processes compounded by his alcohol abuse, Brian believed that Bruce was a mutant child, genetically altered due to the radiation Brian had been exposed to at his workplace. The fact that Bruce exhibited a genius-level intellect from a very early age, exceeding that of most adults, solidified Brian's delusional belief that his son was a monster. In addition, because of the attention Rebecca devoted to her son, Brian saw Bruce as a rival for his wife's affection. Fueled by these hostile sentiments, Brian began to physically abuse both Bruce and Rebecca, eventually causing Rebecca to attempt to flee from the home with her son. This escape attempt pushed Brian over the edge. He went after Bruce and Rebecca and before they could pull away in their car, Brian caught up with them and pulled Rebecca from the vehicle and threw her to the ground, killing her. Bruce watched in horror as his mother was slain at the hands of his father.

As a consequence of this murderous attack on his wife, Brian was confined to a mental hospital and Bruce was left alone with his aunt, Mrs. Drake, who raised him through his teenage years. As a child, Bruce was intellectually gifted, but shy and inwardly angry. He spent much of his time alone, unable to relate to anyone his own age. In order to cope with his loneliness, Bruce created an imaginary friend for himself, named "Hulk," whom he relied on through elementary and high school. Throughout his youth, Bruce harbored intense feelings of hatred and anger towards his father, but he held these feelings inside himself, never expressing them.

Years later, Bruce's father Brian was finally released from the mental hospital in which he had been institutionalized, and he regained custody of Bruce. However, Brian was not fully cured of his insanity, and he still harbored great animosity toward his son. Brian's feelings of hostility mounted over time until one day, while the two of them were visiting Rebecca's grave site, Brian attacked Bruce, intending to kill him. The two men fought, and the struggle ended with Bruce knocking Brian off his feet, causing him to strike his head on Rebecca's gravestone. The impact resulted in this death. With the passage of time, Bruce succeeded in blocking the memory of killing his father from his mind. He only remembered meeting his father at his mother's grave, having a confrontation with him, and then watching his father walk away into the night. Bruce continued to believe this version of events until he was forced later in his life to come to terms with the truth.

Although he hated his father, Bruce eventually followed in Brian's footsteps, becoming a nuclear physicist and going to work for the United States Defense Department nuclear research facility in Desert Base, New Mexico. As a high-level scientist at this facility, Bruce helped to design and construct the "Gamma Bomb," an experimental nuclear device with a high Gamma radiation output and immense destructive power. The development phase of the research went well and Bruce and his fellow investigators were extremely optimistic about the success of the project. However, on the day the bomb was to be tested, a catastrophic accident occurred. As Bruce was preparing for the test from the instrumentation bunker, he noticed a civilian had breached security and entered the test site. Banner commanded his partner, Igor Starsky, to delay the countdown so Bruce could intercept the civilian and escort him to safety. But unknown to Bruce, Igor was operating secretly as a Soviet agent, charged with sabotaging the bomb's construction. Starsky did nothing to interrupt the detonation, believing the explosion would kill Banner and thereby prevent final implementation of the weapon. However, Banner was able to reach the civilian, a teenage boy named Rick Jones, and pull him away from the immediate vicinity of the test site—but in doing so, Bruce was unable to shield himself fully from the Gamma bomb's explosion. When the bomb detonated, massive waves of radioactive energy struck Bruce. Although the radiation from the bomb failed to kill him, the high-level Gamma ray exposure altered his DNA so that, thereafter, circumstances of extreme emotional arousal would cause Banner to change into the fearsome Hulk.

The Hulk is a heavily muscled and emerald-skinned figure with the capacity to lift more than 100 tons when in a fully enraged state. In contrast with Bruce Banner, who is sophisticated, even-tempered, and responsible, the Green Hulk has the temperament and intellect of a child. He is easily agitated and enraged, making him extremely dangerous to society. In the process of protecting himself from harm, the Hulk routinely lays waste to buildings, automobiles, and other public property. In the earliest installments of the Hulk saga, Banner's transformations occurred in a regular daily cycle: Banner would change into the Hulk at sunset and then revert back to human form at dawn. However, as time went by, Banner's transformations came to occur with the release of adrenaline in his body under circumstances of intense emotional arousal—i.e., situations in which Banner became angry, fearful, or highly excited.

The Hulk thus emerges as the personification of intense emotion and unresolved conflicts residing within the troubled psyche of Bruce Banner. What are the origins of these underlying conflicts and the primal rage that emanates from them? In the sections that follow, we consider the evolutionary and neurobiological bases of angry emotion in human beings and factors that contribute to variations in angry responding and aggressive behavior across individuals. An appreciation of the basic mechanisms underlying anger as an emotion and individual differences in anger reactivity can help us to understand not only what drives the destructive behavior of the Hulk, but also what motivates real-life people to commit unspeakable acts of violence.

ANGER AND AGGRESSION: BASIC UNDERLYING MECHANISMS

Anger is in some respects a perplexing emotion because the action it prompts is characteristically destructive, and when turned against members of one's own species, maladaptive from an evolutionary standpoint. In 1920, Freud posited the existence of a "death instinct" (*thanatos*) in humans to account for the destructive side of humanity evidenced so dramatically in the carnage of the first World War. His central idea was that there is a basic drive in each of us that opposes the reproductive life instinct (*eros*), reflecting the unconscious impulse of all living things to return to the inorganic state from which they originated. Freud posited that the death instinct operated at times in a functional manner to promote risk-taking or defensive behavior, but that it was also the basis for murderous and suicidal urges in humans.

Freud's perspective was superseded by neurobiological theories that highlighted the essential evolutionary-adaptive nature of anger and aggressive behavior. In 1927, Walter Cannon introduced the idea of the fight-flight mechanism in mammalian species—namely, that animals such as rats and cats, as well as people instinctively respond with intense physiological arousal when confronted with an immediate threat in order to ready themselves for rapid adaptive action. If escape is feasible, the physiological activation leads to evasive withdrawal (flight); if the animal is cornered and unable to escape, the arousal leads to defensive attack (fight). Later researchers, building on the work of Cannon, developed the idea of emotional reactions as basic survival responses to stimuli governed by specially evolved systems within the brain—in particular, structures comprising the limbic system (amygdala, hippocampus, hypothalamus, cingulate gyrus, and affiliated structures). Other key figures in this emerging science of emotion included Bard (1928), Papez (1937), and Paul MacLean (1952).

In 1939, John Dollard and his colleagues formulated an influential psychological theory of aggressive behavior: the frustration-aggression hypothesis. The core idea of the theory was that aggression is always the result of some form of frustration, defined as the emotional state that arises when an organism or individual is blocked from attaining a goal. Dollard et al. postulated that goal-directed activity entails the arousal of psychic energy that is normally released when a desired goal is achieved or obtained. However, if the individual is prevented from attaining the desired goal, a feeling of pent-up energy is experienced from which the individual seeks release. According to the model, aggressive behavior provides a mechanism for discharging this pent-up psychic energy.

The frustration-aggression hypothesis inspired a good deal of research. Over time, however, various lines of evidence accumulated to challenge this model. In particular, observations of animals and humans across a range of naturalistic and experimental settings revealed that goal blocking represents only one situation in which aggression reliably occurs. Other situations that commonly lead to aggression include: threat posed by an intruder; exposure to uncontrollable pain stimuli; overheating; overcrowding; and noxious noise. Thus, frustration can be viewed as one negative state among many that disposes individuals to aggressive behavior (Berkowitz, 1990). Terms that have been used to describe aggression that arises in response to negative emotional stimulation are: defensive aggression; reactive aggression; angry aggression; and impulsive aggression.

Aggression can also occur in the absence of negative emotional arousal, in the context of coordinated efforts to achieve desired outcomes (i.e., as a means of achieving a goal, rather than as a response to frustration caused by goal blocking). A quintessential example of this form of aggression is the predatory behavior of cats and other carnivorous species, entailing the methodical stalking and killing of prey. In this same general vein, humans rely on aggressive behavior (social as well as physical) in the service of achieving desired goals such as sex, money, or prestige. Terms that have been used in reference to goal-directed aggression of this sort include: instrumental aggression; proactive aggression; predatory aggression; and strategic aggression.

There is evidence that these different forms of aggression are regulated by separate neural systems within the brain (Panksepp, 1998). Reactive aggression is governed by a defensive reactivity system that intersects with, but is also anatomically distinct from, the brain's fear system; this relationship accounts for the fact that similar types of aversive stimuli can evoke either fear or rage reactions, depending upon the overall situational context, and that mixed reactions involving both anger and fear commonly occur. In contrast, the predatory aggression system in animals (and by extension, the brain system that governs instrumental aggression in humans) overlaps substantially with the brain's reward-seeking (appetitive) system. From this standpoint, predatory/instrumental aggression can be viewed as a specific form of reward-seeking behavior.

Which of these forms of aggression is most relevant to an understanding of the motives and behavior of the Hulk? The obvious answer is reactive or defensive aggression—that associated with the underlying psychological experience of anger or rage. Relevant to this, experimental research has shown that when electrical stimulation is applied directly to the medial hypothalamus of a normally docile animal (e.g., a cat), the animal reacts almost immediately with an intense emotional reaction—marked by hissing and spitting, baring of teeth and claws, and vigorous efforts to attack anyone or anything within range. This affective-behavioral response evoked by direct stimulation of the brain's defensive aggression system has been termed "sham rage" (cf. Flynn, 1967). The description of this response in the animal literature fits well with the intense state of anger and destructiveness in which the Green Hulk spends much of his time.

INDIVIDUAL DIFFERENCES IN ANGER AND AGGRESSION

Tendencies toward anger and aggression are fundamentally "hardwired," in that they evolved to serve important survival functions (self-defense; reward seeking; competition for resources) and are governed by specialized neural systems within the brain. The implication is that humans in general are capable of being provoked to anger and exhibiting aggressive behavior under threatening or provocative circumstances. At the same time, our everyday experience tells us that some individuals are more consistently angry and aggressive than others across situations and across time.

At one extreme, social and religious leaders such as Mahatma Ghandi and Martin Luther King, Jr., stand as models of how peacefulness and calm determination can prevail even under circumstances of severe oppression. At the other extreme are commando-style murderers who march into schools or other public places without warning and open fire on innocent victims, claiming multiple lives. Murderers of this sort are chronically hostile individuals with an underlying hatred of society and a yearning for vengeance nurtured by aggressive fantasies and activities ranging from violent computer gaming to the collection and use of weapons. A recent chilling example is that of Seung-Hui Cho, who on April 16, 2007, shot and killed thirty-two people and wounded several others on the campus of Virginia Tech University before killing himself with a gun blast to the head. Cho, a student at Virginia Tech, had no close friends at the university and was described by acquaintances as angry, menacing, depressed, and disturbed. He left behind handwritten notes and homemade videos documenting his hatred of privileged individuals in society whom he felt had belittled and abused him, and announcing his intentions to seek bloody retribution.

Empirical research confirms the existence of stable individual differences in hostility and aggressiveness. Genetic selection studies with animals indicate that aggressive tendencies can be markedly augmented within just a few generations through selective breeding. In the case of humans, the best-known contemporary theories of personality include coverage of traits related to hostility and aggression. (Traits are measurable characteristics of a person that tend to be stable across time and situations.) Eysenck's three-factor model of personality (Eysenck & Eysenck, 1975) includes a dimension of psychoticism that encompasses elements of aggressiveness. Individuals high in psychoticism are hostile, selfish, uncooperative, and socially withdrawn. Another well-known personality framework, the Five Factor Model (FFM; Costa & McCrae, 1985), includes a broad trait of agreeableness among its five major trait dimensions. Individuals low in FFM agreeableness are characteristically antagonistic, suspicious, uncooperative, and callous.

Tellegen's (1982) Multidimensional Model of Personality includes basic traits of aggression and alienation. Individuals high in aggression as defined by this model are physically aggressive, prone to retaliate, and enjoy witnessing violent acts and scenes. Individuals high in alienation feel victimized, mistreated, and exploited by others, and generally unlucky. The tendency to view society and other people as exploitative and untrustworthy (reflected in high alienation) tends to be associated with tendencies toward higher aggressiveness: alienation and aggression are correlated traits that each relate to a broader personality dimension of negative emotionality, reflecting the general tendency to experience negative emotional states. The observed association between aggressive tendencies in this model and the general tendency to experience negative emotions fits with the idea of reactive aggression as a defensive behavioral response associated with the negative experience of anger. In addition, the relationship between an alienated worldview and aggression proneness in this model fits with the characterization of commando-style murderers as embittered, hostile, and vengeful.

In the Hulk comic saga, the character of Bruce Banner is depicted as highly intelligent and sensitive, but plagued by deep-rooted feelings of anger and resentment that are normally held in check. Under circumstances of extreme duress or excitement, however, the hostile feelings buried deep within Banner's psyche find expression in the raging persona of the Hulk. What factors contribute to individual differences in anger and aggressiveness? Why are some individuals able to maintain control of their angry feelings and impulses, whereas others surrender to these feelings and allow their fury to be unleashed upon the world?

ENVIRONMENTAL AND GENETIC CONTRIBUTIONS TO ANGRY/AGGRESSIVE TENDENCIES

The saga of the Incredible Hulk places significant emphasis on events in Bruce's past—his physical and psychological abuse at the hand of his father Brian, the trauma of witnessing his mother's murder, the chronic loneliness and isolation he endured as a youth, and the mortal struggle with his father he experienced as a young man that resulted in his father's death—to account for the various Hulk personas that emerge following Bruce's massive exposure to Gamma radiation. It is natural to attribute the development of deep-seated hostility and resentment to events as powerful and traumatic as these.

Indeed, scientific research indicates that environmental events and experiences contribute importantly to angry and aggressive tendencies. The occurrence of traumatic events in childhood, including physical or emotional abuse, can result in lasting sensitization of circuits within the brain's defensive system that play a crucial role in reactive aggression as well as fear activation. Another mechanism by which experience can influence aggressive behavior is through observational learning, or social modeling. We learn what actions are effective by watching what others do, and with respect to aggression, there is clear evidence that exposure to the antagonistic actions of others can disinhibit or facilitate aggressive behavior among observers. Learning experiences of this kind can operate to modify the expression of aggression because higher brain systems involved in the storage of experiential memories have neural connections with the more primitive brain circuits that directly mediate anger and aggressive responding (Berkowitz, 1990).

However, tracing causal pathways to anger and aggression becomes complicated when the individuals who are inflicting abuse on developing children and modeling aggressive behaviors for them (as was true for Bruce Banner) are parental figures. The reason is that children inherit genes from their parents, as well as being subjected to their behavioral transactions and role-modeling influence. Available evidence indicates a marked contribution of genetic factors (typically around 50 percent) to most behavioral and personality dispositions, including the aggression-related traits mentioned in the preceding section (i.e., Eysenck's psychoticism, FFM agreeableness, and Tellegen's aggression and alienation). Because of this, it is likely that negative feelings and behaviors on the part of children at least in part reflect the transmission of genes that code for these same feelings and behaviors in parents, and that mediate at least in part the negative behaviors of parents.

Bruce Banner was the son of a brutal alcoholic father who was himself the son of an abusive father. What role do genetics and environment play in the transmission of aggression and related problems (e.g., alcohol and drug abuse) from parent to offspring? Recent research involving identical and fraternal twins has demonstrated that the recurrence of *externalizing* problems involving aggressive/antisocial behavior and substance abuse problems from one generation to the next reflects the transmission of a highly heritable underlying vulnerability from parents to their children (Hicks, Krueger, Iacono, McGue, & Patrick, 2004). The presence of this underlying vulnerability puts individuals at general risk for the development of various types of problems involving impulsivity, aggression, and addictions. However, the precise nature and severity of the problems that arise is dependent on other genetic influences and on the unique learning experiences of the individual. In particular, there is evidence that the experience of physical maltreatment at critical early points in life can operate to actuate underlying aggressive potentialities conferred by genes (Caspi et al., 2002).

Other genetic factors and specific learning experiences may in some cases exert a *protective* influence against more malignant expressions of this underlying vulnerability. For example, specific genes exist that cause some individuals to experience an aversive physiological reaction after ingesting alcohol; the presence of such genes may reduce the risk of alcoholism in individuals otherwise disposed to externalizing problems. High general intelligence and high interpersonal sensitivity (qualities evident in Bruce Banner) are examples of other variables that may exert a protective influence. The presence of protective factors of this kind may help to explain why some offspring of parents with severe externalizing problems are able to inhibit or constructively redirect their aggressive and addictive tendencies.

ROOTS OF RAGE: CONCLUDING THOUGHTS

Psychological research with animals, as well as people indicates that the capacity to experience anger and act aggressively reflects the presence of a basic survival instinct in all of us that is governed by specialized neural circuitry in the brain. Nonetheless, individuals in society differ in how prone they are to angry feelings and aggressive actions as a function of variations across people in hereditary makeup and learning history. To understand individuals among us who exhibit repeated, extreme acts of aggression, we need to understand the basic instinctual motivation that drives aggressive behavior in humankind as a whole, and also the distinctive constitutional and environmental influences that contribute to enhanced aggressiveness in particular individuals.

Based on these considerations, it makes sense to think that both environmental and hereditary influences contributed to the tortured psyche of Bruce Banner, the Hulk's alter ego. The experience of abuse inflicted on Bruce by his alcoholic father and the traumatic deaths of his mother and father continued to haunt Bruce through his adult life. However, there is a clear familial pattern to the early abuse that Bruce suffered: Bruce's father Brian was physically abused by his own father as a youth. Available evidence indicates that multi-generational patterns of aggressive-antisocial behavior and substance abuse problems arise at least in part from an underlying genetic vulnerability that is passed along from parents to offspring. From this perspective, the raging Green Hulk can be seen as an outward manifestation of the primal beast that resides within Bruce as a function of malignant genes inherited from his father along with the painful experiences endured in his youth.

As a final point, it is worth noting that despite having the deck stacked against him in these ways from an early age, Bruce Banner managed to achieve a high level of success in his adult life. He avoided alcohol and drugs, established a solid professional career as a scientist, married the woman he loved (Betty Ross) and maintained a healthy relationship with her, and was respected by those around him for his decency and integrity. It was only after the massive radiation exposure he suffered in the Gamma bomb explosion that Bruce's inner demons were unleashed in the form of the Hulk. Scenarios of this kind also occur routinely in everyday life: Whereas some individuals with alcoholic or antisocial parents who suffer abuse or neglect early in life grow up to be addicts or criminals themselves (in some cases even mass murderers), many others do not. This indicates that protective factors exist that can offset these other influences—i.e., separate genes and distinctive environmental experiences that are present for specific individuals. Whatever these factors might be, they give us hope that diamonds can sometimes emerge from even the roughest of backgrounds—and that through continued research and improved scientific understanding, effective methods can be ultimately developed to alter the course of troubled individuals who represent ticking time bombs waiting to explode in society's midst.

Christopher J. Patrick, Ph.D., is Hathaway Professor of Psychology and Director of Clinical Training at the University of Minnesota, where his teaching and research interests focus on emotional and cognitive aspects of crime, violence, antisocial personality, and psychopathic behavior. He is President of the Society for Scientific Study of Psychopathy, and a recipient of early scientific career awards from the American Psychological Association and the Society for Psychophysiological Research. His extracurricular interests include fiction reading and writing, cooking, softball, ocean surfing, and guitar playing.

Sarah K. Patrick is a freshman in high school, and enjoys many activities such as swimming for her school team, listening to music and attending live concerts, surfing, and painting. She also loves to write and is a previously published author.

REFERENCES

P. Bard, "A Diencephalic Mechanism for the Expression of Rage with Special Reference to the Sympathetic Nervous System," *American Journal of Physiology* 84 (1928): 490–513.

L. Berkowitz, "On the Formation and Regulation of Anger and Aggression: A Cognitive-neoassociationistic Analysis," *American Psychologist* 45 (1990): 494–503.

W. B. Cannon, "The James-Lange Theory of Emotions: A Critical Examination and an Alternative Theory," *American Journal of Psychology* 39 (1927): 106–124.

A. Caspi, J. McClay, T. E. Moffitt, J. Mill, J. Martin, I. W. Craig, A. Taylor, and R. Poulton, "Role of Genotype in the Cycle of Violence in Maltreated Children," *Science* 297 (2002): 851–854.

Costa, P. T., & McCrae, R. R. *The NEO Personality Inventory Manual.* Odessa, FL: Psychological Assessment Resources, 1985.

Dollard, J., Doob, L. W., Miller, N. E., Mowrer, O. H., & Sears, R. R. *Frustration and Aggression.* New Haven: Yale University Freer, 1939.

Eysenck, H.J. & Eysenck, S.B.G. *Eysenck Personality Questionnaire.* San Diego, CA: EDITS, 1975.

Flynn, J. P. "The Neural Basis of Aggression in Cats," In D. C. Glass (ed.), *Neurophysiology and Emotion* (pp. 40–60). New York: Rocke-feller University Press, 1967.

Freud, S. *Beyond the Pleasure Principle. The Standard Edition of the Complete Psychological Works of Sigmund Freud, volume XVIII (1920–1922)*. London: Hogarth Press, 1920.

B. M. Hicks, R. F. Krueger, W. G. Iacono, M. K. McGue, and C. J. Patrick, C. J. "The Family Transmission and Heritability of Externalizing Disorders," *Archives of General Psychiatry* 61 (2004): 922–928.

P. D. MacLean, "Some Psychiatric Implications of Physiological Studies on Frontotemporal Portion of Limbic System (visceral brain)," *Electroencephalography and Clinical Neurophysiology* 4 (1952): 407–418.

Panksepp, J. *Affective Neuroscience: The Foundations of Human and Animal Emotions*. New York: Oxford University Press, 1998.

J. W. Papez, "A Proposed Mechanism of Emotion," Archives of Neurology and Psychiatry 38 (1937): 725–743.

Tellegen, A. (1982). *Brief Manual for the Multidimensional Personality Questionnaire*. Unpublished manuscript, University of Minnesota.

THE PSYCHOLOGY OF SUPERHEROES

Kerri L. Johnson, Leah E. Lurye, and Jonathan B. Freeman

GENDER TYPICALITY AND EXTREMITY IN POPULAR CULTURE

Superheroes are, to some extent, caricatures in that their "super" qualities are exaggerations. In this essay, Johnson, Lurye, and Freeman examine the ways that the gender-related qualities of superheroes are similarly exaggerated—specifically their physical proportions and their superhero actions. The essay also describes the results of the authors' creative study investigating gender-related attributes of Mr. Incredible and Elastigirl as well as of their alter egos, Bob and Helen Parr.

"The reason to do animation is caricature. And good caricature picks out the elements that are the essence of the statement and remove[s] everything else. It's not simply about reproducing reality. It's about bumpin' it up."

—BRAD BIRD, WRITER/DIRECTOR OF THE INCREDIBLES

WHAT IS IT THAT'S CARICATURED to make superheroes so exceptional? What made Superman super? Or Wonder Woman wonderful? By definition, superheroes possess some extraordinary capability or skill that renders them super. Such abilities far surpass the physical and perceptual abilities of people—this is the intent of caricature. But caricature in superheroes is not restricted to their strength or skill. In addition to their remarkable abilities, "Supers" are also extreme in other socially meaningful domains—including gender.

The very nomenclature of superheroes suggests that the gender of Supers is a critical aspect of their identity. Supers' names, for example, frequently highlight not only an exceptional talent, but also their sex. This is true for both female (e.g., Wonder-*Woman*, Super-*girl*, *She*-ra, Powerpuff *Girls*, Vampir*ella*, Invisible *Girl*, and Elasti-*girl*) and male (Super*man*, *He-Man*, Spider-*Man*, *Mr.* Fantastic, *Mr.* Incredible) superheroes. Granted, sex is important for identifying the non-superheroes among us too (e.g., Mr., Mrs., Ms., etc.). Yet the manifestation of sex in superheroes is unique. In addition to possessing super-human powers, superheroes possess a super-human gender as well. Indeed, even the Supers whose names do not connote their gender (e.g., Storm from X-Men) remain highly gender stereotyped in form and function. (We should note that we did seek exceptions to this general rule—that whether in name or in form, Supers' gender is noted and caricatured—to no avail. In fact, we would hazard to suggest that there is simply no such thing as an androgynous superhero.)

In this chapter, we will explore how the gender of superheroes is "bumped up" to transform the ordinary into the extraordinary, the so-so to the sublime, to make Superman literally a super man. We propose that certain gendered cues are extremetized to magnify the differences between men and women (e.g., body size and body shape), while others are amplified to accentuate valued gendered traits (e.g., masculinity/femininity). We describe the theoretical underpinnings that make such transformations successful and report empirical evidence to support our claims.

THE PSYCHOLOGY OF SEX AND GENDER

For decades psychologists have recognized that social categories play a critical role in how we perceive others. The moment we see people we effortlessly sort them into social categories (Stangor, Lynch, Duan, and Glass, 1992). Sex, race, and age are the big three. This type of categorical thinking makes perceiving others more efficient and easier (Allport, 1933) because knowing an individual's sex, race, or age is informative—or so we think. Specifically, identifying a person's sex, race, or age calls up existing stereotypes in memory that are connected to each category (e.g., girls like pink; old people walk slowly, etc.). These stereotypes are then used to guide person perception. Initially, these processes were presumed to be inevitable, obligatory (Stangor et al., 1992), and automatic (Bargh, 1999)—to occur without intent. Recent evidence, however, suggests that under certain conditions we may be able to resist categorizing others by age and race (Kurzban, Tooby, and Cosmides, 2001; Quinn & Macrae, 2005), although overriding sex categorization appears to be more difficult. This difference in our ability to resist categorizing others by age and race, but not by sex, is not terribly surprising since sex categories are among the first social categories young children learn (Ruble, Martin, and Berenbaum, 2006), and are arguably the most important social categories in American society. The importance of biological sex is highlighted at birth (e.g., "It's a boy!"; pink or blue booties and bottles), and it remains important throughout our lifespan. Such distinctions dictate where we may go (men's room versus ladies' room), what we may wear (ties versus skirts, with the possible exception of the mini-kilt), and which traits and emotions we are permitted to exhibit (sadness versus anger, assertiveness versus passivity). This has profound implications for how we view and interact with others.

Once perceived, knowledge of another's sex unleashes a cascade of events. Specifically, sex category knowledge activates sex based stereotypes and attitudes that affect how we feel about and interact with others. It also provides a foundation for interaction, influencing how we behave toward others. Finally, sex categories function as a lens through which other gendered cues are perceived—and deemed either compatible or incompatible with the construed biological sex.

Frequently, the sex of a person is fully compatible with other gendered cues (e.g., masculine men and feminine women). Sometimes, however, known sex and gendered cues are at odds (e.g., feminine men and masculine women). In other words, knowing whether someone is a man or a woman also leads to the perception that the individual is either gender typical or gender atypical.

What happens when people appear gender atypical? In general, gender atypicality is penalized quite harshly in our society. Beginning in preschool, *gender nonconformity* (the label that developmental psychologists use to refer to children who possess interests more common in the opposite sex) compels harsh evaluations from parents, peers, and teachers (e.g., Fagot, 1977). And such consequences are not restricted to childhood. In evaluative attractiveness judgments, people who walk in a gender atypical manner (i.e., men who sway their hips or women who swagger their shoulders) are judged to be less attractive than their gender-congruent counterparts (Johnson and Tassinary, 2007), and are frequently presumed to be gay (Johnson, Gill, Reichman, and Tassinary, 2007). Although categorizing gender nonconformists as homosexuals does not necessarily connote harsh evaluations, it relegates the individuals to a minority status.

Interestingly, the adverse effects of gender atypicality are considerably stronger for men and boys than for women and girls. This asymmetry can be partly explained by the traits our society values. Sandra Bem (and others) have argued that what is male or masculine represents the ideal, while that which is female or feminine does not. For example, in American society, it is generally considered better to be assertive (which is associated with males and masculinity) than to be yielding (which is associated with females and femininity). Bem calls this "androcentrism," and proposes that the reason men are punished more harshly than women for gender atypicality is that when men do something feminine, they also do something less valued. A man who exhibits feminine characteristics (be they traits, behaviors, or appearance) is moving away from a societal ideal; a woman who exhibits masculine characteristics, in contrast, is striving to achieve a societal ideal. Thus, although gender atypicality among women is not liked, it is tolerated, and penalized less severely. Women who exhibit agentic traits (masculine traits that are highly valued) in the workplace, for example, are perceived to be competent (consistent with the agentic traits that are deemed necessary for successful business), but they are not liked. In contrast, men who exhibit communal traits (more feminine traits that are less highly valued) are presumed to be incompetent.

What aspects of superheroes' appearance and behavior are likely to be caricatured? Put simply, where should we look? We should probably begin with aspects of appearance and actions that are either truly sexually dimorphic (i.e., men and women *really* differ on the dimension) or are stereotypically sex-typed (i.e., men and women are *presumed* to differ on the dimension). Two cues—bodies and behavior—are likely candidates for caricature.

Bodies differ between men and women, and numerous cues are reliably dimorphic. Compared to women, for example, men are taller, hairier, and brawnier. Women, in contrast, are smaller, softer, and more curvaceous. Many sexual dimorphisms exist in absolute measures (e.g., height and weight), but other differences are more contextualized. Women, for example, are more likely than men to have an hourglass figure, a body shape that can be quantified by dividing the circumference measurements of the waist and the hips, called the waist-to-hip ratio (WHR). Observers rely strongly on this cue to make sex category judgments (Johnson and Tassinary, 2005). Small WHRs have been related to perceptions of attractiveness, and recent evidence highlights that these effects emerge because this body shape is perceived to be feminine (Johnson and Tassinary, 2007). Men are more likely than women to have a tapered torso (think V shaped upper body), a body shape that is quantified by dividing the measurement of the chest and the waist, or chest-to-waist ratio (CWR). Although there is considerably less empirical work relating this body cue to social perceptions, it is a body cue that is sexually dimorphic, and research from our own and others' labs has related it to perceptions of biological sex and masculinity (see e.g., Lippa, 1983; Frederick, Fessler, and Haselton, 2005). Both of these measurements reliably distinguish men from women. Thus, one way that Supers may be exceptional is in their body's physical proportions. If the bodies of superheroes are caricatures of men and women's bodies, the WHR and CWR might be good places to look.

Behavioral norms also differ between men and women, and these correspond to stereotypic notions of sex roles. Compared to feminine individuals, masculine individuals are more likely to describe themselves to be assertive, aggressive, self-sufficient, and independent. Feminine individuals, on the other hand are more likely to describe themselves to be affectionate, gentle, soft-spoken, and warm. These examples come directly from a scale developed to assess adherence to common conceptions of masculinity and femininity, the *Bem Sex Roles Inventory (BSRI*; Bem, 1974). Not surprisingly, men and women tend to differ along these dimensions. Some have argued that the labels *instrumental* and *expressive* might more aptly describe these dimensions (e.g., Spence and Helmreich, 1980), but we will use the more common vernacular—masculine and feminine. Although the BSRI purports to measure attributes that are desirable for both men and women, the masculine items are generally recognized to describe traits and behaviors that are more highly valued in our society. If the behaviors of superheroes are caricatures of men and women's sex roles, the masculine and feminine subscales of the BSRI are likely to reflect those differences.

How can we tell if superheroes possess caricatured bodies or behaviors? Ideally, we could compare non-super individuals with superheroes on measures of bodies and behaviors (i.e, WHR/CWR and masculinity/femininity). One way to achieve this would be to compare the bodies and behaviors of the average man and woman to the bodies and behaviors of super-men and super-women. Such comparisons prove to be quite difficult. Everyday men and women differ from superheroes along many dimensions in addition to those we expect to see caricatured. Real men and women live in corporeality whereas superheroes live in a virtual reality; real men and women's bodies and behaviors are dictated by DNA and experience whereas superheroes bodies and behaviors are limited only by artistic imagination. For these and other reasons, comparing real men and women to superheroes is not only inconvenient, but also imperfect. So we elected to compare the virtual identities of non-super and super characters. Candidates for such a comparison are easy to generate— Clark Kent/Superman, and Diana Prince/Wonder Woman—yet these characters were rendered by different artists and appeared in different mediums. Fortunately, two superheroes (one male, one female) recently emerged on the superhero stage. These Supers achieved fame and fortune (at least for the producers and executives), and their characters provide the perfect opportunity to compare male and female superheroes from a single source. Put simply, they were an incredible find.

In the blockbuster hit *The Incredibles*, all superheroes were forced to shelve their super identities and adopt non-super secret identities to live among the rest of society in anonymity. Although clearly not thrilled with the monotony of regular life, everything was relatively normal until a malevolent pseudo-super, Syndrome, came into the picture. When the evil Syndrome threatened the well being of all humanity, two former Supers abandoned their secret identities to return to their crime-fighting superhero ways. These circumstances led to super transformations: Bob and Helen Parr became Mr. Incredible and Elastigirl. These two characters, linked in identity but different in exceptionality, provided the perfect comparisons for examining how sex differences in bodies and behavior are "bumped up" with super results.

OUR STUDY

We first asked a very simple question: Are the bodies of Supers caricatured or "bumped up" to extremetize the sex typicality of their body shape? Specifically, are the WHRs of female Supers and the CWRs of male Supers more extreme than the WHRs and CWRs of non-super men and women?

To answer this question, we selected static images of the bodies of Mr. Incredible and Elastigirl and their non-super secret identities, Bob and Helen. We measured the chest, waist, and hip breadth for each image. Using these measures, we computed two indices that vary reliably (and stereotypically) between men and women, the WHR and the CWR.

For both physical measures, we made two types of comparisons. First, we compared the body shapes of Helen/Elastigirl and Bob/Mr. Incredible. Next, we compared the body shapes of each character to the anthropometric averages for each sex. We used one of many possible comparison groups—Army recruits. Now, at first blush, it may seem odd that we selected army recruits as a foundation for comparison. Doing so, however, has several distinct advantages that justify these comparisons—some theoretical, others empirical. Theoretically, this comparison group makes perfect sense. In selecting a comparison group, one might hope to identify the closest approximations of non-mutant superheroes with the most conservative of all possible tests. Army recruits, in many ways, are more like superheroes than the average man or woman. After all, the call to duty for superheroes and Army recruits shares considerable overlap. According to the official Army recruitment website, one role of the U.S. Army is "[to] defeat adversaries responsible for aggression that endangers the peace and security of the United States and our allies."

By merely substituting "villain" for adversaries and "evil" for aggression, the goals of the U.S. Army and Superheroes appear to be strikingly similar. This comparison group, therefore, provides a conservative test of our hypotheses. That said, our own research has found few differences between the bodies of the Army recruits in our database and college undergraduates, a fact that makes comparisons with this group warranted from an empirical standpoint. Finally, and perhaps most importantly, we had ready access to a database containing the body measurements of over 5,000 Army recruits. So we used it.

BOB PARR → MR. INCREDIBLE

The shift from Bob Parr to Mr. Incredible brings with it a considerable physical transformation. While both Bob and Mr. Incredible are enormous in sheer physical size, their bodies differ considerably in their relative proportion. Let's begin with the CWR, the male stereotyped V shaped taper of the upper body. As seen in Figure 2, Bob's CWR is 1.19, which is actually quite close to the population mean (1.039). When Bob becomes Mr. Incredible, however, his CWR swells to a whopping 1.54! Prior research indicates that this transformation is likely to increase perceptions of strength, endurance, and masculinity. Thus, Mr. Incredible is not only more manly, physically speaking, than Bob Parr, but also a caricature of the "male" body shape!

Because small WHRs are stereotypically related to femininity, we didn't expect any profound caricature for Mr. Incredible's WHR. We were surprised to learn, however, that the WHR of Bob was the exceptional one, albeit not in a "super" manner whatsoever. Bob's WHR is 1.13, whereas the population average WHR for men is 0.91. Bob's particularly large WHR is consistent with the growth of a beer belly in his sedentary civilian life. We believe that this difference points to one simple fact—Bob is fat. This supposition was underscored by comments made by Edna Mode, who had not seen Bob since the "glory days" of hero work. When Bob arrived seeking Edna's assistance to repair his super suit, Edna's immediate response was, "My god, you've gotten fat!" Thus, Bob's larger than average WHR simply implies that he is fatter than the average man. Mr. Incredible's WHR, in contrast, is a completely gender typical 0.95 and is consistent with a svelte and super physique.

HELEN PARR → ELASTIGIRL

The shift from Helen Parr to Elastigirl brings with it an equally profound physical transformation. For these characters, let's begin with the WHR, the female stereotyped hourglass shape of the torso. As seen in Figure 1, Helen Parr, physically speaking, is indistinguishable from the average woman in our database. Her WHR is 0.77, a measurement that falls well within the normal range, for which the average is 0.84. When Helen becomes Elastigirl, however, her WHR shrinks to a shockingly small 0.42, a caricature of feminine female curves! This WHR, by the way, is so extreme that it does not exist in nature. In fact, it is well beyond the smallest observed WHR in our comparison group, 0.69. Prior research indicates that this transformation is likely to increase perceptions of femininity and even attractiveness. Thus, Elastigirl is not only more womanly, at least physically, than Helen Parr, but also a caricature of the "female" body shape!

Because large CWRs are stereotypically related to masculinity, we didn't necessarily expect any profound caricature for Elastigirl's CWR for theoretical reasons. Because the extreme caricature of the WHR entailed a dramatically small waist, however, it was likely that

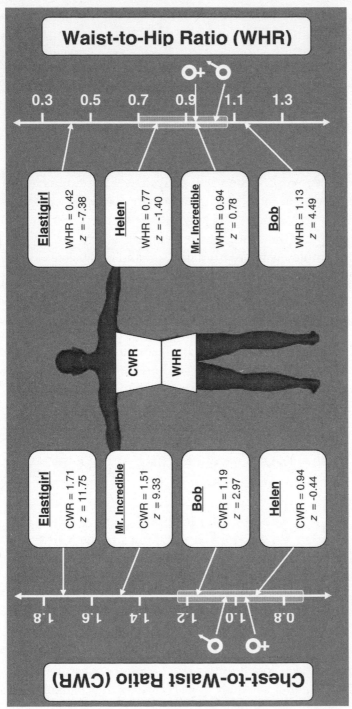

Physical Measurements of Chest-to-Waist and Waist-to-Hip Ratios for Pre/Post Transformation Male and Female Characters. Shaded bars represent the range of human variation for CWR and WHR. Sex symbols represent anthropometric mean for the average man and woman. Z scores indicate the extent of departure from same-sex anthropometric means.

Elastigirl's CWR would also be quite extreme. Indeed, Helen's CWR, 0.94, fell well within the range of normal women, and quite close to the population average, 0.97. When Helen became Elastigirl, however, her CWR became quite large, 1.70. It's important to note that this CWR, in spite of its more masculine measurement, is unlikely to convey masculinity. Instead, within the context of the hip breadth, this CWR is likely to balance the feminine hourglass shape and highlight the extremity of Elastigirl's feminine physique.

Compared to their non-super identities, the bodies of Mr. Incredible and Elastigirl appear to be caricatures of the masculine tapered upper body and the feminine hourglass figure. This is likely to promote favorable social evaluations, based solely on the physical manifestations of masculinity and femininity. Supers, because their bodies are caricatured in a gender-normative manner, are likely to be perceived as quite attractive.

SUPER BEHAVIORS

Whereas the bodies of superhereoes are caricatures of a sexual dimorphism, the sex normative behaviors and traits of those same superheroes are unlikely to be extreme versions of gender-normative roles. Why? If this were so, it would simply not be equally effective for male and female Supers. If male Supers were more extreme on gender-typed behaviors and traits, the result would be, well, super. This would mean that super men possessed greater levels of agentic and instrumental characteristics (e.g., assertive, aggressive, and independent). If female Supers were more extreme on gender-typed behaviors and traits, in contrast, the result would make them kinder and gentler superheroes. This would mean that super-women possessed greater levels of communal and expressive traits (e.g., gentle, soft-spoken, and warm). While these characteristics are generally desirable for women, they are unlikely to be the most effective strategies for battling evil and saving the world. Instead, the stereotypically masculine characteristics seem to be the stuff that superheroes are made of. Therefore, gender roles appear likely to be extreme, but not along gendered lines. Instead, we predicted that Supers, whether they are male or female, were likely to be *masculine*. If correct, this predicts that super men will be *more* gender typical, but that super women will be *less* gender typical (and possibly even more typical of the opposite sex) than their non-super selves.

We asked our participants to evaluate the gendered behaviors and traits for both of the characters in the movie. Participants completed the sixty-item BSRI for each of the four characters. We computed an index of gender typicality by subtracting the average of the gender-incongruent sub-scale from the gender-congruent sub-scale. Thus, for Bob and Mr. Incredible, we subtracted femininity from masculinity; for Helen and Elastigirl we subtracted masculinity from femininity. This gave us a single index of gender typicality. Sex-typed behaviors and traits gave positive values (masculine men and feminine women); Cross sex-typed behaviors and traits yielded negative values (feminine men and masculine women).

The transformation from their non-super to super identities brought about drastically different changes, depending on the sex of the character. As seen in Figure 2, when Bob became Mr. Incredible, the transformation brought with it greater levels of sex-typed behaviors and traits. Put simply, compared to Bob, the extent to which Mr. Incredible is more masculine than feminine is even larger. A different pattern emerged, however, as Helen became Elastigirl. In this case, the transformation brought with it *cross* sex-typed behaviors and traits. Whereas Helen is more feminine than masculine (sex-typed), Elastigirl is more masculine than feminine (cross sex-typed).

This pattern suggests that behavioral caricatures of male and female Supers are decidedly unidirectional—they become more masculine. Within a society that puts such high value on masculine traits, this type of caricature is likely to convey competence, skill, and excellence—the very stuff that superheroes are made of!

SUPER SUMMATION

According to our opening quote, caricature is about taking the essence of a statement and "bumping it up." We found that superheroes are caricatures of gender, but exactly how gender is caricatured varies by domain. The bodies of Supers are caricatures of sexually dimorphic body shapes. Super men have a super physical presence

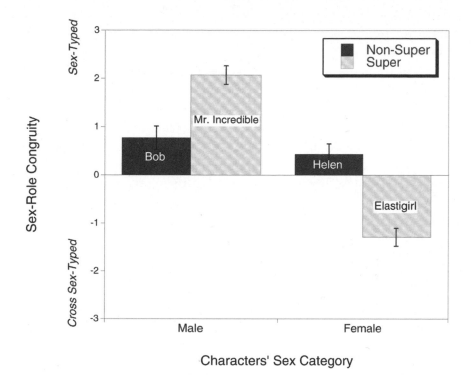

Extent of Sex-Role Typicality for Pre/Post Transformation Male and Female Characters. Error bars depict 95 percent confidence intervals.

with a highly masculine V shaped upper body; super women have a super physique with an exaggerated hourglass figure. The behaviors of Supers, in contrast, are caricatures of masculinity regardless of the super's sex. Both male and female Supers were judged to possess highly valued agentic and instrumental traits, which are advantageous when fighting the forces of evil.

It is worth noting that as extreme and remarkable as their superpowers are, superheroes' gender is at least equally so. It is interesting that when we think about superheroes we tend to think explicitly about their super powers, not their super gender. However, super gender is tightly coupled with super powers, at least in some circumstances. How, for example, could Superman fly "faster than a speeding bullet" or be "stronger than a locomotive" if he did not have the uber-masculine shoulder breadth and muscle mass to do so? Perhaps this is why we readily accept such super gender as part and parcel of superheroes' identities. We suspend disbelief because the extreme gender seems to fit. Yet this premise is complicated by the physical transformations of female Supers, morphological changes that seem unrelated to anything but men's ogling. How, for example, does a small waist and large breasts enable Wonder Woman, and others like her, to perform the death defying feats of which only Supers are capable? But maybe that is part of her charm. Her simultaneous embodiment of the ideal feminine physique and the ideal masculine/agentic attributes allows her not only to be adored and admired as a woman, but also respected and honored like a man. Such an existence is super, indeed.

Kerri L. Johnson is an assistant professor of communication studies at UCLA. She earned her Ph.D. from Cornell University in 2004. Her research examines the causes and consequences of social categorization, often involving perceptions of sex and gender. Together with her students, she aims to "save the world, one bullet point at a time (Mercurio, P. Two Spoons)."

Leah E. Lurye is currently a graduate student in the Social Psychology Program, with a special focus in Developmental Psychology, at New York University. Currently she is interested in what people conceive of as gender typical or atypical, and how they react to those who violate gender norms. She is an enthusiastic Pixar fan and believes *The Incredibles* is one of the coolest movies of all time.

Jonathan B. Freeman recently completed his B.A. in psychology and gender & sexuality studies at New York University, and is currently a doctoral student at Tufts University, earning his Ph.D. in experimental psychology. He is currently interested in the social, neural, cultural, and cognitive processes involved in person construal, first impressions, social evaluation, and interpersonal interaction. In search of nuanced understandings, he tries to work at multiple levels of analysis: social (and cognitive) psychology, social and cultural neuroscience, and critical/cultural studies of gender, sexuality, race, class, and capitalism. Hopefully not having to entirely abandon his delusional ideas about making sense of interesting mental life and its inextricable ties to society and culture, he desperately tries to reconcile a secret infatuation with Mr. Incredible with his varied resistances against heteronormative patriarchy.

REFERENCES

Allport, G. W. and P.E. Vernon. *Studies in Expressive Movement.* New York: Macmillan, 1993.

J. Bargh, "The Cognitive Monster: The Case against the Controllability of Automatic Stereotype Effects," in *Dual Process Theories in Social Psychology*, edited by S. Chaiken and Y. Trope. New York: Guilford Press, 1999.

S. L. Bem, "The Measurement of Psychological Androgyny," *Journal of Consulting and Clinical Psychology* 42: 155–162.

Bem. S. L. *The Lenses of Gender.* New Haven, CT: Yale University Press, 1993.

Fagot, B. I., "Consequences of Moderate Cross-gender Behavior in Preschool Children," *Child Development* 48 (1977): 902–907.

D. A. Frederick, D. M. T. Fessler, and M. G. Haselton, "Do Representations of Male Muscularity Differ in Men's and Women's Magazines?", *Body Image* 2 (2005): 81–86.

K. L. Johnson, S. Gill, V. Reichman, and L. G. Tassinary (in press), "Swagger, Sway, and Sexuality: Judging Sexual Orientation from Body Motion and Morphology," *Journal of Personality and Social Psychology*.

K. L. Johnson and L. G. Tassinary, "Compatibility of Basic Social Perceptions Determines Perceived Attractiveness," *Proceedings of the National Academy of Sciences of the United States of America* 104 (2007): 5246–5251.

K. L. Johnson and L. G. Tassinary, "Perceiving Sex Directly and Indirectly: Meaning in Motion and Morphology," *Psychological Science* 16 (2005): 890–897.

R. Kurzban, J. Tooby, and L. Cosmides, "Can Race be Erased? Coalitional Computation and Social Categorization," *Proceedings of the National Academy of Sciences of the United States of America* 98 (2001): 15387–15392.

R. Lippa, "Sex Typing and the Perception of Body Outlines," *Journal of Personality* 51 (1983): 667–682.

K. A. Quinn and C. N. Macrae, "Categorizing Others: They Dynamics of Person Construal," *Journal of Personality and Social Psychology* 88 (2005): 467–479.

Ruble, D. N., Martin, C. L., & Berenbaum, S. A. (2006). Gender development. In W. Damon (Ed.), *Handbook of Child Psychology* (6th Edition, Vol. 3, pp. 858 - 932). New York: J. Wiley.

J. T. Spence and R. L. Helmreich, "Masculine Instrumentality and Feminine Expressiveness: Their Relationships with Sex Role Attitudes and Behaviors," *Psychology of Women Quarterly* 5 (1980): 147–163.

C. Stangor, L. Lynch, C. Duan and B. Glass, "Categorization of Individuals on the Basis of Multiple Social Features," *Journal of Personality and Social Psychology* 62 (1992): 207–281.

Peter DeScioli
and Robert Kurzban, Ph.D.

CRACKING THE SUPERHERO'S MORAL CODE

Superheroes face moral dilemmas with regularity: An innocent by-stander has been hurt by a criminal. Should the superhero aid the by-stander but let the criminal get away? Or should the highest priority be nailing the criminal? If more lives are ultimately saved by going after the villain but letting the bystander die, what's a superhero to do? DeScioli and Kurzban illuminate some of the psychological aspects of morality that drive superheroes and distinguish them from war heroes, whose morality operates—or doesn't operate—on a different level.

SUPERHEROES SPECIALIZE in within-group conflict, differing markedly from between-group war heroes such as Achilles, Joshua, or Guan Gong. Accordingly, superheroes wield the most devastating weapon of within-group fighting—not heat vision, batarangs, or web-shooters, but rather, the *moral high ground*. In order to excel at moral condemnation, superheroes embody three core features of moral psychology: 1) third-party judgment; 2) moralistic punishment; and 3) moral impartiality. Consequently, superhero lore illuminates patterns in moral thinking (and vice versa).

SUPERMAN'S DILEMMA

In *Superman* #171, the hero finds himself in a predicament that is all too familiar[1] ("Superman's Sacrifice" #171). Rokk and Sorban, super powerful aliens from the planet Ventura, bet on whether they can get Superman to kill someone. Rokk demonstrates to Superman that he can destroy planets with his mind and then gives Superman an ultimatum: "Either you kill someone or Earth will be destroyed! You have twenty-four hours to make your decision." Superman reflects, "What a ghastly choice! Throughout my career I always protected life. Killing someone is against everything I stand for! Yet, if I don't, those vicious aliens will blast the Earth and kill billions of people!"

Superman agonizes over choosing whether to kill one to save many. He tries to kill himself with boulders of kryptonite, but his suicide is thwarted by the aliens, who feel that this solution is too boring. Superman is enraged: "Your conscience doesn't bother you about forcing me to kill someone! All right! I'll kill you!" Superman grips Rokk by the throat while Sorban encourages the homicide. But the hero loses heart: "What am I doing? You upset me so much, I lost my temper and I nearly violated my code. I couldn't kill you, Rokk, even though you deserve death a thousand times!"

We won't spoil the ending.[2] What's relevant here is that Superman is unwilling to kill one person—even an *evil alien* (with a gambling problem)—to save billions of people. From this, we infer that Superman frowns on the utilitarianism of John Stuart Mill and Jeremy Bentham, which holds that it is best to act to maximize welfare—even if this requires killing a few people to save many. Bentham would have strangled Rokk in a second.[3]

---

[1] Not really.

[2] It turns out Rokk is actually a *guy*. Oh, wait. Wrong story. (That was Dil from *The Crying Game*.)

[3] We have no evidence Bentham could have taken Rokk, but then again we have no evidence that Bentham *didn't* have superpowers.

Superman is more of a moral absolutist, like Immanuel Kant. Kant's most famous treatise, *Grounding for the Metaphysics of Morals*, is subtitled: "On a supposed right to lie because of philanthropic concerns." For Kant, welfare gains cannot justify actions like killing or lying, i.e., the ends don't justify the means. On this view, morality is not a means to increase welfare, but instead, consists of what Kant famously termed "categorical imperatives"—categories of actions that are always morally wrong regardless of the consequences.

What about people? Are we more like Mill or more like Kant? If we're like Kant, then we're also like Superman.[4]

DO PEOPLE THINK LIKE SUPERMAN?

Five people stand idly on the tracks as a trolley rapidly approaches. They face certain death if no one intervenes. A skinny engineer sees a large man next to the tracks who is just heavy enough to slow the trolley before it kills the five people. Should the engineer push the man in front of the trolley, killing one to save five? Psychologists have asked this question to thousands of participants from many cultures and religious backgrounds (Hauser 128). People everywhere agree: 90 percent say it would be wrong for the engineer to push the large man. Like Superman, most people think it is wrong to kill one person even when inaction results in more deaths. This has been called the "act-omission effect," in which harmful actions are seen as more wrong than omissions (failures to act) that lead to greater harm. Superman's unwillingness to kill one to save billions is an example.

The act-omission effect also occurs in *Batman Begins*. Batman gains the upper hand against the villain Ra's al Ghul in—fittingly enough—a train headed towards a break in the tracks. The villain asks, "Have you finally learned to do what is necessary?" alluding to Batman's earlier refusal to kill. Batman replies, "I won't kill you, but I don't have to save you," just before jumping out of the train, leaving the villain to plummet to his death. Batman views an action that kills as wrong, but not an omission that results in death. Importantly, the consequences are the same, suggesting that morality is disconnected from welfare outcomes.

---

[4] Absent flight, X-ray vision, and, thankfully, blue tights.

Superheroes fit hand in glove with our moral intuitions. This probably sounds like an unexceptional observation. "Of course, superheroes are designed to be role models for children, to be exemplars of morality and citizenship, just like other heroes such as those found in Greek mythology or the Bible, right?"

That would be right, except it's exactly wrong.

We are so accustomed to superheroes as moral exemplars that we take them for granted. For the vast majority of human history, myths have featured tales of selfish, vengeful, blood-lusting killers rather than upstanding moralists. Across history and cultures, most children have admired a quite different genre of hero—the war hero.

WITHIN- VS. BETWEEN-GROUP CONFLICT

Against the backdrop of world mythology, the most conspicuous feature of superheroes is their focus on within-group criminal activity rather than war. The fighting heroes of history excelled in between-group warfare: Sargon, Gilgamesh, Moses, David, Heracles, Hector, Romulus, Roland, King Arthur, Karna, Arjuna, and so on. In contrast, Superman, Batman, and Spider-Man mark a distinct hero genre—the crime fighter.

From a psychological perspective, within and between-group conflicts are very different. A key difference is uncertainty about who is on which side. In war, opposing sides are usually clear-cut, often separated by geography and culture.[5] From a tactical perspective, morality is largely irrelevant since there is little chance of persuading enemy soldiers to switch to your side.

The heroes of old, specializing in war, were not particularly moral. Moses instructed his army to rape and slaughter women and children (Numbers 31:17), Romulus murdered his brother Remus over a petty argument, and Lancelot committed adultery with King Arthur's wife. This is consistent with attitudes toward real war heroes, such as the WWII Finnish sniper Simo Häyhä who was "credited" with over 500 kills in 100 days. War heroes, in reality and fiction, are known for their number of kills, not their moral character.

Within-group conflict is different. Who is on which side is often

---

[5] Uniforms also help.

opaque and volatile. Here, enemy and ally live intermingled and allegiances shift unpredictably. Caesar's mythical last words, "Et tu, Brute?", symbolize the dismay when friend turns to foe. Among infighters, alliances determine victory, and the moral standing of combatants is a key factor in how people choose sides. In war, victory goes to the strong; within groups, victory goes to the combatant backed by the majority.

Superheroes excel in within-group combat, and accordingly, they deftly wield moral virtue. Superman defends "truth, justice, and the American way" (*Superman*). The "friendly neighborhood" Spider-Man takes to heart Uncle Ben's motto: "With great power comes great responsibility" (*Spider-Man*). Batman follows in the footsteps of his philanthropist father, as he explains to Alfred, "I'm using this monster to help other people, just like my father did" (*Batman Begins*). The moral character of these superheroes is nearly flawless.

In sum, there seems to be a correlation between the kind of conflict a hero engages, war or crime, and the hero types that are admired, furious killer or virtuous fighter. We suggest that this is no accident. Because of the different tactical requirements for being a good warrior and a good crime fighter, humans probably handle warfare and crime with different specialized psychological systems. Each system might be expected to include algorithms for identifying and admiring individuals highly skilled in that domain (war or crime-fighting, respectively). We suggest that psychological systems specialized for war resonate most with stories about furious killers, while systems engineered to handle crime resonate most with tales of virtuous fighters. If we are correct, one might wonder why superheroes didn't appear earlier in human history.

RISE OF THE CRIME FIGHTER

The recent rise of the crime fighter in popular myth is a curious fact of history. Where are the crime-fighting superheroes of old? Where are the masked heroes of impeccable character rushing to condemn and punish moral violators? It is tempting to think that humanity has become increasingly moral in modern times thus creating a cultural market for virtuous heroes. However heartwarming, this explanation is unlikely. Superheroes have by no means displaced war heroes. *Conan the Barbarian*, *Rambo*, Lord of the Rings, and Star Wars all feature deadly warriors who massacre enemies.

Another idea is that successful myths reflect what's on the minds of the people, with more severe dangers better represented in stories and legends. If so, crime fighter myths might be explained by a historical trend characterized by decreasing dangers of bilateral war and/or increasing dangers of multilateral conflict among shifting coalitions.

What we think of as "history" is in its essence a record of intergroup conflict. The classic historical accounts, from the Old Testament to the Iliad, are war stories. In short, for the bulk of human history, people were preoccupied with whether or not their group—band, clan, or city-state—would suffer sudden annihilation by neighbors. In such a context, in which inter-group conflict loomed large, one can imagine a place in the human imagination for deadly warriors. Stories about the hero who prevents merchant carts from being burgled might have been less compelling.

A different milieu was created by rising levels of social organization. Increasingly, wars fought among local lords were determined by alliance networks rather than raw power. Suddenly, morality became a key factor determining outcomes of war. Historian Ernest Gellner argued that this was the niche occupied by the Church, which specialized in moral legitimization, thereby coordinating alliances in conflicts (Gellner 93–100). Under these circumstances warriors became bound by ethical principles such as the medieval code of chivalry. It is telling that chivalry applied only to war among Christians, while the codes were abandoned when sides were clear-cut in battle with non-Christian "infidels."

In parallel, we see the beginning of myths of noble heroes. The knights of Arthurian legend were saints next to older war heroes, but still sinners by superhero standards. Robin Hood, too, was a key development along these lines, and he fittingly became a direct inspiration for Batman's sidekick.

Finally, in modern times, the dangers of war are down while crime is rising. Despite the salience of absolute death tolls in modern wars, archeological evidence indicates that the *fraction* of individuals killed in war during the twentieth century (including two World Wars) was about *ten times smaller* than for most of human history (Keeley 25–40). Meanwhile, the danger of within-group conflict has increased with the growth of large, anonymous communities. Psychological research has shown that as people become more anonymous, they are more likely to behave immorally and selfishly (Diener et al. 178–183). It is probably no accident that superheroes live in large urban centers, precisely where within-group conflict is most acute. Superheroes might have gained a foothold on the human imagination when between-group threats decreased while within-group dangers increased.

In sum, much of human history is characterized by communities which were simultaneously preoccupied with war and sufficiently closely knit to monitor and punish crime. The upstanding crime fighter remained hidden in the shadow of the furious warrior. Perhaps when the threat of sudden annihilation decreased and the hazards of crime increased, a new breed of hero arose. The rise of the crime fighter, as moralist rather than warrior, brought to the fore three character traits: third-party judgment, moralistic punishment, and moral impartiality.

THIRD-PARTY MORAL JUDGMENT

The Book of Matthew recommends, "Do not judge, and you will not be judged. For as you judge others, so you will yourselves be judged, and whatever measure you deal out to others, will be dealt to you" (Matthew 7:1-2). Superheroes fail to heed this warning. Superman has trouble *minding his own business.* Spider-Man is always *snooping around.* Batman is a *busybody* who *butts in* and *interferes* with others' schemes. Daredevil is *nosy and intrusive.* The X-Men are always *prying* into others' affairs. Shaggy and Wilma are *meddling kids.*

A core feature of superheroes is that they engage in third-party intervention in moral infractions. They differ in this respect from war heroes, who typically fight to defend themselves or to directly benefit themselves through conquest. In *300*, for example, Spartan King Leonidas fights the Battle of Thermopylae to defend against Persian invasion.

In contrast, superheroes meddle in interactions that don't directly involve them. In *Superman*, Lex Luther schemes to increase the value of his desert real estate by blasting California into the ocean. Superman—with real estate only in the north pole—has nothing at stake. In *Batman Begins*, the League of Shadows seeks to destroy Gotham because of its crime and decadence. They do not target Batman and, in fact, they try to recruit him. Also, in *Spider-Man*, the Green Goblin has no particular gripe with the hero, and even invites Spider-Man to join forces with him. In *X-Men*, Magneto asks only that Xavier and his students stay out of the way of his war with humans. But in all of these cases, superheroes intervene as third parties, sticking their noses into others' business.

Why do superheroes care? Why don't they do what many of us would do with extraordinary powers—become millionaires, move to a secluded Caribbean island, and breed multicolor lop-eared rabbits?[6] And why do we admire superheroes for this lapse in rationality?

Like superheroes, people everywhere pry into others' business when it comes to moral matters. But superheroes are extreme. They devote their whole lives to crime-fighting. In *Spider-Man*, Peter Parker is a bright student and a budding scientist. However, due to his preoccupation with crime, his grades slip and he can't even hold down a pizza delivery job. These costs are not lost on him and in *Spider-Man 2* he tries, unsuccessfully, to give up crime-fighting.

Perhaps the most conspicuous cost of obsession with crime is the superhero's love life, or rather, lack thereof. Apparently, high-flying heroes find criminals more compelling than the opposite sex. Daredevil's girlfriend Heather breaks up with him saying, "You're never there. At least not for me.... Every time we sleep together, I wake up in the morning alone. I mean, Jesus, where do you go at three in the morning?" In *Superman II*, Superman gives up his powers to be with Lois Lane, but he quickly changes his mind, choosing moral defender over mortal lover. Women swoon over Superman, Batman, and Spider-Man, but their passion is for crime rather than the ladies.

Superheroes might suspend laws of gravity, but when it comes to time they face mortal constraints. Devotion to crime-fighting entails

---

[6] Recall Peter Parker actually moved in this direction, albeit in a smalltime way, on the wrestling circuit.

sacrificing career prospects, financial security, friends, family, and romance. Like superheroes, humans everywhere devote considerable daily resources to monitoring moral violations among others—at the cost of other activities. Why do we care?

MORALISTIC PUNISHMENT

Third-party punishment is another core feature of superheroes. We will see that moralistic punishment is crucially distinct from second-party revenge. Third-party punishment also explains why superheroes have secret identities. Criminals don't take punishment lying down, so superheroes need disguises to protect loved ones from gangland retaliation.

Superhero lore is careful to distinguish moralistic punishment from vigilante revenge; the latter is unbecoming of a superhero. This contrasts with war heroes, who are praised for wrath, rage, and vengeance. For example, Cúchulainn of Irish mythology is known for his ecstatic fits of unbridled fury in which he massacres friends and foes alike. Particularly legendary is the vengeful rage of Achilles, who dragged Hector's dead body behind a chariot for thirteen days. For superheroes, such displays are beyond the pale.

In *Batman Begins*, Bruce Wayne plans revenge against his parents' killer, Mr. Chill, but he is thwarted when a gangster shoots Chill first. When his love interest Rachel learns of his intent, she explains, "You're not talking about justice. You're talking about revenge." Bruce replies, "Sometimes, they're the same." Rachel insists, "No, they're never the same. Justice is about harmony. Revenge is about you making yourself feel better. It's why we have an impartial system." Bruce's martial arts teacher echoes the point: "A vigilante is just a man lost in the scramble for his own gratification. He can be destroyed or locked up. But if you make yourself more than just a man, if you devote yourself to an ideal, and if they can't stop you, then you become something else entirely. . . . Legend, Mr. Wayne." By the movie's conclusion, Batman agrees that "Justice is about more than revenge."

In *Daredevil*, the hero is initially vengeful, murdering a rapist. Subsequently, he talks with a priest in the confessional, arguing, "Justice isn't a sin, Father." The priest replies, "No, but vengeance is. You see it every day on the streets. Violence just begets more violence. Is that how you want to live your life? A lawyer during the day, and then judge and jury at night?" When Daredevil finally has the opportunity to kill the arch-criminal, Kingpin, he instead turns him over to the police, abandoning vengeance for justice.

Even Punisher, perhaps the most vengeful superhero, gives lip service to the key difference between moralistic punishment and revenge: "In certain extreme situations...it is necessary to act outside the law, to pursue natural justice. This is not vengeance. Revenge is not a valid motive, it's an emotional response. No, not vengeance—punishment" (The Punisher). The speech is unconvincing, however, as Punisher is unambiguously vengeful, concluding his campaign by dragging his enemy Howard Saint's dead body behind a car through an exploding parking lot—an echo of Achilles' mutilation of Hector's body. Despite his cheap talk, Punisher falls short of the superhero ideal. This has led to conflict with other superheroes, most notably Daredevil, e.g., Daredevil vs. Punisher (Lapham).

Moralistic punishment carries special costs that explain why superheroes need a secret identity. In war, adversaries are separated by geographic boundaries, but crime fighters live among their enemies. This means that criminals are well-positioned for surprise attacks on crime fighters and their loved ones. To preclude retaliation, superheroes hide behind masks and costumes. Among war heroes, such behavior would be counter to the aim of personal glory and would likely be viewed as cowardly.

Because superheroes themselves are formidable, criminals often target their loved ones. Spider-Man laments, "No matter what I do. No matter how hard I try. The ones I love will always be the ones who pay" (Spider-Man). Secret identities help protect friends and family. Superman's father Jor-El insists, "You must keep your secret identity," and when Superman asks why, Jor-El explains, "Your enemies will discover their only way to hurt you—by hurting the people you care for" (Superman).

Bruce Wayne realizes the danger to his loved ones when he is threatened by the gangster Carmine Falcone: "You think you got nothing to lose. But you haven't thought it through. You haven't thought about your lady friend in the DA's office. You haven't thought about your old butler. Bang!" When Bruce mentions the concept of Batman to Alfred, the butler asks, "This symbol is a persona to protect those you care about from reprisals?" Bruce responds, "You're thinking about Rachel?" Alfred admits, "Actually, sir, I was thinking of myself" (*Batman Begins*).

Even a disguise might not be enough. Spider-Man's girlfriend Gwen Stacy was murdered by the Green Goblin ("The Night Gwen Stacey Died" #121). Three of Daredevil's lovers were slain by his enemies. A particularly gruesome instance occurred when Green Lantern found the dismembered body of romantic partner Alex DeWitt in his refrigerator, handiwork of the villain Major Force ("Deadly Force" #54). This incident gave rise to the popular culture term and Web site, "Women in Refrigerators", signifying the severe threat to crime fighters' loved ones. Crime-fighting is risky business.

MORAL IMPARTIALITY

A third property of human morality is *impartiality*. Like Daredevil, justice is blind. Moralists are expected to enforce moral principles regardless of who is helped or harmed by condemnation. This can require moralists to ignore kinship, friendship, or alliances, as well as requiring moralists to show restraint with personal enemies.

Superheroes often demonstrate impartiality by turning on their friends in response to a moral violation. In *Batman Begins*, Bruce Wayne trains in martial arts for seven years with Ra's al Ghul's League of Shadows. In his final test, Bruce is asked to demonstrate commitment to justice by executing a murderer. Bruce refuses to execute the helpless prisoner, instead turning on his teacher in a spectacular battle that leaves the League of Shadows in ashes. Later, Bruce's teacher returns to Gotham saying, "When I found you in that jail, you were lost. But I believed in you. I took away your fear, and I showed you a path. You were my greatest student. It should be you standing by my side." Bruce declines, threatening, "I'll be standing where I belong, between you and the people of Gotham."

In *X-Men*, Xavier and Magneto are old friends, but they differ on how mutants should deal with humans. Magneto believes humans and mutants will inevitably fall out in war, and in order to ensure mutant security he doesn't mind killing people. In contrast, Xavier teaches his mutant students to use their powers to benefit humans, even when that means fighting other mutants. The tension between friendship and morality is vividly captured in the final scene of *X-Men*, in which Magneto is visited in prison by Xavier. Magneto says that he will escape and that "the war is still coming, Charles, and I intend to fight it...by any means necessary." Xavier becomes stern, leans forward aggressively, and warns, "And I will always be there, old friend."

In the movie *Spider-Man*, Peter Parker learned the ideal of impartiality the hard way when he let a thief escape because the victim was a personal enemy. Later, the thief killed Parker's beloved Uncle Ben.

Superheroes also demonstrate impartiality by showing restraint with their enemies. Superheroes rarely kill. Instead they turn criminals over to the authorities (no matter how incompetent). They fail to kill evildoers even when they know the villains will escape prison and that innocent lives will be lost in the next round of capture. Like Superman faced with Rokk's dilemma, superheroes don't kill even when their restraint risks others' lives. Yet somehow we all admire superhero restraint, despite the reckless endangerment to humanity entailed by leaving villains like Lex Luthor or Kingpin alive.

PULSE OF THE SUPERHERO

Superheroes have many characteristic features. To a psychologist, the question is: Which features explain the powerful response among human audiences? To answer this question, it is necessary to distinguish essential superhero qualities from properties common to all heroes (Campbell), and from accidental conventions peculiar to the genre.

Many superheroes are orphans (e.g., Superman, Spider-Man, Batman), many undergo a period of training with a knowledgeable teacher (e.g., Superman, Batman), and many possess a trademark weapon (e.g., Wonder Woman's lasso, Captain America's shield). But the same properties are common among war heroes. For example, Achilles was an orphan, he was trained by Chiron the centaur, and he killed with a special spear.

Other features of superheroes, like spandex tights and comic book origins, are probably accidental conventions. Japanese comics contain soap opera stories rather than crime-fighting, suggesting that there is no intrinsic link between comics and superheroes. Spandex tights worn beneath shorts was a convention modeled after trapeze artist costumes at a time when traveling circuses were in vogue.

Crime-fighting and moral condemnation set superheroes apart. Superheroes confront within-group conflict, which involves ambiguity about who's on which side. Indeed, superheroes themselves are often pursued by law enforcement, and they sometimes doubt their own virtue. Daredevil worried to himself, "I'm not the bad guy. I'm not" (*Daredevil*). Such concerns are not found among war heroes. As crime fighters, superheroes devote their time to uncovering and stopping moral violations. They punish wrongdoers, risking retaliation against themselves and loved ones. They even turn against close friends and show restraint with enemies.

Superpowers, too, might have moral significance. In many cultures, the most serious moral accusations are charges of witchcraft or sorcery. Witches and sorcerers are widely viewed as the epitome of evil, and people believe that their black magic can only be countered by opposing white magic. Interestingly, these figures possess the same occult powers attributed to superheroes. Witches and sorcerers are thought capable of flight (like Superman, Wonder Woman, Icarus), weather control (like Storm, Iceman, Red Tornado), animal transformation (like Wolverine, Spider-Man, Animal Man), telekinesis (like Phoenix, Doctor Fate, Raven), teleportation (like Nightcrawler, Magik, Blink), astral projection (like Doctor Strange, Madame Web, Trance), and telepathy (like Xavier, Psylocke, Marvel Girl).

In sum, superheroes are not war heroes; they are moral heroes. It is no accident that Superman won't kill Rokk even to save the world, that Batman refuses to kill directly but allows Ra's al Ghul to die, that Spider-Man neglects his personal life to stop the Green Goblin, that Daredevil restrains his vengeance against Kingpin, or that Xavier turns on his friend Magneto to defend human strangers. These common moral themes form the pulse of the superhero. Much more than children's entertainment, superhero myths represent a deep shift in the hero genre, marking a historical transformation in the relative dangers of war and crime. Perhaps most importantly, superheroes provide a unique window into our moral minds.

Peter DeScioli is a doctoral candidate at the University of Pennsylvania in the Department of Psychology. He received his B.A. in philosophy and anthropology at the University of Delaware. He is broadly interested in how psychological systems employ principles of strategy. His research topics include morality, third-party condemnation, moralistic punishment, moral impartiality, friendship, and loyalty.

Robert Kurzban, Ph.D., is currently an Assistant Professor at the University of Pennsylvania in the Department of Psychology. He received his Ph.D. at the University of California Santa Barbara, and received postdoctoral training at Caltech, UCLA, and the University of Arizona. His research focuses on evolved cognitive adaptations for navigating the social world in domains such as mate choice, friendship, morality, and cooperation.

ACKNOWLEDGEMENTS

We thank Bryan Bencomo, Brendan Ryan, and Chris Taylor for helpful comments on previous drafts of this chapter.

REFERENCES

300. Dir. Zack Snyder. Perf. Gerard Butler, Lena Headey. Warner Bros., 2007.

Batman Begins. Dir. Christopher Nolan. Perf. Christian Bale, Michael Caine. Warner Bros., 2005.

Campbell, Joseph. *The Hero with a Thousand Faces*. Princeton: Princeton University Press, 1949.

Conway, Gerry (w), Gil Kane (p), and John Romita and Tony Mortellary (i). "The Night Gwen Stacey Died." *The Amazing Spider-Man* #121. Marvel Comics: June 1973.

Daredevil. Dir. Mark Steven Johnson. Perf. Ben Affleck, Jennifer Garner. Twentieth Century-Fox Film Corporation, 2003.

Diener, Edward, Scott C. Fraser, Arthur L. Beaman, and Roger T. Kelem. "Effects of Deindividuation Variables on Stealing Among

Halloween Trick-or-treaters." *Journal of Personality and Social Psychology* 33, 1976: 178-183.

Dorfman, Leo (w), Al Plastino (p), and Uncredited (i). "Superman's Sacrifice." *Superman* #171. DC Comics: August 1964.

Gellner, Ernest. *Plough, Sword and Book*. Chicago: University of Chicago Press, 1989.

Hauser, Marc D. *Moral Minds*. New York: HarperCollins, 2006.

Kant, Immanuel. *Grounding for the Metaphysics of Morals*. Trans. James Ellington. Indianapolis: Hackett Publishing Company, 1993.

Keeley, Lawrence H. *War Before Civilization*. Oxford: Oxford University Press, 1996.

Lapham, Dave. *Daredevil vs. Punisher*. New York: Marvel Comics, 2006.

Marz, Ron (w), Darryl Banks and Carr Aucoin (p), and Romeo Tanghal (i). "Deadly Force!" *Green Lantern* #54. DC Comics: 1994.

Spider-Man 2. Dir. Sam Raimi. Perf. Tobey Maguire, Kirsten Dunst. Columbia Pictures, 2004.

Spider-Man. Dir. Sam Raimi. Perf. Tobey Maguire, Willem Dafoe. Columbia Pictures, 2002.

Superman II. Dir. Richard Lester. Perf. Gene Hackman, Christopher Reeve. Warner Bros., 1981.

Superman. Dir. Richard Donner. Perf. Christopher Reeve, Gene Hackman. Warner Bros., 1978.

The Oxford Study Bible. New York: Oxford University Press, 1992.

The Punisher. Dir. Jonathan Hensleigh. Perf. Thomas Jane, John Travolta. Lions Gate Films, 2004.

X-Men. Dir. Bryan Singer. Perf. Hugh Jackman, Patrick Stewart. Twentieth Century-Fox Film Corporation, 2000.